# LIVING WITHOUT DOMINATION

*Living Without Domination* defends the bold claim that humans can organise themselves to live peacefully and prosperously together in an anarchist utopia. Clark refutes errors about what anarchism is, about utopianism, and about human sociability and its history. He then develops an analysis of natural human social activity which places anarchy in the real landscape of sociability, along with more familiar possibilities including states and slavery.

## ASHGATE NEW CRITICAL THINKING IN PHILOSOPHY

The *Ashgate New Critical Thinking in Philosophy* series brings high quality research monograph publishing into focus for authors, the international library market, and student, academic and research readers. Headed by an international editorial advisory board of acclaimed scholars from across the philosophical spectrum, this monograph series presents cutting-edge research from established as well as exciting new authors in the field. Spanning the breadth of philosophy and related disciplinary and interdisciplinary perspectives *Ashgate New Critical Thinking in Philosophy* takes contemporary philosophical research into new directions and debate.

# Living Without Domination

## The Possibility of an Anarchist Utopia

SAMUEL CLARK

ASHGATE

Published by
Ashgate Publishing Limited
Gower House
Croft Road
Aldershot
Hampshire GU11 3HR
England

Ashgate Publishing Company
Suite 420
101 Cherry Street
Burlington, VT 05401-4405
USA

Ashgate website: http://www.ashgate.com

**British Library Cataloguing in Publication Data**
Clark, Samuel
Living without domination : the possibility of an anarchist utopia. - (Ashgate new critical thinking in philosophy)
1. Anarchism 2. Utopias
I. Title
321'.07

**Library of Congress Cataloging-in-Publication Data**
Clark, Samuel, 1974-
Living without domination : the possibility of an anarchist utopia / Samuel Clark.
p. cm. -- (Ashgate new critical thinking in philosophy)
Includes bibliographical references and index.
ISBN 0-7546-5461-3
1. Anarchism. 2. Utopias. I. Title. II. Series

HX833.C563 2007
335'.83--dc22

2006008833

ISBN-13: 978-0-7546-5461-2
ISBN-10: 0-7546-5461-3

Printed and bound by Antony Rowe Limited, Chippenham, Wiltshire.

# Contents

# Preface

This book has its roots in a doctoral thesis written from 2000 to 2003, in the Politics Department at the University of York. During my time at York and since, I've had help from friends, fellow-students, teachers, colleagues and family. Thankfully, these aren't mutually exclusive categories.

Friends outside the academy, including especially Eric Howard, Vix Lowthion, David Martin and Nick Spicer, friends and fellow-students inside it, including Alex Bavister-Gould, Derek Edyvane, Sarah Marshall, Matt Sleat and Rob Wavre, and my sisters Alex and Verity Clark, gave of their company, conversation and various expertises.

Teachers including Matt Matravers, Sue Mendus and Jon Parkin disagreed with me, pushed for clarity, and helped create a rigorous but friendly working culture. Peter Nicholson, who was my supervisor until his retirement, made doing a PhD psychologically possible for me. Alex Callinicos, who then took over, was thoughtful, supportive, and a pleasure to work with.

My parents Gillian and Stephen Clark gave generous personal, professional and financial support, despite their occasional misgivings about my joining the family firm.

Finally, my wife Emily supported us both, put up with my lows and absences, and gave of her good sense, determination and love. This would have been impossible without her; so would everything else.

Sam Clark, York and Glasgow, 2006

# Introduction

This book is an exercise in practical utopianism. I shall show, by an analysis and some examples of human sociability, that an anarchist utopia is within the bounds of social possibility. We really could live together peacefully and prosperously without domination.

Twentieth-century anarchist texts frequently open by noting that anarchism has long been thought dead, but that *now* is the time when it is (again) vital and relevant.[1] Few other movements have been buried so often or so impermanently, and these corrections and recoveries are therefore needed. However, they are incomplete. The importance of anarchism does not lie wholly in its relation to current circumstances, however propitious or demanding. It lies also at the level of theory, in anarchism's comprehensive challenge to domination and assertion of radical social possibility.

Several kinds of work are needed to take advantage of these virtues. We must reread central texts and, in connection with this, we must clear away accumulated misrepresentations. Most importantly here, we must extend, correct and supplement the discovered anarchist theory: that is, we must continue to do anarchist philosophy in the tradition of William Godwin, Peter Kropotkin and many others.

Denials of the utopian claim with which I began have often been grounded in mistakes about what anarchists want, about utopianism, and about human sociability. I reach my conclusion partly by considering and refuting them, beginning with some common mistakes about the nature of anarchism.

## Anarchism: Marginalisation and Variety

This book is both anarchist and about historical anarchism. But it is not immediately obvious what anarchism in general is, and it may be too marginal or too flawed to be worth such consideration. As James Joll remarks, 'Anyone who has tried to write about anarchism sometimes comes to a point at which he wonders just what it is he is writing about'; elsewhere, Joll feels the need to justify writing about the subject by appeal to the thought that 'if the aim of the historian, like that of the artist,

1 For instance: George Woodcock, *Anarchism: A history of libertarian ideas and movements* (Harmondsworth, 1963); David Goodway ed., *For Anarchism: History, theory, and practice* (London, 1989).

is to enlarge our picture of the world … then the study of failure can often be as instructive as the study of success.'[2]

There are five common but mistaken reasons for marginalising anarchism. The first two are culturally sanctioned images of anarchists which distort our perception. There is an image immortalised and satirised by Joseph Conrad in *The Secret Agent*. Conrad's 'Professor' expresses his pathological hatred for everything with calculated violence. He carries a bomb so as never to be taken alive by the police; he hands out explosive to anyone who asks, for whatever purpose; he devotes his life to a search for 'the perfect detonator'.[3] His only interests are destruction and its techniques. There certainly have been anarchist terrorists (Francois-Claudius Ravachol, Emile Henry, perhaps Alexander Berkman), even if they do not quite match up to the Professor's single-minded competence. However, they are in the minority, their activity was largely confined to the period between 1890 and 1930 (particularly in France and the United States),[4] and many other anarchists repudiated their actions. In any case, few political positions can claim that no one has ever committed violence in their names. Supporters of states, in particular, must recognise that far more violence, including terrorist violence, has been done by states, through their institutions, and in their names, than by anarchists: 'For every bomb manufactured by an anarchist, many millions are manufactured by governments, and for every man killed by anarchist violence, many millions are killed by the violence of states.'[5] Violence, including symbolic violence for ideological ends, is neither typical of, nor exclusive to anarchists. The image of the wild-eyed, bearded anarchist with the Molotov cocktail persists, but it is not an accurate picture of most anarchists, nor of the claims and results of anarchist theory.

The second false image is immortalised and satirised by the Sex Pistols in 'Anarchy in the UK':[6] the anarchist as pathetic and ineffectual nihilist, who violently rejects everything, but lacks any idea of how to replace it. She has no answer when asked what a better world would be like. Again, there have been self-described anarchists who are like this. But again, they are in the minority. Anarchist texts (the work of William Godwin, Peter Kropotkin, Colin Ward or Murray Bookchin, for

---

2 James Joll, 'Singing, Dancing and Dynamite: Review of Jean Maitron', *Le Mouvement Anarchiste en France*, *Times Literary Supplement*, 10 September 1976: pp. 1092–3, p. 1092. Joll, *The Anarchists* (2nd edn, London, 1979), p. vii.

3 Joseph Conrad, *The Secret Agent: A simple tale* (Ware, 1993), p. 61.

4 For sensationalist contemporary accounts, see Michael J. Schaack, *Anarchy and Anarchists: A history of the red terror and the social revolution in America and Europe* (Chicago, 1889) and Ernest Alfred Vizetelly, *The Anarchists: Their faith and their record including sidelights on the royal and other personages who have been assassinated* (London, 1911). For the era of propaganda by deed in historical context, see for instance Joll, *The Anarchists*, Chapter 5.

5 Bertrand Russell, *Roads to Freedom: Socialism, anarchism, and syndicalism* (London, 1918), p. 38.

6 The Sex Pistols, 'Anarchy in the UK', on *Never Mind the Bollocks: Here's the Sex Pistols* (Sex Pistols Residuals/Virgin Records), track 8.

instance) show that anarchists have not typically lacked ideas about what they want, nor advocated destruction for its own sake.

The third reason for marginalisation is the belief that anarchism is extreme political scepticism, and that therefore, like epistemological scepticism, it can immediately be rejected. Scepticism and anarchism can be useful heuristic devices, and 'the sceptic' and 'the anarchist' useful imaginary interlocutors, but their positions cannot reasonably be endorsed. The analogy between anarchism and scepticism has been made by, amongst others, Jeffrey Reiman, Rex Martin, Jonathan Wolff[7] and Robert Ladenson:

> An analogy more appropriate than the [Kantian] one drawn by [Robert Paul] Wolff would be between his doubts about the existence of morally legitimate political authority and the radical doubts about the existence of an external world which Kant was also concerned to refute. The parallel with radical scepticism in the realm of epistemology is almost exact. According to this kind of scepticism, even after we have checked all the considerations which, even in the widest sense, count as evidence for empirical knowledge, it still does not follow that the existence claims one makes about physical objects, presumably on the basis of this evidence, are well founded. If one asks the sceptic what would be needed in order to have good grounds for such claims, over and above the normal evidence of sight, touch and so forth, he tells us that nothing would or even could do the job. Likewise with Wolff, if asked what would be needed to establish the moral legitimacy of a given state's authority, over and above showing that it does a tolerably good job of serving purposes such as those enumerated in the Preamble to the United States Constitution (i.e., the sorts of things one would naturally think of as relevant for deciding the issue) he would say that nothing could do this. On his view, no state, in principle has had or could have the right to rule. Now the beliefs which the radical sceptic about the external world seeks to undermine are so basic that they cannot be rejected. Accordingly, the fact that a given epistemological theory leads to radical scepticism about the external world is a sufficient reason for rejecting it. The same is true of Wolff's account of legitimate political authority. The fact that it leads to the kind of scepticism that it does shows his account to be unacceptable.[8]

This argument rests on several dubious claims: that we have a good idea what 'one' (who?) would 'naturally' think relevant to the question of legitimacy; that belief in the legitimacy of the state is as basic as belief in the legitimacy of observational statements about the world; that difficulties in putting a conclusion into practice refute the argument which led to it. However, my interest in Ladenson is not the cogency of his argument, but the understanding of anarchism which it expresses. For this false image of anarchism, the paradigm anarchist is Robert Paul Wolff, and

---

7 Reiman, *In Defence of Political Philosophy* (New York, 1972); Martin, 'Anarchism and Skepticism' in J.R. Pennock and J.W. Chapman (eds), *Nomos XIX: Anarchism* (New York, 1978), pp. 140–49; Wolff, 'Anarchism and Skepticism' in John T. Sanders and Jan Narveson (eds), *For and Against the State* (Lanham, 1996), pp. 99–118.

8 'Legitimate Authority', *American Philosophical Quarterly* vol. 9 (1972): 335–41, p. 337.

anarchism is the doctrine expressed in his *In Defence of Anarchism*.[9] Wolff is, in his own term, a 'philosophical anarchist'.[10] For him, 'the fundamental problem of political philosophy' is 'how the moral autonomy of the individual can be made compatible with the legitimate authority of the state'.[11] That is, how can someone obey a state's authority, order or law, because it is the state's and not for any prudential or further moral reason, and remain autonomous? Wolff's answer is that she cannot. There is a logical contradiction between autonomy and authority, and therefore 'legitimate authority' is analogous to 'round square' or 'married bachelor'. Wolff's book sparked a brief, heated burst of counterargument, but it is not my business here to consider that. My point is that Wolff's philosophical anarchism has little to do with other anarchisms. Whether or not it is just a version of scepticism, and whether or not scepticism can be refuted, few anarchists are sceptics. Philosophical anarchism was a moment in the recent history of professional political theory, and a minority interest in the discipline at around the same time that John Rawls was revolutionising it.[12] To tar other anarchists with the same brush is a mistake.

These false images are easily refuted but less easily removed, because myths have their own historical momentum, and an argument that one is mistaken is not always enough to exorcise it. The other two reasons for marginalisation are harder to refute; responses to them will run through much of the rest of this book. The fourth is that anarchists are primitivists: nostalgic for a mythical golden age, or over-optimistic about human nature, or both. This position is supposed to be so obviously wrong that it and anarchism can immediately be rejected, but I show in Chapter 1 that it is misattributed. Anarchists are not typically primitivists.

The final reason for marginalisation is perhaps the most obvious and I think the most interesting, and is the main target of this book. It is the belief that anarchist utopianism is unacceptable, both because of the weakness of utopian argument-forms, and because of the unavailability to us of the anarchist utopia. Anarchists are relegated to the margins of political discourse because they use a marginal form of political argument and work for something we cannot attain. Anarchism is *unrealistic*: we just cannot live like that. This is an accusation which some anarchists have gleefully appropriated. In Paris in 1968, 'street posters declared … "Be Realistic: Demand the Impossible".'[13] I shall argue, on the contrary, that utopianism is a reasonable mode of political thought and intervention, and that the anarchist utopia is possible. Humans are capable of organising ourselves in the way that anarchists typically demand, and utopianism is one reasonable way of arguing and working for that possibility.

---

9 2nd edn, Berkeley, 1998.

10 Ibid., p. xxviii.

11 Ibid., p. xxvii.

12 On the Rawlsian revolution, see for instance H. Gene Blocker and Elizabeth S. Smith, Preface to Blocker and Smith (eds), *John Rawls's Theory of Social Justice: An introduction* (Athens, 1980), pp. vii–xii. On Wolff's interaction with Rawls, 2nd edn Preface to *In Defence of Anarchism*, pp. vii–xxv.

13 Peter Marshall, *Demanding the Impossible: A history of anarchism* (revised edn, London, 1993), p. xii.

Even if we suppose, for a moment, that these mistaken reasons for marginalisation are removed, we still have the question of what anarchism is. Characterisations of anarchism and of anarchists have varied in the common character they identify, in the claims they suppose central, and in the individuals and movements they include or emphasise. Given that range of generalisation and taxonomy, the terms 'anarchist' and 'anarchism' might turn out to be nothing more than catch-all names for a disparate collection of fringe theorists, extremists and cranks, with little in common.[14]

Anarchism has been identified with a wide variety of mental, social and physical pathologies: a 'common conviction of superiority'; the desperate psychology of medieval millennialism; Cesare Lombroso's claim that 'anarchists possessed certain well-defined physiological characteristics which were easily discernible; for example, exaggerated plagiocephaly, facial asymmetry, cranial abnormalities (ultra-brachycephaly), large jawbone, exaggerated zygomas, enormous frontal sinus, anomalies of the eyes, ears, nose and teeth, anomalous colouration of the skin, and neuro-pathological anomalies.'[15] However, these unsympathetic commentators may just be confused. In 1897, E.V. Zenker noted that 'since the extraordinary danger of anarchist doctrines is firmly fixed as a dogma in the minds of the vast majority of mankind, it is apparently quite unnecessary to obtain any information about its real character in order to pronounce a decided, and often a decisive, judgement upon it.'[16] John Clark made a similar point nearly a century later, regretting that 'it is not unusual for academic "scholars" to gather no more evidence about the nature of anarchism than the derivation of the term, after which they can ascend to the heights of abstraction, paying attention neither to social history nor to the history of ideas.'[17] Accounts of anarchism have frequently lacked evidence and understanding; but this does not solve our problem, because sympathetic commentators, and even anarchists themselves, have disagreed just as much as have their enemies about how to characterise anarchism.

---

14 Noam Chomsky could be right that 'it would be hopeless to try to encompass all of these conflicting tendencies [of anarchism] in some general theory or ideology' (Introduction to Daniel Guérin, *Anarchism: From theory to practice*, trans. Mary Klopper (New York, 1970), pp. vii–xx, p. vii). Or, as Michael Freeden expresses the point, perhaps 'anarchism' is merely an 'umbrella term that covers a cluster of concepts whose totality can be made to pull in entirely different ideological directions' in *Ideologies and Political Theory: A conceptual approach* (Oxford, 1996), p. 311.

15 Isaac Kramnick, 'On Anarchism and the Real World: William Godwin and radical England', *American Political Science Review*, 66 (1972): 114–28, pp. 114–15. Joll, *The Anarchists*. A.R. Carlson, *Anarchism in Germany*, vol. 1: *The Early Movement* (Metuchen, 1972), pp. 6–7.

16 *Anarchism: A criticism and history of the anarchist theory* (New York, 1897), p. v. Why anarchism so often excites not merely disagreement, but hatred and contempt, is a question which could support some study.

17 'What is Anarchism?' in *The Anarchist Moment: Reflections on culture, nature and power* (Montréal, 1984), pp. 117–40, p. 117.

Anarchism 'may be described as *the doctrine that all the affairs of men should be managed by individuals or voluntary associations, and that the State should be abolished*'.[18] Or then again, a 'mental shift into a timeless world, out of progress and freed from material temptations' has been seen as 'the necessary leap of faith for the true black anarchist'.[19] According to Alan Ritter, anarchists seek 'to combine the greatest individual development with the greatest communal unity. Their goal is a society of strongly separate persons who are strongly bound together in a group. In a full-fledged anarchy, individual and communal tendencies, now often contradictory, become mutually reinforcing and coalesce.'[20]

Peter Kropotkin introduces anarchism as 'the no-government system of socialism';[21] Eric Hobsbawm, as 'the libertarian tradition of communism'.[22] According to Alan Carter, anarchism centres on 'normative opposition to certain substantive political inequalities and the empirical belief that they principally derive from, are preserved by, or are embedded within, certain centralized forms of power'.[23] Or, according to commentators including the influential Paul Eltzbacher, the only thing anarchists have in common is 'that they negate the State for our future', and this negation 'has totally different meanings'[24] for different anarchists!

Some analysts present anarchism as a permanent feature of human life. Max Nettlau, for instance, believes that anarchism is part of a history of 'continuous struggle to shake off authoritarian chains and restraints': 'The history of anarchist ideas is inseparable from the history of all progressive developments and aspirations towards liberty. It therefore starts from the earliest favourable historic moment when men first evolved the concept of a free life.'[25] His expansiveness allows him to include, amongst many others, Zeno of Citium (336–264 BCE), the founder of the Stoic school, as a proto-anarchist. Peter Marshall spreads his net as widely, and grounds the permanence of anarchism in human nature. He traces anarchism's 'origins and development from ancient civilisations to the present day', hopes that 'a study of anarchism will show that the drive for freedom is not only a central part of our collective experience but responds to a deeply felt human need',[26] and includes Lao Tzu (born around 604 BCE). Both may have been influenced by Peter

---

18 Benjamin Tucker, 'State Socialism and Anarchism: How far they agree and wherein they differ' in *State Socialism and Anarchism and other essays* (Colorado Springs, 1972), pp. 11–25, p. 16.

19 Woodcock, *Anarchism*, p. 344.

20 *Anarchism: A theoretical analysis* (Cambridge, 1980), p. 3.

21 'Anarchist Communism: Its basis and principles' in George Woodcock (ed.), *Fugitive Writings* (Montréal, 1993), pp. 72–94, p. 72.

22 'Bolshevism and the Anarchists' in *Revolutionaries* (London, 1999), pp. 67–83, p. 67.

23 'Analytical Anarchism: Some conceptual foundations', *Political Theory* vol. 28 (2000): 230–53, p. 232.

24 *Anarchism: Exponents of the anarchist philosophy*, trans. Steven T. Byington, ed. James J. Martin (New York, n.d.), p. 189.

25 *A Short History of Anarchism*, trans. Ida P. Isca, ed. Heiner M. Becker (London, 1996), p. 1.

26 Marshall, *Demanding the Impossible*, pp. xiii, xiv.

Kropotkin's article 'Anarchism' in the eleventh (1911) edition of the *Encyclopaedia Britannica*, in which he argues that anarchism's 'conception of society … and the tendency which is its dynamic expression, have always existed in mankind, in opposition to the governing hierarchic conception and tendency'.[27]

This account of anarchism as a permanent human tendency has been attacked by a number of authors. George Woodcock, for one, argues that 'anarchist historians have confused certain attitudes which lie at the core of anarchism … with anarchism as a movement and a creed appearing at a certain time in history and having specific theories, aims and methods.'[28] Andrew Vincent, for another, suggests that those 'who claim that anarchism is … an all-pervasive universal and ahistorical libertarian disposition' betray 'an intellectual weak-mindedness … that ignores historical and sociological factors'.[29] Both trace the myth of permanence to a desire for an authoritative ancient lineage for a modern phenomenon. These and other authors have presented anarchism as distinctively modern: a political discourse which emerged with other modern ideologies around the time of the French Revolution, and was first clearly expressed by William Godwin in 1793, when *Enquiry Concerning Political Justice* was published. Or, perhaps, not until the European Revolutions of 1848, in which working-class political movements were born; or not until 1880, by which time there was a self-consciously anarchist wing of the International.

Even if we ignore supposed forerunners like Lao Tzu, Zeno or the Anabaptists, there is still a difficulty about who counts as an anarchist. Eltzbacher, for instance, bases his largely negative characterisation on seven anarchist sages: William Godwin, Peter Kropotkin, Michael Bakunin, Pierre-Joseph Proudhon, Leo Tolstoy, Max Stirner and Benjamin Tucker. His 'assumption that anarchist theoretical wisdom is crystallised in his seven subjects'[30] has both influenced and been challenged by later analysts. R.B. Fowler replaces the sole American, Tucker, with Alexander Herzen, but otherwise leaves the list unchanged.[31] Ritter limits himself to Godwin, Proudhon, Bakunin and Kropotkin, 'whose contributions to anarchist theory are universally recognised as most seminal'.[32] George Crowder follows him.[33] April Carter invokes Eltzbacher's seven, but insists on the importance of Errico Malatesta, Josiah Warren, Henry David Thoreau, Elisée Reclus and Emma Goldman, and of anarchist

---

27 'Anarchism' from *The Encyclopaedia Britannica*, 11[th] edn, 1911, in M.S. Shatz (ed.), *The Conquest of Bread and other writings* (Cambridge, 1995), pp. 233–47, p. 236. Kropotkin is particularly concerned to show this tendency at work in Christian heresy, as is James Joll, who begins his survey in *The Anarchists* with Gnosticism.

28 Woodcock, *Anarchism*, p. 37.

29 *Modern Political Ideologies* (Oxford, 1992), p. 116.

30 Editor's note to Eltzbacher, *Anarchism*, p. 182. To be fair to Eltzbacher, he does not *assume* this: he attempts a logical proof of it.

31 'The Anarchist Tradition of Political Thought', *Western Political Quarterly* vol. 25 (1972): 738–52.

32 Ritter, *Anarchism*, p. 5.

33 *Classical Anarchism: The political thought of Godwin, Proudhon, Bakunin, and Kropotkin* (Oxford, 1991).

movements in Russia with Nestor Makhno and Spain with Buenaventura Durutti.[34] Any complete account of anarchism (if such a thing is possible) ought also to take into account more recent work by, for instance, Colin Ward, Paul Goodman, Murray Bookchin and Hakim Bey.

However widely the net is cast, many taxonomies have been developed to categorise the anarchisms it catches, which can be split along various faultlines between different movements, individuals and episodes. There is an often rancorous division between libertarian (right-wing) and socialist (left-wing) anarchists: 'There has always been a conflict within anarchism between the two traditions of determinism and utopianism.'[35] We can identify fractures between millennialist and progressivist, violent and pacifist, sacral and atheist, activist and philosophical, gradualist and revolutionary, and conspiratorial and educational anarchisms. Irving Horowitz distinguishes anarchism into utilitarian, peasant, anarcho-syndicalist, collectivist, conspiratorial, communist, individualist and pacifist forms.[36]

Another possible division is geographical. According to Gerald Brenan, American and non-industrial European anarchisms are entirely different, because they are grounded in different economic circumstances: while American anarchism is 'an ultra-liberal doctrine suited to industrial countries with a middle-class standard of life', the anarcho-communist Bakunin 'is the creator of the peasant anarchism of Southern and Eastern Europe'.[37] Similarly, according to Nettlau, 'there was very little mutual knowledge' between the American and European anarchists until fairly recently, and 'ample room for both movements to function without any interference on either side, so that one was hardly aware of the existence of the other'.[38] Specifically *Spanish* anarchism has sometimes been presented as radically different from other anarchisms, much as Spain has sometimes been presented as radically different from the rest of Europe.

Once we have started to play this game of splitting, it is difficult to stop, because anarchists differ so much from each other, even down to the level of individuals. Godwin's proto-utilitarian, gradualist anarchism, shaped by dissenting Christianity, is a world away from Bakunin's revolutionary rhetoric, love of conspiracy and pan-Slavic nationalism. Stirner's egoism has little in common with Kropotkin's evolutionary communism, and indeed the former is 'the epitome of almost everything which revolutionaries of Kropotkin's tradition came to oppose';[39] 'Stirner's consuming egoism, Herzen's elegant ambiguities, and Kropotkin's breathless

34 *The Political Theory of Anarchism* (London, 1971).

35 Lawrence Otter, 'Determinism and Utopianism in the Anarchist Tradition', *Anarchy* 68 (1966): 305–18, p. 305. I shall argue in Chapter 1 that William Godwin, who seems a prime candidate for pigeonholing as a determinist, can fruitfully be understood as a utopian.

36 (ed.), *The Anarchists* (New York, 1964).

37 *The Spanish Labyrinth: An account of the social and political background of the civil war* (2nd edn, Cambridge, 2000), pp. 131–2.

38 Nettlau, *A Short History of Anarchism*, p. 39.

39 Marie Fleming, *The Anarchist Way to Socialism: Elisée Reclus and nineteenth-century European anarchism* (London, 1979), p. 20.

positivism apparently lie far apart.'[40] Once we realise that we have to accommodate not only this variety, but also the Japanese anarchist movement, anarchist involvement in working-class activism in Brazil during the First World War, and many other movements, episodes and fleeting appearances, we may decide that anarchism is not, after all, a single phenomenon. Perhaps there are many anarchisms, sharing little but the name.

Indeed, even the name may be problematic. Godwin never used it, and many of Proudhon's followers have preferred to call themselves 'mutualists'. The pacifist Tolstoy rejected the label, on the grounds that 'the anarchists' preached violent revolution and attempted, he thought paradoxically, 'to destroy violence by violence, by terrorism, dynamite bombs and daggers'. Worse, acceptance of the term has often been temporary, ironic or unwilling. As Daniel Guérin points out, Proudhon took 'malicious pleasure'[41] in the confusion he caused by using 'anarchy' and 'anarchist' in both positive and pejorative senses, and he abandoned the terms entirely in later life. James Guillaume spoke for many when he argued, in 1876, that 'the terms "anarchist" and "anarchy" expressed only a negative idea "without indicating any positive theory" and led to "distressing ambiguities".'[42]

The point of accumulating this contradictory collection of generalisations, taxonomies and divisions is to indicate the difficulty of assigning single, unambiguous meanings to 'anarchism' and 'anarchist'. It may be argued, in response, that I am needlessly complicating the issue by ignoring the most obvious characterisation of anarchism: anarchists are anti-statists. This claim is often grounded on the observation that the words 'anarchism', 'anarchy' and 'anarchist' are derived 'from Medieval Latin *anarchia*, from Greek *anarkhia*, from *anarkhos* without a ruler, from AN- [not; without] + *arkh-* leader'.[43] So, anarchy must be the condition of lacking a ruler, anarchism the position which demands and works for that condition, and an anarchist a person who holds that position. But etymology does not govern meaning. That anarchism has come to be called 'anarchism' by some long series of borrowings, baptisms, extensions and creative misunderstandings does not tell us anything about the beliefs and activities of the people who are now called anarchists. Consider how little can be discovered about modern western liberals by noting that 'liberal' derives 'from Latin *liberalis* of freedom', or about the Pope by observing that 'Catholic' derives 'from Latin *catholicus*, from Greek *katholikos* universal, from *katholou* in general, from *kata-* according to + *holos* whole'.[44] This etymological information does not entail the Pope or the Catholic Church's positions on the trinity, gay marriage

40 Fowler, 'The Anarchist Tradition of Political Thought', p. 739. 'Breathless positivism' is a bizarre characterisation of Kropotkin's measured, empirically grounded writing, as I hope to show in subsequent chapters.

41 *Anarchism: From theory to practice*, p. 12.

42 Fleming, *The Anarchist Way to Socialism*, p. 16.

43 *Collins English Dictionary*.

44 Ibid.

or any other particular issue. Similarly, that 'anarchy' and its related terms have the etymology they do tells us next to nothing about anarchism or anarchists.

That the 'obvious' answer is often derived in this faulty way does not prove it false. However, there are other reasons to think that it is, at best, not very useful. Anarchists very often are opposed to states, but they are not the only ones: many Marxists look forward to states' obsolescence and destruction; recent anti-capitalist and anti-globalisation protesters attack states amongst other institutions.[45] So, anti-statism is not a distinguishing characteristic of anarchism. Anarchists are often opposed to states as (currently large and important) examples of some more general category, such as 'oppressive institutions', which could also include capitalism and organised religions. Alternative ways of organising domination often have been, and I shall argue should be, just as important to anarchists as states.[46] So, anti-statism is an incomplete characterisation of anarchism. Further, although anarchists do perform the negative act of opposing states, they also spend a great deal of time and effort on the positive acts of discovery, analysis and celebration of alternative social forms (a practice which I take up in later chapters), and of working for anarchic organisation and justice. So, even if all and only anarchists could be characterised as anti-statists, that would again be an incomplete characterisation. It would be no more useful than a characterisation of humans as featherless bipeds:[47] true, but uninteresting.

The 'obvious' answer that anarchists are anti-statists fails because it is non-distinguishing and doubly incomplete. Finally, it may also be suspect because it has not always seemed so obvious. Until comparatively recently, the 'intuitively obvious' characterisation was the *Secret Agent* image, discussed above, of the anarchist as nihilistic terrorist. Zenker in 1897, Eltzbacher in 1900 and Bertrand Russell in 1918 all felt the need to warn against this error. That the supposedly obvious answer to the problem of characterising anarchism has such a short history should make us wonder how firmly grounded it is.

To characterise anarchism as anti-statism is unhelpful. I do not mean to make the peculiar claim that anti-statism has nothing to do with anarchism, but only to argue that 'anti-statism' is not a particularly good answer to the complex historical question, What is anarchism? It does not catch enough of anarchists' concerns, claims or activity.

I have sketched the variety of anarchism, by noting some of the various and contradictory characterisations and taxonomies of anarchism which have been given, and then argued that one common solution to the problem of variety fails. I have not offered an alternative solution. Anarchism is various, and there may be no clear central claims that one must accept, or activities she must take part in, in

---

45 'The core institutions of global capitalism are the multinational corporations, the leading capitalist states and the international institutions that reflect their interests' in Alex Callinicos, *Against the Third Way: An anti-capitalist critique* (Cambridge, 2001), p. 111.

46 See Chapter 3.

47 So far as I can discover, the phrase is (the economist, psychologist and pioneering artificial intelligence researcher) Herbert Simon's.

order correctly to be labelled 'an anarchist'. So, this book cannot be about anarchism in the same way that it could, perhaps, be about being a member of the Church of England (a partial account of the authoritative claims and activities of which can be found in *The Book of Common Prayer*). However, that is not a problem unique to anarchism. Being a liberal or a socialist involves similar ambiguities, and there is no *Book of Common Liberalism* either. The negative claim that it is not obvious what anarchism in general is, is intended as a starting point. I have not claimed that there is no unity to the anarchist tradition, only that we should not be confident that we know in what that unity consists. I shall have more to say in later chapters about general characterisations of anarchism.

Finally in this section, I have stated an ambition to continue to do anarchist philosophy; but it might be thought that we cannot join or continue such a fragmentary tradition, and that the *authority* of tradition, in any case, can have no purchase on an anarchist. So, my ambition cannot be fulfilled. However, both of these claims rest on a crude understanding of the continuity of a tradition, as consisting in a chain of acceptance of a single body of authoritative assertions. Perhaps some traditions are like this (religious traditions have often been so understood, although I suspect inaccurately). However, all certainly are not. In many cases, continuing a tradition is a matter of going on with some complex practice in one of the many ways it could convincingly be continued. My own practice, I believe, is one such way, but I do not claim to discover some 'real' or 'core' anarchism, opposed to other pretenders to that crown. I intend to come to a negotiated settlement with, and thereby to extend, the tradition, not to present myself as its one true heir.

## A Defence of Utopianism

I have taken on the task of defending the possibility of an anarchist utopia. However, because the terms 'utopia' and 'utopianism' have such polemical heft, I need to defend (my) utopianism against some expected attacks and misunderstandings. A defence of utopianism implies a direct clash between arguments for and against utopianism. I wish it were so: but attacks on utopianism too often talk past it; they fail to take notice of what actual utopian texts are like and what actual utopists use them to do. The contest between utopist and anti-utopist is less like a duel than like ships passing in the night. So, my initial defence is a description of utopian texts and tactics in general, and a demonstration that several common attacks fail to engage with them. I then discuss some of the purposes of utopists in writing and publishing utopias, and consider some more telling criticism. I conclude that utopianism, properly understood, is one of a range of reasonable ways of carrying out what I call a political intervention.

The title of this section alludes to a series of articles by G.K. Chesterton, published under the byline 'The Defendant', and including for instance 'A Defence of Rash

Vows'.[48] Chesterton's defensive strategy is often to show that a widespread belief that his subject has long ago been disproved, shown to be ridiculous, or rendered obsolete – that nobody who is anybody could *now* believe, worry about or do *that* – is false. I intend something similar here: despite a widespread belief to the contrary, no one has shown that utopianism is a bad idea. Utopianism is in much the same position as anarchism, in having been marginalised but not actually refuted. Their opponents are still drifting in fog, and have rarely fired on a real target. Once we understand what utopists do with utopias, we can see utopianism as one reasonable form of political action.

For my purposes, *utopianism* is the creation and use of utopias, and a *utopia* is a text which makes use of a historically developed and developing vocabulary of tropes, story-fragments, and rhetorical and argumentative tactics.[49] The utopian vocabulary includes a previously undiscovered land; a framing story of a traveller who has visited it; an imaginary community; a story within the story of its foundation; a built environment in which its members are fully at home; a travelogue which reveals the lineaments of the utopia; peace, harmony and human flourishing; and an often satirical comparison with our own land and living arrangements. Example utopias include Thomas More's *Utopia*, Francis Bacon's *A New Atlantis*, William Morris's *News From Nowhere*, H.G. Wells's *A Modern Utopia* and Ursula Le Guin's *The Dispossessed* and *Always Coming Home*.[50]

One major utopian trope is the description of an *ideal* way of life, and it is worth considering the meaning of 'ideal'. It might mean a *perfect* way of life. However, utopias more often describe something less than perfection: either a life which is better than ours (without the claim that nothing even better is possible), or an ideal in the weak sense of something which is as good as possible *for us*. That is, as good as is possible for flawed humans in a not entirely friendly world.

One can write a utopia just by making use of, modifying or even alluding to, or satirising the utopian vocabulary, and this has a number of consequences. The boundaries of the genre are extremely fuzzy. We might or might not choose to include, for instance, Samuel Butler's *Erewhon* or Iain M. Banks's 'culture' novels. This problem is made worse by anachronistic, but sometimes useful, extension of the genre back into the period before its explicit invention: we might or might not

48 In *Stories, Essays, & Poems* (London, 1935), pp. 113–18.

49 That is, I exclude from consideration real experimental communities of the kind which briefly flourished, especially, in the United States in the nineteenth century. See for instance Donald E. Pitzer (ed.), *America's Communal Utopias* (Chapel Hill, 1997).

50 Thomas More, *Utopia*, ed. and trans. Robert M. Adams (2nd edn, New York, 1992). Francis Bacon, *A New Atlantis*, in Henry Morley (ed.), *Ideal Commonwealths* (London, 1889), pp. 171–213. William Morris, *News From Nowhere*, in Clive Wilmer (ed.), *News from Nowhere and other writings* (London, 1993), pp. 41–228. H.G. Wells, *A Modern Utopia*, in *Tono-Bungay and A Modern Utopia* (London, n.d.), pp. 307–504. Ursula Le Guin, *The Dispossessed* (London, 1975); *Always Coming Home* (London, 1986). For many more examples, see for instance Marie Louise Berneri, *Journey Through Utopia* (London, 1982); F.E. and F.P. Manuel, *Utopian Thought in the Western World* (Oxford, 1979).

include *Republic*. The boundaries are rendered even less secure by the possibility of combining the utopian vocabulary with other vocabularies and tactics. Science-fiction, in particular, provides a rich resource for such cross-fertilisation.[51]

Most importantly: because one can write a utopia just by making use of the vocabulary, we cannot completely specify in advance for what particular purposes, by whom, nor to express what particular ideal, the vocabulary might be used. It has been used for purposes of satire, criticism, experimental community design, moral polemic and sheer creative game-playing, by Christians, behaviourists, anarchists, socialists, libertarians and others. The ideals it has been used to express include monastic communism, enlightened technocracy, arts-and-crafts federalism, and shamanic anarchy. It is still available to innumerable other users for innumerable other purposes.

However, one limitation we can make to the range of tasks to which utopias have been put is that typically, they have been political interventions. By calling utopias *interventions*, I mean to emphasise that they are *public* acts: attempts to do something to and with others by writing and publishing, whether it is to debate, to motivate, to shock or to delight. I mean 'political' in a wide sense, covering not only parliamentary activity, for instance, but all human sociability and interaction. Whatever particular purpose and ideal it is meant to serve and present, we can expect that a utopia will be a political intervention in this sense. I argue below that we can make some further specifications of the typical (although perhaps not the universal) purposes of utopias.

Given the variation of utopias, if by a defence of utopianism we mean a defence of all the particular purposes and ideals elaborated in examples of the genre, then the project is probably impossible and certainly unwise. It would end in trying to defend both Thomas More and L. Neil Smith:[52] both communism and (right-wing) libertarianism; both deism and secularism; both regimentation and laissez faire. It would also require me to defend things I have no wish to defend. I find B.F. Skinner's ideal unappealing, but cannot deny, without implausible stipulation, that *Walden Two*[53] is a utopia: Skinner explicitly says it is, uses many elements of the utopian vocabulary, and has discussed the strand of the tradition with which he identifies himself.[54] The defence or criticism of this and other particular utopias must be a matter of local analysis. So, rather than make the mistake of trying to defend all utopias at once, I shall identify and defend some major purposes and characteristic features of utopian writing: criticism, imagination, storytelling and construction.

---

51 See, for instance, the work by Wells, Le Guin and Banks already mentioned. On the general relationship between utopian and science-fictional writing, see for instance William H. Hardesty, 'Mapping the Future: Extrapolation in utopian/dystopian and science fiction' in Gorman Beauchamp et al. (eds), *Utopian Studies One* (Lanham, 1987), pp. 160–72.

52 See for instance *The Probability Broach* (New York, 1980).

53 B.F. Skinner, *Walden Two* (new edn, New Jersey, 1976).

54 B.F. Skinner, 'Utopianism: The design of experimental communities', in David L. Sills (ed.), *International Encyclopedia of the Social Sciences* (New York, 1968), vol. 16, pp. 271–5.

First, however, I must parallel the first section of this chapter and deal with some common but mistaken attacks.

Perhaps the most common attack on utopias and utopianism is the simple use of the adjective 'utopian'. Used to describe a utopia, or any radical proposal, it means unrealistic, impractical, weird, lunatic or unlikely to come true. 'Utopian' is used as the opposite of 'realistic'. The critic often then acts as though a telling point has been made, but it has not. Not all utopias are intended to describe realistic possibilities or practical manoeuvres. Some describe an unreachable goal, on the basis that even halfway there would be better than here. Others describe a moral ideal against which current arrangements can be judged. Even if we cannot possibly ensure that *no one* starves, that is no reason not to describe a world without starvation, to take that ideal as morally demanding, and to work towards it. Fewer deaths by starvation would be better than what we have now, even if there were more than none. It might be the case that action intended to move us in that direction would in fact makes things worse (either as measured by levels of starvation, or on some other scale): but that bare *possibility* is not a criticism of such action. Reasons to think that this will *in fact* be its consequence are required. Even where a utopia is intended to describe a real (even if distant or difficult) possibility, the criticism that it fails to do so again requires reasons in order to be telling. Calling something 'utopian' in this sense, without showing that and why it is dangerous or unrealistic, is not an argument but an example of what Martin Buber calls 'annihilation by labels'.[55]

'Utopian' is also an attack made by Marxists, in two distinct senses. In the first, respectful sense, a utopian socialist is one of a group of pre-Marxian socialists including Robert Owen, Henri de Saint-Simon and Charles Fourier. Marxists to an extent share the utopians' ideals, and give some credit for their unscientific expression. However, Marx and Engels influentially argued that the utopians were hamstrung by their historical position: lacking both Marxian science and a developed proletariat, the utopians could not avoid becoming 'lost in pure fantasy',[56] and could not be politically effective. 'Utopian' is used here as the opposite of 'scientific'. In a second, contemptuous sense, a utopian is a socialist who does not share the Marxian theory of history, or whom Marx and Engels wanted to discredit in the eyes of their contemporary socialist and communist movements. The first are 'utopians as forerunners'; the second, 'utopians as obscurantists'.[57]

In both cases, the claim is a political tactic internal to the European socialist movement, and in many ways specific to its late nineteenth-century debates and schisms. Marx and Engels used the epithet in its first sense in *The Communist Manifesto*, to claim Owen and the rest as *their* forerunners, and thereby to present themselves as early socialism's true heirs. They used or alluded to it in its second sense against many rivals for influence, including, for instance, Proudhon and

55 *Paths in Utopia*, trans. R.F.C. Hull (Boston, 1958), p. 6.

56 Friedrich Engels, *Socialism: Utopian and scientific* (London, 1993), p. 64.

57 Buber, *Paths in Utopia*, p. 6.

Wilhelm Weitling, and their disciples have often followed their example.[58] The Marxist use of this charge of utopianism is significant for two groups. Non-Marxist socialists in movements with strong Marxist wings must find ways to avoid or transform it. The rest of us must resist the polemical force given to it by Marx's genius for contemptuous rhetoric. However, the charge is only a matter of deep theoretical concern for those who accept Marx's account of history.

The third common attack is the use of 'utopian' as a label for a political intervention which presents an ideal without suggesting any means for reaching it. 'That sounds wonderful', says the critic, 'but what are we to do now, or at any time, to get there?' As with the first attack, the critic often then acts as though a telling point has been made; as with the first attack, it has not. It may be that this is simply an appropriation of 'utopian' as a technical term unrelated to the utopian genre, and I shall deal with that possibility in a moment. First, we should note that if the critic supposes that utopian texts typically sketch ideals without any means to reach them, then she is mistaken. More's *Utopia*, Morris's *News From Nowhere*, Smith's libertarian utopia in the sequence of novels beginning with *The Probability Broach*, and many others, all provide detailed accounts of how we might realise their ideals. Whether these means would actually work is another question: the point is that 'utopian', if the word is to have anything to do with actual utopian writing, cannot be used to mean an ideal without means.

Suppose, then, that what is signalled by this third use of 'utopian' is just that some ideal (whether expressed in the utopian vocabulary or not) can be disregarded because it lacks an account of the means for achieving it. This is an odd criticism: the fact that some political intervention is incomplete does not obviously mean that we can disregard it. An ideal without means is not a complete system, but not only complete systems are worth reading. 'All ideal, no means' might be a telling criticism of an individual actor, but it is no criticism at all of a text. John Rawls provides no account of how to get to the ideal just society he describes in *A Theory of Justice*, because that is not the task he had set himself. To attack him as 'utopian' is to misunderstand his project, which is to derive a coherent and appealing standard of judgement for societies from a version of the social contract. I do not provide an account of how to get to the ideal described in this book either, because that is not the task I have set myself. My argument is that the anarchist utopia is a possible social form for humans. To attack that argument as 'utopian' would, again, be to miss the point (although I do give some consideration, below, to the idea that the typically utopian project of expanding the assumed bounds of possibility might in itself be one way of starting the journey from here to there). This defence also applies to other utopias, and to other ideals without means: there is nothing as such wrong with

58 Although E.P. Thompson, for instance, has come close to a rehabilitation of utopianism, especially as represented by William Morris. See Thompson's 1976 postscript to *William Morris: Romantic to Revolutionary* (2nd edn, London, 1976), pp. 763–810. But it does a disservice to Thompson's independence and critical imagination to describe him as a 'disciple'.

essays, as opposed to systems; and this is lucky, because if there were, most of us who write would be subject to the same criticism.

These three kinds of attack are likely to come up whenever utopias or utopianism are mentioned. I have argued that none is telling, but more is needed in a defence of utopianism. Having seen what utopias are not, we need to see what they (historically and typically) are, and I therefore now identify and discuss some important features of utopian political interventions.

*Criticism* is an important element of many political acts, including political writing, and a significant feature of much utopianism. Utopian criticism can be distinguished by locating it in the wider map of critical types, and the first of that map's dimensions which we should note is that criticism can be internal or external. Internal criticism claims that its subject is internally flawed, perhaps by containing 'contradictions', as Marxists have claimed of capitalism; or by being self-defeating, as Derek Parfit has claimed of some moral theories;[59] or by not living up to its own standards, as a social critic might complain of her society. External criticism attacks its subject by unfavourable comparison with something else, and this is the kind of criticism which utopian texts typically enact.

External criticism can further be divided according to the kind of 'something else' with which its object is compared. I doubt that there could be a complete list of possible comparisons, but we can note some common types. Comparison can be with a theoretical structure or ideal, as when Rawls constructs a description of a just society, against which our arrangements can be measured; or with a set of statements about what would be right, perhaps in the form 'everyone has a right to x'; or with some real alternative which exists now or has existed in the past; or with some imaginary better thing. Utopias typically perform an external criticism of the fourth type, and condemn our politics and society by unfavourable comparison with an imagined alternative.

A utopia, then, is often a broad external criticism in the form of a story. That is, it criticises a large subject (an entire social form, society or world) by unfavourable comparison with a narrative fiction about an equally large subject. In *Utopia*, Thomas More uses Raphael Hythloday's travelogue and reports of discussions with the inhabitants of Utopia to make a broad external criticism of his society (indeed, it is so broad that it also applies to our society). We the readers are continually invited to compare our own arrangements with the Utopians', and to find ours wanting. In their efficiency, justice, security, philosophy, art, technology and piety, the Utopians are intended as a standing rebuke of ours. One of the central things that *Utopia* does is criticise. Similarly, William Morris attacks what is wrong with his society by dramatic comparison with the future England where William Guest wakes up one morning, after an argument with his comrades about 'what would happen on the morrow of the Revolution';[60] H.G. Wells, by comparison with the other planet, physically identical with ours, where his lecturer and botanist inexplicably find

59 *Reasons and Persons* (Oxford, 1985).

60 *News From Nowhere*, p. 43.

themselves after descending from the Alps; Thomas Campanella, by comparison with the City of the Sun.[61] In general, a utopian political intervention constructs and dramatises a model of an ideal alternative to our own arrangements, and thereby criticises those arrangements.

The second major feature of utopias which I want to emphasise is the *expansion of imagination*. Clearly, a utopist exercises imagination in inventing and picturing her ideal, but what I want to point out is that one typical purpose of utopias is to expand the political imaginations of their readers. That is, to attack our acceptance of the here and now as inevitable, inescapable and as good as we can get: 'Things in the past could not have worked out any differently; having got here, we cannot get away; and this is as good as things will get.' In this explicit form, it should be clear how strong and strange this assumption is, but it is none the less widespread. Not all utopias are intended to describe real possibilities; but some are, and one of their purposes is to assert and defend the possibility of better alternatives to what we have now.

We are contained in and to some extent constructed by our local circumstances and ways of thinking, and it is therefore easy to believe that nothing could be much different. There are several ways in which we might attack this belief. One is to show that what we have here and now has a history: that things were not always like this, and that our arrangements were preceded by other social forms. Utopias use another tactic. They expand the political imaginations of their readers by giving an account of a better life somewhere else (in place or time), and by defending its possibility. They are intended to show that current arrangements, far from being obvious, are startling and unlikely; and that, far from being the best we can expect, they are worse than imaginable alternatives. False assumptions about the limited possibilities of human sociability can stand in the way of movement towards a better way of life: Kropotkin believed that the claim that human limitations prevent the realisation of communism did so, for instance.[62] So, the expansion of political imagination may have a revolutionary potential of its own. It has been argued by Miguel Abensour that part of the point of William Morris's utopianism (and, by extension, of many utopias) is the 'education of desire'.[63] A utopia can crack open the imaginations of its readers, and thereby not only show that what was thought impossible is possible, but also be a first step towards its realisation.

For this attempt at the transformation of imagination to be successful, the possibility of utopia must be defended rather than merely asserted, and that can be done in many different ways. For example: More initially asserts the possibility of the Utopians' social form by having Hythloday say that they are no more intelligent than us: 'As a matter of fact, I believe we surpass them in natural intelligence, but

61 *The City of the Sun*, in Henry Morley (ed.), *Ideal Commonwealths* (London, 1889), pp. 217–63.

62 See Chapter 1.

63 As translated by Thompson, *William Morris*, p. 793.

they leave us far behind in their diligence and zeal to learn.'[64] The suggestion is that, since the Utopians have no special advantage over us, and started, as it were, in the same place as we did, we could have done, and still could do, what they have done with the endowments we share. The difference between us and the Utopians is not that they are of a different and better natural kind from us, but that they have invented better ways of living together, and 'what ingenuity has discovered or chance hit upon could have turned up just as well in one place as the other.'[65] Utopians are humans, not angels; Utopia is a place on Earth, not in heaven; we can do as well as the Utopians.

This way of defending the possibility of utopia for us, by grounding it on shared nature and capacities, is common to many utopias. They need not be set literally on Earth. Wells's utopia is set on a planet 'out beyond Sirius, far in the deeps of space, beyond the flight of a cannon-ball flying for a billion years', but that planet is completely Earth-like: 'the same continents, the same islands, the same oceans and seas, another Fuji-Yama is beautiful there dominating another Yokohama',[66] and its inhabitants are only humans who have done better than us at creating a common life for themselves. Again, the implication is that if these familiar people, in this familiar place, can do so well, then so can we. Utopias are typically far away in terms of distance, but close in terms of who lives there. This does not preclude, indeed often implies, that their inhabitants have built better selves for themselves than we have; but they built out of the same materials.

The defence of these possibilities is rarely explicit in utopias, but utopists often describe people like us, in a place like our place, successfully creating an ideal social form, at least in the minimal sense of one better than ours. The intended implication of this display is the real possibility of that ideal society, grounded on a human nature which we share with its inhabitants. Showing other people acting in ways which are not completely alien to our endowments and capacities, but which are involved in, and give rise to a better life than ours, implicitly defends the possibility of that life.

We can now say of utopias that they are typically political interventions intended not only to criticise here and now, but to assert and defend the possibility of better alternatives to here and now. The expected response to a utopia is not just to say 'that sounds wonderful', but to change one's beliefs about what is really possible for us: that is, to expand one's political imagination. However, this second purpose is in tension with the critical purpose of utopias. Utopias typically enact a broad external criticism by comparison with an imaginary ideal social form. This can be polemically effective, just because the comparison can be so extreme: an imaginary ideal can be designed precisely to foreground what is thought wrong with our current circumstances, and to make them look unpalatable by contrast. However, the defence of possibility which is also typical of utopias depends for its plausibility on realism, at least about the shared nature of humans, and the messy reality of that nature is

64 More, *Utopia*, pp. 29–30.

65 Ibid., p. 29.

66 Wells, *A Modern Utopia*, p. 318.

unlikely to throw up neat ideals for comparison unless it is seriously misdescribed. It appears that there is a tension at the heart of utopianism: its purposes pull in opposite directions. Criticism pulls us towards the construction of imaginary ideals, the better to contrast with our own arrangements; the expansion of political imagination, towards realistic description of human life and nature. This is a problem to which I shall return in later chapters.

I have so far described two major features typical of utopias and utopianism. I now want to consider a third, their rhetorical form. Unlike many other kinds of political intervention – manifestos, monographs in political philosophy, speeches – utopias are typically stories. That is, they are both narrative and (openly) fictional. By 'narrative', I mean structured by a plot (even if it is rudimentary: a character finds herself in a strange place, meets friendly natives, is shown around, and comes home to tell us) and around characters (even if they are also rudimentary), as opposed to being structured, for instance, by an analytic division of subject matter. By 'fictional', I mean that their narratives are literally false, known to be false by their authors, and paradigmatically intended to be known to be false by their readers.[67]

Utopian stories are often structured, as already noted, by the visit of a traveller or travellers from the author's world to the utopia. In More, Campanella and Bacon, who were all influenced by contemporary real-world journeys and discoveries, this traveller is an explorer and sailor.[68] In Morris and Wells, someone who finds himself transported, without explanation, to the utopia. This plot is a useful device for describing the utopia, since the traveller, a stranger, can be shown things and have things explained which a local would find obvious or uninteresting. The stranger is the reader's representative in utopia, and as 'one of us', is used to focus attention on what we find interesting. The traveller form is also a dramatisation of criticism. By juxtaposing the utopia with someone strange to it but familiar to us, the author emphasises the comparison between us and them and between here and there, and thereby emphasises the criticism which that comparison is intended to make. The criticism is further emphasised by the return of the traveller to tell us what she has seen. Her travel and return typically frame utopian stories: she is our representative there, and then the representative of the ideal which *there* represents when she comes home.

---

67 I say only *paradigmatically* intended to be known to be false, because there is room for play, and utopists often have played, with presenting fiction as fact. More scattered his *Utopia* with coded indications that his story is not true (the river running through the main Utopian city, for instance, is called 'Anyder', which means 'no water') but convinced many of his contemporaries, and probably enjoyed the joke. Utopists are not alone in playing with fiction-as-fact: the Coen brothers, for instance, prefaced their film *Fargo* (1996) with the statement 'This is a true story.' It is not, and the Coens later said that the truth-claim, which appears in the screenplay, was part of the fiction.

68 Travel-narratives in early modern utopias are often reminiscent of those collected in the sixteenth century by Richard Hakluyt, *Voyages and Discoveries* [*The Principle Navigations, Voyages, Traffiques and Discoveries of the English Nation*], ed. Jack Beeching (London, 1972).

Not all utopias use this device. In Le Guin's *Always Coming Home*, for instance, the main characters live in the utopia, and the narrative which structures our discovery of it is not a travelogue but a web of biography, fable and children's stories. In these cases, we take on the role of the traveller: the reader is the stranger. However, in both cases, the utopist invites us to compare here with there, and to find *here* wanting.

The device of the stranger's visit also relates to the imaginative purpose of utopias. That the stranger is able to talk and live with the utopians implies that she is not as strange to them, or they to us, as all that. The utopians are humans, not angels or aliens. That she got from here to there and back again emphasises that the utopia may be physically far away, but is also close to us. Utopia is in this universe, not heaven. Where the traveller device is not used, and we are the strangers, we are typically encouraged to the same conclusions by identification with the viewpoint character or characters. Le Guin's Stone Telling, Pandora and others in *Always Coming Home* are strange people, but ones with whom we can come to empathise.

Whatever its particular plot, the fact that a utopia is introduced to us in a story, not an analysis, can be rhetorically powerful. A story requires concrete and small elements as well as the general ones on which a political theory, for instance, would focus. The traveller or viewpoint character is shown living day to day in utopia, and so encounters not only justice but the judge; not only economics but the sounds and smells of a market; not only the necessity of producing clothes, but 'a brown leather belt around his waist, and I noticed that its clasp was of damascened steel beautifully wrought'.[69] The concreteness which is required and encouraged by the story form can be persuasive in furthering both the critical and the imaginative purposes of utopias.

Despite its rhetorical advantages, I do not intend to emulate this feature of utopianism. I shall develop my utopia in another direction, following the final feature that I want to emphasise in utopias: *construction*. A utopist constructs her ideal out of elements derived from imagination, contemporary and historical example, and other texts including other utopias. The demands of presenting that construction are in tension with the demands of storytelling: the first is structured by balance, mutual support, logical consistency and (the illusion of) completeness; the second, by character and plot development. This tension is most apparent, perhaps, in *Utopia*. More's narrative Book One tells the story of the meeting and conversation between More, his friend Peter Giles and the Portuguese traveller Raphael Hythloday, in Antwerp. It is dramatic and filled with incidental and particular detail. His constructive Book Two describes the island of Utopia: its geography, cities, laws, history and people. This Book is filled with descriptions of types rather than particulars: slaves, wrongdoers, infants, householders, cities, clothing, syphogrants and tanibors.[70] Activity is ritualistic, rather than the product of individual character.[71] The whole

69 Morris, *News From Nowhere*, p. 47.

70 The last two are types of elected official.

71 The point is Northrop Frye's: 'Varieties of Literary Utopia', in More, *Utopia*, pp. 205–11.

has the interest of a role-playing game background rather than of a novel, in being satisfyingly complete and well-balanced, but static. As that last point implies, it is also more exciting to read than descriptions of imaginary legal procedures, for instance, might be expected to be.

This last typical feature of utopias raises a last objection: the utopian construction looks worryingly like a blueprint for society, intended to be dictatorially and violently imposed. It looks like this because it is presented as coming from outside, because it differs radically from the society it is presented to, and because the device of the returned traveller apparently dramatises the attempt of one person to impose her vision on everyone else. This objection is powerfully made by Karl Popper. He attacks 'utopian engineering',[72] which he defines as a view about rationality in action, and especially action for social and political goals. According to this view, an actor must have a known end (a blueprint, ideal or utopian construction), must choose means according to that end, and must not act until the end is fully worked out, on pain of being irrational. Popper prefers 'piecemeal engineering', which requires the political actor to 'adopt the method of searching for, and fighting against, the greatest and most urgent evils of society, rather than searching for, and fighting for, its greatest ultimate good'.[73] His argument for this strategy and against utopian engineering is that the latter will lead to an 'intolerable increase in human suffering',[74] to totalitarian dictatorship, and to a brutal process of 'canvas-cleaning'.[75] The utopian politician must 'eradicate the existing institutions and traditions. He must purify, purge, expel, banish, and kill.'[76] The utopist's attempt to state an ideal, and her advocacy of action for its realisation, will have disastrous consequences if anyone listens to her. It is worth noting just how different this objection is from others I have considered: the claim here is not that utopias lack means, but that they advocate unacceptable means; not that they are unrealisable, but that their (attempted) realisation would be too costly.

Some utopias certainly are *radical* in this way. Like other radical texts, they advocate the total destruction of the old, to leave the stage clear for building the new. Some advocate the forcible imposition of a political and social blueprint on that stage. However, these two kinds of advocacy are not necessarily linked: one could advocate destruction to leave space for natural growth rather than imposition; or one could think, like Marx, that both destruction and subsequent rebuilding are parts of a single inevitable process, and that an attempt at imposition would therefore be pointless, because ineffective (this is part of Marx's objection to utopian socialism). More importantly, neither kind of advocacy is a universal feature of utopias. If Popper's claim is that, as a matter of psychological or historical fact,

---

72 Karl Popper, *The Open Society and its Enemies* (2 vols, London, 1966), vol. 1, p. 157.

73 Ibid., p. 158.

74 Ibid.

75 Ibid., p. 166.

76 Ibid.

the construction of ideals is always linked to radical canvas-clearing means, then he is mistaken. William Godwin, for instance, constructs an ideal and explicitly argues that progress towards it should and will be gradual and by the improvement of individual judgement, not revolutionary.[77] Popper could instead be arguing that the construction of ideals *entails* such means whether their authors realise it or not, and that theories like Godwin's are therefore self-contradictory. However, if this is his claim, then it is unargued. Popper's association of utopian engineering with canvas-clearing proceeds by assertion and historical example, not by deduction. And in general, no such entailment could hold: one could follow Rawls and construct an ideal involving the priority of the right over the good, which requires that certain means, including the violent means which Popper rejects, are always impermissible regardless of their predicted good consequences. It is possible to imagine someone irrationally attempting to impose this ideal by violence; but it is not possible to make a theory advocating both such an ideal and such right-violating means coherent, and there can therefore be no entailment from ideal-construction to right-violating, canvas-clearing means.

Although Popper presents his attack on utopian engineering as an attack on a theory about rational action, his actual target is not that theory, but rather the radicalism or romanticism he associates with it. That is, he objects to the *content* of *particular* utopian ideals, not to their general *form*. Even if he is right to do so, that is not a refutation of utopianism, but of those particular political ideals.

In this section I have described utopianism as political intervention carried out by writing and publishing utopias, which are texts making use of a historically developed vocabulary of tropes and tactics, and which therefore cannot be defined by any one particular purpose or ideal. I then distinguished four typical (but not necessarily universal) features of utopianism: criticism, imagination, storytelling and construction. I shall return to them, consider past anarchists' enactment of them, and explain my own use of them in subsequent chapters. Of course, there are other ways than utopianism of criticising here and now, expanding political imagination, telling stories and constructing ideals. I have not argued for this particular way of doing things to the exclusion of these other ways. I advocate not the replacement of political philosophy, speeches, manifestos or arguments in pubs with utopias, but the acceptance and use of utopias as part of our repertoire of modes of political intervention.

I shall end this chapter by anticipating my conclusion and briefly setting out the utopian ideal I argue for in this book. Kropotkin defines the term 'anarchism' in his *Encyclopaedia Britannica* article as follows. Anarchism is:

> … a principle or theory of life and conduct under which society is conceived without government – harmony in such a society being obtained, not by submission to law, or by obedience to any authority, but by free agreements concluded between the various groups, territorial and professional, freely constituted for the sake of production and

77 *Enquiry Concerning Political Justice and its Influence on Modern Morals and Happiness*, ed. Isaac Kramnick (3rd edn, London, 1985). See Chapter 1.

> consumption, as also for the satisfaction of the infinite variety of needs and aspirations of a civilized being. In a society developed along these lines, the voluntary associations which already now begin to cover all the fields of human activity would take a still greater extension so as to substitute themselves for the state in all its functions. They would represent an interwoven network, composed of an infinite variety of groups and federations of all sizes and degrees, local, regional, national and international – temporary or more or less permanent – for all possible purposes: production, consumption and exchange, communications, sanitary arrangements, education, mutual protection, defence of the territory, and so on; and, on the other side, for the satisfaction of an ever-increasing number of scientific, artistic, literary and sociable needs.[78]

I have given reasons above to be suspicious of Kropotkin's confidence that anarchism can be summed up this or any other way, but his account is a good beginning description of my anarchist utopia. It consists of multiple interwoven networks of social humans pursuing their huge variety of interests, from the most basic in making a living to the most subtle in art, science and communication. There is no domination within or between these networks. Coordination between individuals and networks is achieved, not by an attempt to unify them into a single territorial hierarchy, but by federalisation and agreement. Conflict is not absent, but is limited and resolved by mediation and negotiation.

Much of this sketch is at present unclear: it will be examined and further characterised in subsequent chapters. All I intend, by giving it here, is to indicate where we are going. I must also indicate how we are going to get there: in Chapter 1, I correct one deeply entrenched misreading of anarchism, which takes anarchists to be primitivists. I explain this mistake, and discover in the explanation a common anarchist rhetorical trope of critical and exemplary juxtaposition of social forms. This trope suggests a form of utopian argument, which I go on to use to prove my main thesis, that my anarchist utopia is possible. However, there is a serious problem with that argument-form, and its solution requires some theoretical apparatus. Chapter 2 provides it by developing and arguing for a theory of human sociability. Chapter 3 puts that theory to use in displaying some of the non-anarchic ways of life – states and slavery – which humans can create for themselves. Chapter 4 does the same with examples displaying the possibility of anarchic alternatives. Finally, a Conclusion draws my argument together, constructs a possible utopia out of these fragments, and considers its implications.

---

78 Kropotkin, 'Anarchism', pp. 233–4.

## Chapter 1

# Primitivism

Anarchists are commonly supposed to hold deeply optimistic views about human nature, and to be nostalgic for 'primitive' (as opposed to 'civilised') societies: 'Traditionally, anarchists are seen to possess an optimistic conception of human nature, an optimism essential to the success of their vision of a stateless society.'[1] According to James Joll, 'The fundamental idea that man is by nature good and that it is institutions that corrupt him remains the basis of all anarchist thought.'[2] For him, anarchists share the mental pathology of heretical Christians who demand and expect 'a return to the Golden Age of the Garden of Eden before the Fall'.[3] Roger Scruton claims that 'typical anarchist beliefs' include that 'men are benign by nature and corrupted by government.'[4] Irving Horowitz, that 'Anarchism has as its theoretical underpinning an idealization of natural man in contrast and in opposition to civilized man … What is offered is a belief in "natural man" as more fundamental and historically prior to "political man".'[5] Norman Barry, that 'Communitarian [as opposed to libertarian] anarchism depends upon an optimistic view of human nature as essentially benign and cooperative.'[6] These examples could easily be continued; but, as I argue here, they are false generalisations.

Claims that anarchists think like this have often been used to ground criticism. Robert Dahl, for instance, offers as 'a critique of anarchism' the thought that 'While some romantic anarchists may imagine our returning to the tiny autonomous groups of some preliterate societies, short of a cataclysm that no sane person wants, a return to the infancy of the species looks to be impossible or, if not impossible, highly undesirable.'[7] Benjamin Barber attacks anarchists because 'their view of actual men is wildly romanticized. Hunger, greed, ambition, avarice, the will to power, to glory, to honour, and to security which have played some role in all traditional ethnologies find no place in the anarchist portrait of man.'[8] Barber directs this attack specifically against twentieth-century American anarchists like Abbie Hoffman, but is explicit

---

1 David Morland, *Demanding the Impossible? Human nature and politics in nineteenth-century social anarchism* (London, 1997), p. vii.

2 Joll, *The Anarchists*, p. 16.

3 Ibid., p. 6.

4 *A Dictionary of Political Thought* (London, 1983), p. 15.

5 Horowitz, *The Anarchists*, p. 16.

6 'Anarchism' in Nigel Ashford and Stephen Davies (eds), *A Dictionary of Conservative and Libertarian Thought* (London, 1991), pp. 4–7, p. 5.

7 *Democracy and its Critics* (New Haven, 1989), pp. 43, 46.

8 *Superman and Common Men* (Harmondsworth, 1972), p. 18.

that he believes the tradition from Godwin onwards to be implicated in this wild romanticism. His evidence in fact consists of unsupported claims about the elitist psychology of individual anarchists and a few, out-of-context quotations. Similarly, the only support Horowitz can give for his characterisation (quoted above) comes from Denis Diderot, who, in Horowitz's own words, 'advocated a parliamentary monarchism in which representation would be elected by the propertied classes',[9] and was therefore clearly not an anarchist. In the face of evidence this weak, it is tempting to dismiss the whole line of attack as a self-sustaining polemic.

There are, however, two forms of this criticism which require a more detailed response. I call them accusations of 'primitivism', for convenience and because each can be related to one of the various meanings of 'primitive'. This chapter will display, analyse and refute two important forms of the assertion that anarchists are primitivists.

'Primitive' is a complex term. It can mean unsophisticated, savage, stupid or childish; pure; original or primary; low or simple; an early stage of evolution or progress; a relic or survival in a world that has moved on. It can refer to people or societies without our technology or without institutions like our states. 'Primitive' stands in some complex relation to a cluster of terms including 'savage', 'native', 'aboriginal', 'undeveloped', 'unevolved' and 'prehistoric', and also to opposing terms like 'civilised', 'developed', 'complex', 'sophisticated' and 'modern'. We should note the term's ideological weight: calling societies or people 'primitive' has often been involved in, and even stood in for, justifications of marginalisation, oppression and extermination. It can also be used in a less extreme but still polemical way, to indicate a comfortable value judgement: 'we are civilised, they are primitive.'

The two meanings of the term which relate to the criticisms of anarchism under discussion here are primitive as *pure*, and primitive as *original* or *primary*. The criticisms which involve these meanings are, respectively: the claim that anarchism depends on an unrealistic notion of uncorrupted human nature ('human nature primitivism'), and the claim that anarchists are nostalgic for a mythical golden age ('golden age primitivism'). I shall define and respond to each in turn.

## Anarchism and Human Nature Primitivism

Ideas of human nature are various, important and contested. The range of such ideas includes, for instance, Christian, liberal, conservative individualist, Rousseauian, Darwinian, Freudian, existentialist and feminist human natures.[10] They are important because so much can depend on them. For an individual, an answer to the question about the human nature she shares will shape how she understands the meaning of her life, what she ought to do, what she might be able to achieve or become, and

9 Horowitz, *The Anarchists*, pp. 65–6.

10 See Norman Chaney, *Six Images of Human Nature* (Englewood Cliffs, NJ, 1990); Peter Loptson, *Theories of Human Nature* (Peterborough, Ontario, 1995); Leslie Stevenson and David L. Haberman, *Ten Theories of Human Nature* (3rd edn, New York, 1998).

what limits she must respect or accept. For groups, it will shape our understanding of our history, the changes we ought to make, and the vision of the future we can reasonably hope to realise. That is, ideas of human nature are important because very different, and often very powerful individual and political aims and understandings can be based on different accounts of human nature. They are also important because claims about human nature are often an effective means of criticism, both of current arrangements and of schemes for their reform. Current arrangements can be condemned as corrupting or not living up to human nature; suggested reforms, as not taking human nature into account. Ideas of human nature are contested because of both their variety and their importance. Human nature is the locus of a continuing argument, both in its own right and as a battleground of ideologies which involve particular claims about it. Existentialist and other negative claims about human nature (at the limit, that there is no such thing) can also perform these functions of grounding aims and analysis, and of criticism.

Historically and typically, an idea of human nature is a set of claims that a specified character is *real* or permanent or transhistorically present in humans; is *shared* by all humans; *distinguishes* humans by kind, and not merely by degree, from the rest of the world, and especially from (other) animals; is *separate* from the distortion and masking which can be created by current circumstances; and stands as a moral, social or political *norm* for all humans. These five components are not necessarily connected. What is real or permanent, rather than merely apparent or transitory, in some one human might not be shared by all or only other humans. What is shared by all humans might not have any normative force. What distinguishes humans from other animals might *be* the distortion caused by current circumstances. However, these five claims do form a group which repeatedly appears in the history of thought. Different ideas of human nature make this set of claims about different characters; negative ideas deny that some or all of them are true of any character. Some ideas have both positive and negative elements: some post-Darwinian thinkers, for instance, have made the negative claim that humans are *not* distinct in kind from other animals, because all evolved by natural selection, and the positive claim that what is shared by all such creatures is being vehicles for 'selfish genes'.[11]

If anarchists are human nature primitivists, then their shared idea of human nature must be that what is real, permanent, ahistorical, shared, distinguishing, separate and normative in humans is a nature which is wholly pure and good. That is, which is virtuous, benevolent, altruistic, reasonable, peaceable, cooperative or loving (or some combination of some or all of these), and not vicious, malicious, selfish, irrational, aggressive or hateful. Even if this is the anarchist idea of human nature, that is a criticism of anarchism only if it is inaccurate, and its inaccuracy is such as to make it unusable as a norm. The second criterion is needed because the fact that a claim or story is literally false does not, by itself, disqualify it as morally useful: it need not be the case that someone called Raphael Hythloday really visited a place called Utopia for the idea of Utopia to be a standard of criticism for the real world.

11 See Richard Dawkins, *The Selfish Gene* (Oxford, 1989).

Similarly, that an account of human nature is literally false does not necessarily mean that it is unusable.

There are three ways of defending anarchism against the critical accusation of human nature primitivism: to show that anarchists do not, in fact, share that idea of human nature; to show that the idea is true; or, to show that although it is false, it is still useful as a moral, social or political norm. I take the first path, and defeat the accusation by counter-example.

Some anarchists think it enough, when stating their views on human nature, to distance themselves from other anarchists who, they suppose, *do* hold the primitivist view. Jacques Ellul, for instance, distinguishes himself from (what he believes is) mainstream anarchism on two grounds: he is a Christian, and he does not believe that 'an anarchist society – with no state, no organisation, no hierarchy, and no authorities – is possible'.[12] This 'anarchist vision or hope of a society with neither authorities nor institutions rests on the twofold conviction that people are by nature good and that society alone is corrupt',[13] but Ellul does not accept that primitivist account of human nature. He thinks that the 'anarchist fight'[14] is worth fighting, but that its goal is unreachable, because of flawed (that is, fallen) human nature. Ellul shows that his Christianity distinguishes him from other anarchists with a concrete example. Guy Debord and his situationist comrades refused to let him join them: 'since I was a Christian I could not belong to their movement.'[15] But in the case of Ellul's view of human nature, the parallel evidence is unsupported attribution of the view with which he disagrees to the un-named 'true anarchist'.[16]

Other anarchists, who perhaps wrote before the accusation of human nature primitivism became widespread, simply state quite different ideas of human nature. The accusation is the generalisation that anarchists, as a group, share and use the particular idea of human nature defined above. One counter-example is enough to falsify a generalisation, but to make the point more strongly, and for further reasons which will become clear below, I give two: the ideas of human nature in the work of Godwin and of Kropotkin.

William Godwin was born in 1756, brought up a Calvinist, and initially followed his father and grandfather into Independent ministry. During periods as minister to congregations in Ware, Stowmarket and Beaconsfield, he lost or transformed his faith. He moved to London in 1782, and spent the rest of his life there, supporting himself by writing novels, plays, political journalism and philosophy. He married Mary Wollstonecraft in 1797, when she became pregnant (they had been openly a couple, although maintaining separate households, for some years). She died a few days after giving birth to their daughter Mary, later Mary Shelley. Godwin lived until

12 *Anarchy and Christianity*, trans. G.W. Bromiley (Grand Rapids, MI, 1991), p. 19.

13 Ibid.

14 Ibid.

15 Ibid., p. 3.

16 Ibid., p. 19.

1836, and gradually modified or repudiated much of the radicalism of his earlier work.[17]

*Enquiry Concerning Political Justice*, published in 1793, made Godwin first famous, then caricatured, and finally, in combination with his frank memoirs of Wollstonecraft, reviled. It presents several problems of interpretation, the first of which is how to understand its project and claims as a whole. It can be read as utilitarian; as extreme rationalist; as the effort of a lapsed Christian to restate his faith in secular terms; as a celebration of the French Revolution; as an abstract mirroring of working-class social radicalism; as a product of the enthusiasm of a recent convert to Enlightenment atheism and determinism; as the philosophical expression of beliefs current in the intellectual and social circles of late eighteenth-century Rational Dissenters; and as the gospel of anarchism.[18] I shall not attempt a resolution of these tensions: what is important here is the idea of human nature which the book asserts.

Godwin's idea of human nature is twofold, and essentially critical. He makes two claims, and the point of each is that it refutes an objection to his prescription for and prediction of future human sociability. 'I shall attempt to prove two things: first, that the actions and dispositions of mankind are the offspring of circumstances and events, and not of any original determination that they bring into the world; and, secondly, that the great stream of our voluntary actions essentially depends, not upon the direct and immediate impulses of sense, but upon the decisions of the understanding.'[19] That is, first, 'the characters of men originate in their external circumstances',[20] and not in any innate characteristics; secondly, 'our prospects of melioration depend on the progress of enquiry and the general advancement of knowledge.'[21] Knowledge is motivating;[22] future knowledge about human good will motivate people to act

17 William Godwin, *Collected Novels and Memoirs of William Godwin*, vol. 1: *Memoirs*, ed. Mark Philp (London, 1992). Peter Marshall, *William Godwin* (New Haven, CT, 1984) and Editor's Introduction to William Godwin, *The Anarchist Writings of William Godwin* (London, 1986), pp. 9–48. William St. Clair, *The Godwins and the Shelleys: The biography of a family* (London, 1989). George Woodcock, *William Godwin: A biographical study* (London, 1946).

18 For discussion of these readings, see Mark Philp, *Godwin's Political Justice* (Ithaca, NY, 1986), especially Part One. The last interpretation, with its cultish overtones, has been popular amongst non-anarchist historians of anarchism: Isaac Kramnick, for instance, calls Godwin the 'prophet' of anarchism (Editor's Introduction to Godwin, *Enquiry Concerning Political Justice*, pp. 7–54, p. 7).

19 Godwin, *Enquiry Concerning Political Justice*, p. 97.

20 Ibid., p. 96.

21 Ibid., p. 116.

22 John Stuart Mill and his father James seem to have held a similar anti-Humean view that judgements about the truth, not just desires, can motivate. For them as for Godwin, this had the consequence of giving education and free discussion immense political import, since what people learned would give rise to action (see especially John Stuart Mill, *Autobiography*, ed. Harold J. Laski (London, 1926) and *On Liberty* in John Gray (ed.), *On Liberty and Other Essays* (Oxford, 1991), pp. 5–128). Thomas Scanlon's argument that reasons rather than desires are motivationally basic, in *What We Owe to Each Other* (Cambridge, MA, 1998),

for it; and there are no bars to the gradual creation of people capable of this radical transformation of human life. This means that through progress in moral, social and political science, through the exercise of individual judgement, and through the consequent transformation of human thinking and political institutions, Godwin's anarchic utopia is realisable.

That this claim is perhaps unconvincing is irrelevant here. According to the accusation of human nature primitivism, anarchists are supposed to hold a particular idea of human nature, but Godwin's stated idea is utterly unlike it. For him, the only things which are permanent and shared in humans are the absence of innate limitation and the possibility of true and motivating judgement. This idea of human nature does work morally and politically only in that it supports the practical possibility of a utopia of rational, sincere, mutually censorious neighbours always working without partiality, but using their own individual judgement, for universal human flourishing. That utopia does further work in providing both a target for social change, and a critical comparison with our current arrangements. Godwin not only makes no assertions about the innate purity and goodness of humans, but explicitly denies that such a claim could be true.[23] For Godwin, pure humans exist only in the imagined future, and only then as a result of the transformation of current humans, and their institutions, by the progress of knowledge. Anarchists are supposed to be human nature primitivists: but the Godwin of *Enquiry*, at least, was not. We have our first counter-example.

Peter Kropotkin was a younger son of the Russian aristocracy born in 1842. A geographer, naturalist and mathematician, at nineteen a personal page of Tsar Alexander II, and in the 1860s a military administrator in Siberia, he repudiated his privilege and scientific career to become a revolutionary, political exile and anarchist writer. The major influences on his life and theory were his older brother Alexander; the serfs on his family estate; the socialist movements, and in particular the Bakuninite Jura Federation, which he encountered in Europe; and, most importantly here, Charles Darwin, as understood through the Russian evolutionist tradition which rejected Darwin's Malthusian metaphor of individualist struggle.[24]

Kropotkin approaches the idea of human nature in two main ways: as a defender of the possibility of anarchism and communism, and as a Darwinian naturalist.

---

is a more recent contribution to this philosophic radical tradition. I hope to pursue this topic elsewhere.

23 Godwin later changed his mind about this conclusion, and does assert innate human goodness in the 1831 essay *Thoughts on Man* (in Mark Philp (ed.), *Political and Philosophical Writings of William Godwin* (6 vols, London, 1996), vol. 6, pp. 31–292). Even there, however, he emphasises the changeability of humans and our *potential* for good, grounded on the proper and private exercise of shared rational capacity.

24 Paul Avrich, 'Kropotkin's Ethical Anarchism' in *Anarchist Portraits* (Princeton, NJ, 1988), pp. 53–78. Peter Kropotkin, *Memoirs of a Revolutionist* (2 vols, London, 1899). Martin A. Miller, *Kropotkin* (Chicago, IL, 1976). Daniel P. Todes, 'Darwin's Malthusian Metaphor and Russian Evolutionary Thought, 1859–1917' in *Isis* vol. 78 (1987): 537–51. George Woodcock and Ivan Avakumović, *Peter Kropotkin: From Prince to Rebel* (Montréal, 1990).

In the first case, Kropotkin notes that it is a common objection to 'communism, and socialism altogether' that:

> the idea is so old, and yet it has never been realised. Schemes of ideal states haunted the thinkers of ancient Greece; later on, the early Christians joined in communist groups; centuries later, large communist brotherhoods came into existence during the reform movement. Then, the same ideals were revived during the great English and French Revolutions; and finally, quite lately, in 1848, a revolution, inspired to a great extent with socialist ideals, took place in France. 'And yet, you see,' we are told, 'how far away is the realization of your schemes. Don't you think that there is some fundamental error in your understanding of human nature and its needs?'[25]

We might expect a human nature primitivist to respond to this pseudo-historical derivation of an idea of human nature – the idea that it renders us incapable of communism – with a positive counter-assertion. We might expect an *anarchist* primitivist to reply that real, pure and good human nature, which is capable of anarchist communism, has been corrupted and thwarted by state reaction.

Kropotkin does nothing of the sort. Instead, he suggests a more careful reading of history, which leads him to argue that 'hundreds of millions of men have succeeded in maintaining amongst themselves, in their village communities, for many hundreds of years, one of the main elements of socialism – the common ownership of the chief instrument of production, the land, and the apportionment of the same according to the labour capacities of the different families.'[26] The historical evidence does give partial support to the possibility of communism, and certainly does not support the sweeping anti-communist generalisation about human nature and potential. So, 'all we are authorized to conclude is, that mankind has not yet found the proper form for combining, on communistic principles, agriculture with a suddenly developed industry and a rapidly growing international trade.'[27] Far from asserting any permanent characteristic of human nature, Kropotkin tentatively interprets the empirical evidence of human history. His interest is not in such permanent characteristics at all, but in some temporary, changing and potentially changeable features of human social activity, as they have appeared. Human nature appears only in a criticism of communism, in order that Kropotkin can refute it. This concern with history, and with the tentative conclusions that can be drawn from it, runs throughout his work.

In the second case, Kropotkin approaches human nature as a naturalist and Darwinian. In his theory, humans are seen as part of the wider natural world, and in *Mutual Aid*,[28] he attempts to show that cooperation within species, including the

---

25 Peter Kropotkin, *The Conquest of Bread and other writings*, ed. M.S. Shatz (Cambridge, 1995), p. 4.

26 Ibid.

27 Ibid., p. 5.

28 Peter Kropotkin, *Mutual Aid: A factor of evolution* (Montréal, 1989). *Mutual Aid* was first published in book form in 1902, after appearing as a series of articles in the periodical *Nineteenth Century*.

human species, is a major factor in evolution (not, as has sometimes been asserted of him, the only factor: Kropotkin wanted to correct Thomas Huxley's over-emphasis of a gladiatorial struggle for existence). The details and force of this argument are not relevant here. What is important is that, far from asserting a permanent and pure human nature, Kropotkin uses detailed empirical evidence of change and its causes to derive tentative conclusions about current humans and their social characteristics. He presents humans as part of the wider and changing system of nature.[29] In an evolutionary world, there can be no human nature in the strong sense defined above, because *nothing* is permanent or transhistorically present in humans. Kropotkin is interested in what humans and other creatures have come to be, and how. His central conclusion is that humans, as they have evolved, have tendencies both to egalitarianism and mutual aid (good characteristics, for him) and to hierarchy and selfishness (bad ones). That is, that we are not wholly pure and good, but have both good and bad tendencies, 'now the one and now the other taking the upper hand at different periods of history'.[30]

Kropotkin is not particularly interested in permanent, shared, distinguishing, separate and normative characteristics in either of his approaches to human nature. Nor does he assert that human nature is pure and good. He investigates the nature of current humans as an empirical fact and as a moment in a long transformation, discoverable by research in biology and history, and admitting only tentative conclusions. We have our second counter-example to the generalisation that anarchists are human nature primitivists: Kropotkin emphatically was not.

It is unlikely that partisans of the accusation of human nature primitivism literally and formally mean the generalisation 'all anarchists are human nature primitivists'. If any do, they have been proved wrong twice over, unless they are prepared to argue that neither Godwin nor Kropotkin was really an anarchist. If, as is more likely, they mean only that most anarchists are human nature primitivists, or that anarchism tends to partake of such primitivism, then the formal way to test their claim would be to go through all anarchists, testing each. However, given the problem of identification discussed in the Introduction, how are we to list 'all anarchists'? The two counter-examples given above must, at least, throw doubt on the accusation. Godwin and Kropotkin are widely recognised to be anarchists, and among the most important of anarchism's theorists. If they were not human nature primitivists, stronger evidence than I can find will be needed to make the general accusation, and derived criticisms, stick. In the absence of that further evidence, we must accept that anarchists are not, in general, human nature primitivists.

---

29 And, in typical nineteenth-century evolutionist's terms, as high in a hierarchy of development. See Chapter 2.

30 Kropotkin, 'Anarchism', p. 236.

## Anarchism and Golden Age Primitivism

Golden age primitivism centres on a value claim about a picture of human historical development. In this picture, humanity or human society is envisioned as having changed from some primary, natural or foundational state to some elaborated or artificial one. This change is understood as both qualitative and quantitative. The qualitative change, at its simplest, is from 'primitive' to 'civilised', but has been further divided in various ways. The quantitative change is typically measured on a scale of complexity (from simple to complex) or of height (from lower to higher forms), or both. I consider this kind of 'evolutionary' picture further in Chapter 2, but for the moment, we should note that such pictures are common and used for a wide variety of purposes. Various kinds of evidence can be used to characterise the primary state, but most often the theorist will use historical and archaeological evidence about past social forms, or anthropological evidence about current social forms which are conceived as relics of the primary state, or both.

A golden age primitivist claims that 'the highest degree of excellence or happiness in man's life existed at the beginning of history.'[31] The qualitative and quantitative change was for the worse, whether thought of as gradual (the golden age lapsing into silver) or sudden (the fall and expulsion from Eden). This type of primitivism's central normative metaphors are *return* (or its tragic impossibility) and the *dismantling* or *destruction* of the elaboration which moved us away from the primary state. Its normative focus is on an ideal past. Golden age primitivism is in direct competition with theories or stories which use the same picture of history, but make the opposite value claim: the qualitative and quantitative change was for the better.

We can now see that although human nature and golden age primitivism are analytically distinct, it is possible to hold both positions, or a position involving elements of both. Apart from archaeological and anthropological evidence, another way of supporting a characterisation of a golden age is to use claims about an uncorrupted human nature, which was fully expressed before whatever elaboration produced our current arrangements occurred. Or we might support a characterisation of human nature as wholly good with claims about how humans lived in a primary, natural or undistorted state.

The possible practical results of accepting golden age primitivism are various. We might, for instance, try to return to the golden age, whether individually or collectively; or lapse into quietist nostalgia; or take the ideal as reason for bitter rejection of the current world. Whatever practical conclusions anarchists are supposed to draw from their alleged primitivism, the critics' central assertions must be that anarchists hold such an idea of a past golden age or Eden, and use the metaphors of return and dismantling or destruction; and that this idea invalidates their theories because it is false in such a way as to make it useless as a norm.

---

31 Arthur O. Lovejoy and George Boas, *Primitivism and Related Ideas in Antiquity* (New York, 1973), p. 2.

As with the accusation of human nature primitivism, there are three ways of defending anarchism against this accusation: to show that anarchists do not, in fact, share such an idea; to show that it is true; or, to show that, although false, it is still useful as a norm. And, as above, I take the first path and disprove the critics' generalisation by counter-example.

Godwin begins his scattered consideration of history by repeating the 'old observation that the history of mankind is little else than a record of crimes'.[32] If we consider the continuous war, torture, slavery and despotism which historians record, we may believe that little has changed or will change:

> An opinion has been extensively entertained "that the differences of the human species in different ages and countries, particularly so far as relates to moral principles of conduct, are extremely insignificant and trifling; that we are deceived in this respect by distance and confounded by glare; but that in reality the virtues and vices of men, collectively taken, always have remained, and of consequence," it is said, "always will remain, nearly at the same point."[33]

However, this opinion is shown to be false by 'a summary recollection of the actual history of our species',[34] which, according to Godwin, shows 'man' gradually improving 'as an intellectual being'.[35] His deduction from the conjunction of this intellectual improvement with the motivating power of knowledge of the good (discussed above) is that human *moral* improvement has kept and will keep pace with it. 'Man in his original state' was 'a being capable of impressions and knowledge to an unbounded extent, but not having as yet received the one or cultivated the other'.[36] Godwin contrasts the history of pain and oppression that he has noted with 'all that science and genius have effected',[37] and emphasises the examples of language and writing. Far from harking back to a golden age from which we have descended, Godwin pictures history as recording upward progress in knowledge and consequently in value.

The conclusion Godwin finally draws from this record of progress is that humans are 'susceptible of *perpetual* improvement'.[38] This derivation is surely invalid, but that is not the criticism we are dealing with here, and Godwin is only one of many who have made that perfectionist claim.[39] Godwin, as an anarchist, is accused of golden age primitivism, but what he actually says is that:

> There is no science that is not capable of additions; there is no art that may not be carried to a still higher perfection. If this be true of all other sciences, why not of morals? If this

32 Godwin, *Enquiry Concerning Political Justice*, p. 83.

33 Ibid., p. 156.

34 Ibid., p. 156–7.

35 Ibid., p. 157.

36 Ibid.

37 Ibid.

38 Ibid., p. 156, my emphasis.

39 See John Passmore, *The Perfectibility of Man* (3rd edn, Indianapolis, IN, 2000).

> be true of all other arts, why not of social institution? … This is the temper with which we ought to engage in the study of political truth. Let us look back, that we may profit by the experience of mankind; but let us not look back as if the wisdom of our ancestors was such as to leave no room for future improvement.[40]

That is, he gives as explicit a rejection of golden age primitivism as could be expected from someone who had not had the criticism put to him. The central normative metaphors of golden age primitivism are return and dismantling or destruction; Godwin's are (perpetual) improvement and further building. Where its normative focus is an ideal past, his is an ideal future. So, we have our first counter-example to this second sense in which anarchists are supposed to be primitivists. Godwin was no more a golden age primitivist than he was a human nature primitivist.

We have already noted Kropotkin's interest in natural and social history. In *Mutual Aid* he treats the two as continuous, and moves from mutual aid amongst animals, to 'savages', 'barbarians', and in medieval cities, to mutual aid amongst 'ourselves'. This natural and social history has a double purpose. Kropotkin intends to show that mutual aid is a factor in evolution. That is, to show that one of the things which must be taken into account in order to explain the facts of current animal and human nature, and their development, is mutual aid. According to this account, our current world cannot be explained only as the evolutionary result of ruthless individual struggle (as Huxley supposed). Secondly, Kropotkin intends to display and celebrate the successes and continuing existence of the tendency towards mutual aid, despite undeniable division, self-assertion and oppression.

Kropotkin concludes *Mutual Aid* with two claims, one general and the other more specific. The general claim is that:

> The animal species, in which individual struggle has been reduced to its narrowest limits, and the practice of mutual aid has attained the greatest development, are invariably the most numerous, the most prosperous, and the most open to further progress. The mutual protection which is obtained in this case, the possibility of attaining old age and of accumulating experience, the higher intellectual development, and the further growth of sociable habits, secure the maintenance of the species, its extension, and its further progressive evolution. The unsociable species, on the contrary, are doomed to decay.[41]

Evolution by natural selection has given rise to a tendency to mutual aid, because that tendency is adaptive, while the opposite tendency is maladaptive. The more specific claim is that:

> The periods where institutions based on the mutual-aid tendency took their greatest development were also the periods of the greatest progress in arts, industry, and science. In fact, the study of the inner life of the mediaeval city and of the ancient Greek cities reveals the fact that the combination of mutual aid, as it was practised within the guild and the Greek clan, with a large initiative which was left to the individual and the group

40 Godwin, *Enquiry Concerning Political Justice*, p. 163.

41 Kropotkin, *Mutual Aid*, p. 293.

> by means of the federative principle, gave to mankind the two greatest periods of its history – the ancient Greek city and the mediaeval city periods; while the ruin of the above institutions during the State periods of history, which followed, corresponded in both cases to a rapid decay.[42]

The expression of the mutual aid tendency has good consequences, and its eclipse by the equally real opposing tendency has bad ones, measured by human social progress and flourishing. In this second conclusion, Kropotkin certainly does claim that there have been better times than now (or rather, than the late nineteenth century). However, he does not locate these better times at the beginning of history or of a single value-gradient, either for the better or for the worse. He does not appear even to recognise the notion of a beginning to specifically *human* history, since he treats it as continuous with natural history. Instead, Kropotkin pictures history as a dialectical process between egalitarian mutual aid and hierarchical self-assertive tendencies and social forms, sometimes the one and sometimes the other gaining the upper hand. That first tendency, although now in eclipse, has not disappeared: 'Neither the crushing powers of the centralized state nor the teachings of mutual hatred and pitiless struggle … could weed out the feeling of human solidarity, deeply lodged in men's understanding and heart, because it has been nurtured by all our preceding evolution.'[43] The continuing existence of this mutual aid tendency entitles us to (cautious) optimism about the future.

Again: the central normative metaphors of golden age primitivism are return and dismantling or destruction; its focus is an ideal past. Kropotkin does not recommend return to any earlier social form, but the expression of one continuing tendency of human life over another. He does recommend dismantling one set of social forms – states and capitalism – but he wants to replace it with another, better one, not to dig down to some simple or primary foundation. His focus is a better future, not an ideal past. So, we have our final counter-example: Kropotkin was not a golden age primitivist, either.

As with my argument above against the accusation of human nature primitivism, it is unlikely that the partisans of this accusation literally and formally mean the generalisation '*all* anarchists … '. And again, my counter-examples throw doubt on, but cannot completely disprove, the weaker claim they probably do mean.

These interpretations of Godwin and Kropotkin are not intended as defences of their arguments. I have no brief here to show that either is right. All I need to show, and have shown, is that they do not hold the views attributed to them by the accusations of human nature or golden age primitivism. This must, at minimum, make us doubt that these accusations are true in general, and, I suggest, ought to make us reject them altogether. Anarchists are neither human nature nor golden age primitivists.

42 Ibid., p. 296–7.

43 Ibid., p. 292.

## Generalisations about Anarchism

In my Introduction, I sketched the variety of anarchism by noting some taxonomies, internal distinctions and generalisations, and argued that a common solution to the problem of that variety (the claim that anarchists are essentially anti-statists) fails. I have shown here that two further common generalisations also fail: anarchists are not, in general, primitivists of either of the two kinds I have identified.

I want to emphasise that these negative claims are about generalisations. I have not argued that *no* anarchist is a primitivist: anarchism is various, and some self-described anarchists may hold an idea of human nature as wholly pure and good, or admire and desire to emulate 'primitive' (primary, natural or foundational) social forms.[44] It is also open to future anarchists to do so. However, many anarchists, including two of the most important anarchist theorists, are not primitivists in either of these ways, and therefore being an anarchist does not entail being a primitivist. According to Sébastien Faure, 'There is not, and there cannot be, a libertarian *Creed* or *Catechism*.'[45] However, if we imagine for a moment that there could be, it would not include a statement of primitivist belief.

Nor would the imagined catechism include *any* particular claims about human nature. The point of giving two counter-examples to the accusation of human nature primitivism was to make the point more strongly than a single, possibly exceptional example could, but also to suggest that anarchists do not share some other, non-primitivist account of human nature. Godwin and Kropotkin not only do not share the primitivist idea, they share *no* idea of human nature. For Godwin, humans are rational and motivated by their judgement, have no innate bars to transformation through education, and perpetually improve. For Kropotkin, in contrast, humans are evolved creatures, related to the rest of the natural world, and as a result of that evolution have opposed tendencies towards different kinds of sociability. So, there is no orthodox anarchist view of human nature. Even if accepting some set of claims is necessary if one is to be an anarchist in the ordinary sense of the term, that set does not include any claim about human nature.

Similarly, the catechism would not include a particular view of the shape and moral direction of human history. For Godwin, history is a gradual upward process driven by the increase of knowledge; for Kropotkin, a dialectic of anarchic against hierarchical tendencies. Both focus more on the future than on the ideal past of the golden age primitivist, but where Godwin celebrates an inevitable and ideal future, Kropotkin merely argues for the possibility of a better one. So, again, even if an anarchist must accept some orthodox claims, they do not include a view of history. Anarchism cannot be generally characterised by particular positions on either human nature or history.

---

44 Two examples are Fredy Perlman and John Zerzan: see John Moore, *A Primitivism Primer*, at <http://www.primitivism.com/primer.htm> (accessed 3 August 2005).

45 Extract from *Encyclopédie Anarchiste* in George Woodcock (ed.), *The Anarchist Reader* (Glasgow, 1977), p. 62.

These rereadings of Godwin and Kropotkin have more general consequences for how we should think about anarchism. Both were intensely involved in major intellectual currents of their times. Godwin was shaped by nonconformist and Calvinist Christianity and by (one strand of) Enlightenment thought; Kropotkin, by the political and theoretical ferment which followed the publication of *Origin of Species* in 1859. So, anarchists are not, in general, the marginal or isolated figures they are sometimes painted.

Our conclusion that anarchists are not primitivists also has consequences for how we should think about anarchism. The force of primitivist arguments of both kinds is that they hold out the promise that, if only our current institutions and arrangements (however conceived) could be removed, then everything would be fine. Human nature primitivism promises that once some distorting influence is removed, real and good humanity will express itself; golden age primitivism, that once the elaboration of the decline or fall is removed, we will be left with a simple, good life; combinations of the two, that the distortion *is* the elaboration, and that once it is gone, we will return to the good and natural life with which we began. I call this powerful form of polemic 'post-apocalyptic', for convenience and after fictions which imagine the aftermath of the destruction of current social forms and institutions.[46] Post-apocalyptic rhetoric, in general, proposes a politics of *absence*: the absence of power, institutions, organisation and political compromise. Anarchists are not primitivists, and do not typically share the post-apocalyptic faith. The anarchist utopia is one specific social form among many possible ones, not merely the absence of states, or capitalism, or any of the other features of our current arrangements which anarchists criticise. Anarchists do not propose to remove politics or power to reveal something pure or primary beneath; rather, they reject some particular ways of organising power (which I shall call 'domination' in later chapters), and particular forms of politics, in favour of a peaceful, prosperous and egalitarian utopia. They claim that this anarchic utopia is a possible social form, not that it is a golden age to which we might return, nor that it would be the result of the undistorted expression of a wholly good human nature. Much of the rest of this book will be devoted to theorising and supporting that claim about possibility.

However, first: given that anarchists are not primitivists, the obvious question is, why have they so often been accused of primitivism? I now consider this question.

## Why Anarchists are Accused of Primitivism

It is difficult to explain why anarchists have so often been characterised as human nature primitivists, when they have so often denied it and so often given clearly

46 I do not mean to suggest that post-apocalyptic literature in general claims that everything would be fine after the disaster. Algis Budrys's *Some Will Not Die* (London, 1964), for instance, is extremely pessimistic; Pat Murphy's *The City, Not Long After* (New York, 1990) offers both good (anarchist) and bad (militaristic) possibilities. For analyses of the apocalyptic trope in its usual home, science-fiction, see David Seed (ed.), *Imagining Apocalypse: Studies in cultural crisis* (Houndmills, 2000).

non-primitivist accounts of human nature. I tentatively offer three possible explanations.

The accusation may derive from misinterpretation of anarchist correctives to extreme pessimism about human nature. Someone who believes that humans are wholly and irredeemably self-interested may read anarchist claims that we are also or sometimes altruistic as expressing unbounded optimism. However, as shown above, that reading is a mistake. Kropotkin believes that humans have evolved both self-interested and altruistic tendencies. Godwin, that whether humans are selfish or benevolent depends on their education and rational judgement, not on any innate character. While these claims do not entail human nature primitivism, the misreading is understandable in the context of extreme pessimist assumptions about human nature.

The accusation may derive from a tacit assumption that *only* a picture of human nature as wholly good could justify belief in the possibility of the anarchic utopia. As I noted above, ideas of human nature are important for many political purposes and theories. However, that does not mean that all such purposes and theories need to invoke some picture of human nature, and I shall show in later chapters that belief in that possibility can be justified by a theoretical and empirical investigation of human sociability as it has historically appeared, rather than human nature. So, this mistake rests on a failure of argumentative imagination. Further, even if an anarchist did base her position on some rich and normative account of human nature, it is not obvious that it would have to be wholly good. An anarchic utopia need not involve a total absence of conflict or selfishness (Godwin's does; Kropotkin's does not). Even an anarchist who did base her belief in the possibility of utopia on a picture of human nature would not have to picture it as wholly good.

Finally, that the accusation of human nature primitivism is so widespread may be to do with the way characterisations of anarchism have been written. Perhaps most such accusations are based, not on readings of anarchist texts, but on characterisations in earlier textbooks, themselves based on still earlier ones. If this is the case, then the accusation is just an artefact of scholarship: a meme[47] rather than a misreading *of anarchism* at all.

These three possibilities are not mutually exclusive, and particular accusations may be grounded on combinations of some or all of them. However, their problem as explanations is that all lack conclusive evidence. Below, I shall suggest an explanation of the accusation of golden age primitivism which may also help here, but for the moment, I leave it as an admitted puzzle.

There are better reasons for the mistaken accusation of golden age primitivism: its reasonable element is the recognition of a rhetorical trope which is widely

47 'Meme' is Dawkins's term, in *The Selfish Gene*, for putative units of cultural transmission, analogous to genes, which are supposed to explain cultural 'evolution' by their differential survival. I use it here only as shorthand for the idea that the apparently high *survival* value of the belief that anarchists are human nature primitivists may be to do with how it 'reproduces' itself, not with its *truth* value.

used by anarchists. In the style which appears to support the accusation, this trope characterises some past or contemporary non-hierarchical, non-urban 'primitive' social form or group in rosy terms, and unfavourably compares our own current arrangements with it. Kropotkin, for instance, characterises 'savage' sociability by using both the archaeology and the anthropology of his day.[48]

In the archaeological case, Kropotkin argues against Hobbes and Huxley that past, stateless humans did not, as a matter of fact, live in a state of war of each against all.[49] According to Kropotkin, past stateless humans did not live as isolated individuals and families fighting each other for survival, but as tribes and clans with complex ethics and institutions of mutual support:

> Now, if we take into consideration that this complicated organization developed among men who stood at the lowest known degree of development, and that it maintained itself in societies knowing no kind of authority besides the authority of public opinion, we at once see how deeply inrooted social instincts must have been in human nature, even at its lowest stages. A savage who is capable of living under such an organization, and of freely submitting to rules which continually clash with his personal desires, certainly is not a beast devoid of ethical principles and knowing no rein to its passions … The very persistence of the clan organization shows how utterly false it is to represent primitive mankind as a disorderly agglomeration of individuals, who only obey their individual passions, and take advantage of their personal force and cunningness against all other representatives of the species.[50]

As this passage makes clear, Kropotkin does hold an 'evolutionary' picture of human history, involving a developmental scale starting at 'low' or 'primitive'. He also believes that this 'primitive' life was in some ways better than his and our own: 'Unbridled individualism is a modern growth, but it is not characteristic of primitive mankind.'[51]

---

48 It is worth repeating the point made above, that 'evolutionary' pictures of history are typically supported by archaeological evidence about past social forms, or anthropological evidence about current ones conceived as relics, or both. However, it is also worth noting that the combined use of these forms of evidence is also common practice in modern archaeology, without commitment to 'evolutionary' pictures, and is known as 'ethnoarchaeology' (see Brian M. Fagan, *People of the Earth: An introduction to world prehistory* ($8^{th}$ edn, New York, 1995) and Nicholas David and Carol Kramer, *Ethnoarchaeology in Action* (Cambridge, 2001)). Kropotkin's use of these forms of evidence therefore does not, in itself, convict him of golden age primitivism.

49 Hobbes need not be read as making this claim about a historical past: but the point is that both Kropotkin and Huxley did read him in this way. See James Paradis, '*Evolution and Ethics* in its Victorian Context' in T.H. Huxley et al., *Evolution and Ethics: T.H. Huxley's Evolution and Ethics with new essays on its Victorian and sociobiological context* (Princeton, NJ, 1989), pp. 3–55. Note, however, that Paradis perpetuates the false image of Kropotkin as a primitivist.

50 Kropotkin, *Mutual Aid*, pp. 86, 88.

51 Ibid., p. 88.

In the anthropological case, Kropotkin uses contemporary research and travellers' reports on Bushmen and Hottentots,[52] amongst other groups, further to characterise 'primitive' sociability. The first 'used to hunt in common, and divided the spoil without quarrelling'; 'they never abandoned their wounded, and displayed strong affection to their comrades'; they were 'goodhearted, distinterested, true to their promises, and grateful'.[53] On the second, Kropotkin quotes the early anthropologist Peter Kolben: 'If anything is given to a Hottentot, he at once divides it amongst all present'; a Hottentot 'cannot eat alone, and, however hungry, he calls those who pass by to share his food'.[54]

As a general characterisation of 'primitive' life on the basis of both of these forms of evidence, Kropotkin says that 'When Kolben wrote that [Hottentots] "are certainly the most friendly, the most liberal and the most benevolent people to one another that ever appeared on the earth" … he wrote a sentence which has continually appeared since in the description of savages.'[55] Again, it is clear that Kropotkin thinks this 'savage' way of life superior, when measured by mutual support and benevolence, to his and our own.

Kropotkin is not a primitivist. He does not have the required view of human nature; does not think that the past social forms he considers represent a lost golden age; does not recommend return to them; does not believe that the contemporary social forms he also considers are relics of such a golden age. He does think that the anarchic mutual aid tendency which past and contemporary 'savages' display still exists, even though currently eclipsed by the opposing hierarchical and oppressive tendency. However, when he and other anarchists write in this style, it is easy to see how they might be mistaken for primitivists. Kropotkin's description of 'savages' sounds like golden age primitivism, and if we add the assumption that people at the start or low point of a scale of human development also have an uncorrupted human nature, then it may also sound like human nature primitivism.

However, this is only part of the story. Anarchists use the same rhetorical trope with non-'primitive' social forms both past and present, and with imagined future social forms, for several important purposes. So, in order to read such rhetorical as primitivist, we would have to read it out of context. Before showing this to be true specifically of Godwin and Kropotkin, I shall analyse the trope in general.

## The Comparative Trope as Utopian Practice

The rhetorical habit of comparison between social forms is common in anarchism, and particularly in Kropotkin's work. He displays it, for instance, in a remark

52 'Bushman' is a generic term, originally from Afrikaans, for the hunting and gathering peoples of southern Africa, and especially of the Kalahari region. 'Hottentot' is the English name for a now mostly dead people who occupied the area around the Cape of Good Hope.

53 Kropotkin, *Mutual Aid*, p. 89.

54 Ibid., p. 90.

55 Ibid., p. 91.

about modern division of labour: 'The division and subdivision – the permanent subdivision – of functions has been pushed so far as to divide humanity into castes which are almost as firmly established as those of old India.'[56] His point is an attack on a widely-accepted feature of his and our current arrangements, by a comparison which discovers a similarity with a social form for which, he assumes, his readers share his dislike. The remark's argumentative tactic is to criticise our social form by comparing it with a disapproved one, and thereby extending that disapproval. In other instances of this rhetoric, the comparison discovers a difference instead of a similarity, and the argumentative tactic is to attack our social form by displaying its poverty compared to some real or imagined alternative.

Kropotkin's description of 'savages' is of this second type, which typically has the following structure: describe some different social form, and then compare it with our own, with the triple purpose of dramatising criticism of our social form, asserting the variety of human sociability, and giving an example of the possibility, and availability to us, of a different social form (or of particular features of it). Kropotkin uses a description of the 'savage' social form (whether accurate or not) to criticise his and our current arrangements, to assert that ours is just one among many varied social forms, and to give an example of (what he claims is) a real alternative to our social form, or at least to particular features of it (he recommends abandoning modern self-aggrandisement and hierarchy, but not modern technology, for instance).

This trope appears in a variety of styles throughout anarchist writing and argument; one obvious way to distinguish these styles is according to what kind of social form is described and used by them. I have already given one instance of the trope, and am about to give two more. They divide as follows. In the first instance, which can be mistaken for primitivism, the social form which Kropotkin describes and uses is non-urban, non-hierarchical and 'primitive', and involves mutual aid. It existed in the past and still exists on the margins of states and other current institutions. In the second, the medieval guild city, Kropotkin describes and uses an urban, technically sophisticated social form which is also non-hierarchical and also involves mutual aid. It existed in the recent past, and left its mark on our social and urban landscape. In the third, Godwin describes and uses an imaginary future social form, which is non-hierarchical and non-coercive, and is inhabited by rational, impartial maximisers of the good. The fundamental distinction is between those instances of the trope which use (supposedly) real and those which use (openly) imaginary social forms. These two major forms are both used by anarchists for the three purposes of criticism, assertion of variety and exemplification of alternative possibility. I shall now consider the second and third examples noted above, in order to show that this, and not primitivism, is the context in which Kropotkin and other anarchists' descriptions of 'primitive' peoples ought to be read, and to display the trope as a fragmentary utopian practice.

---

56 Peter Kropotkin, *Fields, Factories and Workshops Tomorrow*, ed. Colin Ward (2nd edn, London, 1985), p. 23.

Kropotkin pictures history as a dialectical process involving two opposing tendencies, the anarchic and the hierarchical, 'now the one and now the other taking the upper hand at different periods of history'.[57] The 'free mediaeval city'[58] is the last time the anarchic tendency had the upper hand:

> Wherever men had found, or expected to find, some protection behind their town walls, they instituted their 'co-jurations', their 'fraternities', their 'friendships', united in one common idea, and boldly marching towards a new life of mutual support and liberty. And they succeeded so well that in three or four hundred years they had changed the very face of Europe. They had covered the country with beautiful sumptuous buildings, expressing the genius of free unions of free men, unrivalled since for their beauty and expressiveness; and they bequeathed to the following generations all the arts, all the industries, of which our present civilization, with all its achievements and promises for the future, is only a further development. And when we look to the forces which have produced these grand results, we find them – not in the genius of individual heroes, not in the mighty organization of huge States or the political capacities of their rulers, but in the very same current of mutual aid and support which we saw at work in the village community, and which was vivified and reinforced in the Middle Ages by a new form of unions, inspired by the very same spirit but shaped on a new model – the guilds.[59]

Kropotkin recommends and celebrates 'the very same spirit' and the victory of the anarchic over the hierarchical tendency, here and now.

The purpose of this celebration of the last time that happened, and perhaps of the whole of *Mutual Aid*, is threefold. Kropotkin foregrounds what is wrong with our current arrangements by comparing them with the creativity and resistance to authority of these past arrangements. He asserts the variety of human sociability: not long ago, people lived very differently from us. Finally, he uses the example of the guild city to urge the possibility of a better, alternative social form for us. Because we had it once, we can have it again. That is, Kropotkin performs the trope I described above: he describes medieval guild cities' social form, and then compares it with our own, with the triple purpose of dramatising criticism of our social form, asserting the variety of human sociability, and giving an example of the possibility and availability to us of this life of 'mutual support and liberty', with its appealing results.

This use of the trope is clearly not primitivist. Medieval guild cities were not 'primitive' in any ordinary sense of that term. They were not a golden age at the start of an 'evolutionary' hierarchy, nor a relic of such a golden age. Kropotkin does not conceive them as expressing a pure and good human nature. They did not lack sophisticated technology (Kropotkin suggests that our 'arts' and 'industry' are grounded on theirs). Kropotkin's account of medieval guild cities, then, is a non-primitivist instance of the trope, which makes use of a real past social form,

57 Kropotkin, 'Anarchism', p. 236.

58 Ibid.

59 Kropotkin, *Mutual Aid*, pp. 163–4.

for purposes of critical comparison, assertion of human social possibility and exemplification of the possibility of an alternative to our social form.

As with Kropotkin's accounts of 'savage' sociability, of human nature and of history, it does not matter here whether his description of the guild city is accurate. The question is, what is Kropotkin doing argumentatively with this material? The answer is that he is not performing primitivist argument or polemic, but is using it to enact some of the features of utopianism which I identified in the Introduction. Kropotkin is carrying out an external criticism by comparison, attempting to expand the political imaginations of his readers, and drawing together elements for utopian construction (he is also telling stories, but he does not believe them to be false or intend his readers to think them so). Kropotkin's method of supporting the possibility of his (implied) utopia is particularly important in relation to my purposes: he argues for it by giving accounts of real humans living in the ways he recommends. He therefore makes his argument as a whole suited to the imaginative more than to the critical purpose of utopias.[60]

Godwin's faith in the perfectibility of humans is at the centre of his theory, and all of *Enquiry Concerning Political Justice* orbits his imagined perfect future. His purpose is, in part, to convince his readers to work towards their own perfection, but that future also stands in critical comparison to our own arrangements, as an assertion of the variety of human social possibility, and as an exemplar of one alternative possibility, just as the guild city does for Kropotkin.

Godwin's account of the 'dissolution of government'[61] is one of many instances of this use of his imagined future utopia. He considers the question of whether a future national assembly, and by extension future district assemblies and juries, would command or only suggest, and answers that 'The former of these might at first be necessary. The latter would afterwards be sufficient.'[62] 'Authority and violence'[63] are necessary evils for current humans, but continuing improvement will remove that necessity. Our current arrangements encourage one 'to conceive that, while his neighbour, his parent, and his political governor, pretended to be actuated by a pure regard for his interest or pleasure, they were, in reality, at the expense of his, promoting their own'.[64] In the imagined future society, everyone will know that this is not the case, and will accept and act on reasonable arguments about what she should do, from neighbours or whomever else, without compulsion. Here and all through *Enquiry*, Godwin criticises our current arrangements (in this case, the necessity of force to compel just action) by foregrounding what is wrong with them by comparison with his imagined future.

The second part of Godwin's point is to assert the possibility (indeed, the inevitability) of a better society as one among a variety of humanly possible social

60 See my Introduction.

61 Godwin, *Enquiry Concerning Political Justice*, p. 552.

62 Ibid.

63 Ibid., p. 553.

64 Ibid.

forms (ranged across time from past to future). That assertion is supported by arguments that humans are perfectible and that the source of action is rationally modifiable opinion, as already discussed. It is made again and again throughout *Enquiry*, and in the case of assemblies and juries, Godwin is particularly rapturous in making it:

> If juries might at length cease to decide, and be contented to invite, if force might gradually be withdrawn and reason trusted alone, shall we not one day find that juries themselves and every other species of public institution may be laid aside as unnecessary? … This is one of the most memorable stages of human improvement. With what delight must every well informed friend of mankind look forward to the auspicious period, the dissolution of political government, of that brute engine which has been the only perennial cause of the vices of mankind, and which, as has abundantly appeared in the progress of the present work, has mischiefs of various sorts incorporated in its substance, and no otherwise removable than by its utter annihilation![65]

As in my discussion of Kropotkin, it does not matter whether this account of our future is true (or even slightly believable). The question – what is Godwin doing argumentatively with this material? – and its answer, are the same. Godwin is making use of an imagined future to criticise our arrangements by extreme external comparison, asserting the variety of human social possibility, and attempting to expand our political imaginations by exemplifying a better social possibility. That is, he is engaging in a utopian rather than a primitivist practice. However, unlike Kropotkin, he has chosen an object of comparison more suited to criticism than to convincing us of its possibility.

Over the course of this chapter, I have displayed three instances of a common anarchist rhetorical trope. In the first, Kropotkin deploys past and contemporary 'savage' social forms; in the second, medieval guild cities; in the third, Godwin deploys an imagined future. All three describe some social form and compare it with our own in order to dramatise criticism, assert human social variety and expand our political imaginations by arguing for the possibility of radical alternatives. That is, all three make the same argumentative and polemical move using different social forms, whether real or imagined.

So, the context in which anarchists' use of accounts of 'primitive' peoples ought to be read is not primitivism, but this utopian rhetorical trope. Anarchists typically make use of real and imagined social forms to perform a radical external criticism of current arrangements and to celebrate the 'social genius'[66] of humans, both in general and in its specific capacity for anarchic forms of life.

In subsequent chapters I make a similar utopian argument. I argue that we can construct an anarchic utopia from real examples of human sociability which, because they *are* real examples, provide evidence for that utopia's possibility. However, that

---

65 Ibid., p. 554.

66 Kropotkin, *Mutual Aid.*, p. 154.

claim is problematic as it stands. In a different context, Martin Hollis and Steven Lukes write that:

> It is as if scientific paradigms and theoretical frameworks were strung out in time like islands across an archipelago. Other minds, other cultures, other languages and other theoretical schemes call for understanding from within. Seen from within, they make us doubt whether there is anything universal under the sun. This doubt is also a challenge to the very idea of a single world. Is not the world, as interpreted in our scheme of things, but one of many?[67]

Similarly, different social forms might be strung out like islands, and there might be no meaningful way to bring them together for comparison and construction: they might be incommensurable given our culture-dependent capacities. In Chapter 2, I set out and refute what I take to be the strongest version of this criticism. For reasons I explore there, that requires me to develop a theory of human sociability. That theory forms the background of Chapters 3 and 4, which explore some landmarks in the human social landscape: states and slavery in Chapter 3, and anarchic possibilities in Chapter 4.

67 Editors' Introduction to *Rationality and Relativism* (Oxford, 1982), pp. 1–20, p. 1.

## Chapter 2

# The Human Landscape

My ambition is to carry out a Kropotkinite utopian argument, by constructing an anarchist utopia from parts found in various real human social forms; but that ambition must face a powerful objection. Utopian texts, including this book, perform external criticism and expand political imagination; but it has been argued by Michael Walzer that only internal criticism is possible, and that since our only moral resources are in our shared 'social meanings',[1] the shared meanings and ways of life of others are not available to us.

For Walzer, there is no transcultural point of view from which we could judge all, or even our own institutions. All one can do is 'interpret to one's fellow citizens the world of meanings that we share'.[2] So, all *criticism* of ways of life is internal criticism, which shows us that we are not living up to our own best understanding of the good life.[3] Comparison with some other social form is irrelevant to that task, and delusive in its pretence that we could stand back from our own and compare it with another's understanding. 'A given society is just if its substantive life is lived in a certain way – that is, in a way faithful to the shared understandings of the members';[4] it is unjust if not. It cannot be praised or condemned according to how it compares to values or understandings external to it. A caste society cannot be criticised for not living up to egalitarian ideals (nor vice versa). The moral and political understandings of other societies are not available to us, and so the cherry-picking of exemplary elements for construction which I propose is equally delusive. Kropotkin attempts to expand our political imaginations by showing us mutual aid in action in 'savage' societies: but there are no moral resources there for us. Our imaginations must be expanded, if at all, by the discovery and interpretation of our own best selves. The politics which Walzer discovers and interprets for us is radically egalitarian, pluralist and

1 Michael Walzer, *Spheres of Justice: A defence of pluralism and equality* (New York, 1983), p. 9. See also Walzer, *Interpretation and Social Criticism* (Cambridge, MA, 1987). Walzer's views have changed somewhat since the publication of *Spheres of Justice*. In *Thick and Thin: Moral argument at home and abroad* (Notre Dame, IN, 1994), Walzer wants 'to endorse the politics of difference and, at the same time, to describe and defend a certain sort of universalism' (p. x). However, since my target is a widely held view of which *Spheres of Justice* is a particularly elegant statement, not Walzer himself, this complication need not detain us here.

2 Walzer, *Spheres of Justice*, p. xiv.

3 Walzer is in fact more narrowly concerned with the particular good of justice, but I cannot see why the point would not be generalisable if true.

4 Ibid., p. 313.

democratic, but his methodology is 'radically particularist', and so 'If such a society isn't already here – hidden, as it were, in our concepts and categories – we will never know it concretely or realize it in fact.'[5]

If Walzer is correct, my project is unworkable. I shall argue that his argument fails. Our criticism is not limited to the internal, and the elements Kropotkin and I use to construct anarchist utopias are available to us and to everyone.

Walzer's argument requires that there are such things as 'shared meanings' which can be interpreted for critical and political purposes. The possibility of shared meanings depends on the fact of human society: a permanently isolated human could not *share* meaning. Walzer's argument further depends on a particular understanding of the sharing of meaning, and therefore of society. For Walzer, *we* share some set of meanings (democratic, pluralist, egalitarian), and *they* share some different set, such that our goods are different and incommensurable. There must be at least two distinct human societies, and therefore at least two distinguishable sets of meanings, if there are to be examples of human sociability which are not available to *us* for comparison and example. It seems obvious, of course, that this is the case: I shall argue that it is not. Although individual humans are certainly different from one another, there are no discrete, mutually exclusive societies to make discrete, incommensurable meanings possible. Walzer's argument fails, because its foundation is a faulty theory of society. I shall now set out and argue for the alternative theory which refutes Walzer's.

## A Theory of Society[6]

A theory of society could be an attempt at a complete general account, or even a complete explanation, of society. I do not intend anything so ambitious here. My theory's scope is best understood via a useful metaphor: mapmaking. A *projection* is a technique for representing the Earth's spherical surface, or a portion of it, on a flat surface.[7] The properties a map needs to represent include the direction any point bears to another, the distance between given points, and the shapes and areas of regions: 'When *small* areas are being mapped, it is possible to obtain sensibly accurate representation of all properties, but in the case of *large* areas, something must be sacrificed.'[8] Any projection of a sufficiently large area will accurately represent some properties at the expense of distorting others. There are many possible

5 Ibid., p. xiv.

6 The theory I develop here is deeply indebted, as ongoing citation should make clear, to the work of Eric Wolf in *Europe and the People Without History* (Berkeley, CA, 1997) and Michael Mann in *Sources of Social Power* (2 vols, Cambridge, 1986 and 1993).

7 The other element of mapmaking is scaling: a map needs not only to be flat, but to be small enough to carry. I ignore this complication here, and assume, following George P. Kellaway, *Map Projections* (2nd edn, London, 1949), that projection is carried out from a scaled globe of the earth.

8 Ibid., p. 5.

projections, and different projections have different advantages and disadvantages. In gnomonic zenithal projections, for instance, the relative positions of places are clearly shown and direction from the centre is always true; however, away from the centre, distances become distorted, the shapes of regions are distorted, and their areas exaggerated, the more so the further from the centre they are: 'The problem is thus really a matter of selecting the projection which best satisfies the requirements in each particular case.'[9]

All flat maps of the Earth distort some of its properties. This is not a problem, so long as we know what and how they distort, and have chosen the right mapping for our purposes. The analogy I want to draw is that my theory of society performs a mapping of the landscape of human sociability. It distorts at least in focussing on some features (capacities for domination and resistance; the logistics of social interaction) at the expense of others (culture, subjectivity and their hermeneutic interpretation), and in largely avoiding consideration of the causes or explanations of the social forms I describe.

It may be, at best, that a non-distorting mapping of human sociability is unlikely because it would have to cover such an immense number and complexity of features. It may be, worse, that all mappings – all interpretations – are *necessarily* distorting, because they are carried out using tools (concepts, theories, perceptual and cognitive mechanisms) which structure the data in some way. That is, because some version of the 'neo-Kantian postulate'[10] that we have no transparent, unmediated access to a world outside us, is true. Again, though, this is not a problem to the extent that we can be aware of the distortions and structures imposed by our own tools of thought, and to the extent that we can design such tools. That my mapping of human sociability distorts it is not a problem, so long as we know what and how it distorts and what it accurately represents, and have chosen the right mapping for our purposes. That there are alternative possible mappings, which are better suited to other purposes than mine, does not mean that there is nothing to choose between mappings. It especially does not mean that there are no wrong maps: there are many ways to map a territory, and some of them are dangerously mistaken.

The negative point of using this metaphor is to emphasise that I am not involving myself in a reductive project. I do not claim that the features of human sociability on which I focus are real, fundamental or deep in comparison to other features, nor that they are finally explanatory. In particular, I claim only that society makes shared meaning possible, not that shared meaning is an epiphenomenon of society. Shared meanings may well have independent causal powers (I do not need to consider whether or not they do, here). My argument is that the possibility of shared human meaning depends on human society;[11] that the truth of a theory of society which

9 Ibid.

10 Eric R. Wolf, *Envisioning Power: Ideologies of dominance and crisis* (Berkeley, CA, 1999), p. 3.

11 That is, the possibility of shared meaning has society as a necessary, but perhaps not a sufficient, condition.

makes Walzer's appeal to incommensurable meanings impossible therefore refutes his theory, and that this refutation removes the major obstacle to my utopian plan. Now that we have described what kind of theory is presented here, we can proceed to describe the theory itself.

Humans, pursuing a wide variety of interests, create, discover, modify and destroy social organisations. These organisations consist of networks of humans interacting in modes including cooperation, negotiation, production, exchange, coercion, hierarchy, friendship, enmity, violence, ritual and play. Interactions are carried out both face-to-face and through various media. Almost all humans are involved in many such networks, in many roles, and these networks overlap, interpenetrate and sometimes include one another. Networks change in response to changes in, or discoveries of interests, to the effects of other networks, and to changing environments and the opportunities and demands they create.

Although it is perhaps possible that some humans could organise themselves into a single, unified and discrete organisation in and through which they carried out all of their social activity, this has never in fact happened. There are, and have been, no social totalities: 'We can never find a single bounded society in geographical or social space.'[12] 'Society' names not a kind of organism, but an activity, apparently natural for humans as for many other animals. It importantly involves the cooperative creation and assignment of capacities (especially capacities to attain and distribute goods, manage conflict, dominate others and resist domination). Human social life consists of 'overlapping networks of social interaction' which are also 'organisations, institutional means of attaining human goals'.[13]

Human social life has historically been both various, and sometimes quite stable, and I therefore use 'social form' as a term of convenience for any relatively stable and persistent bundle of networks, where it is useful to have a shorthand for such a distinguishable way of life. I refer to the Ik social form below, for instance. However, I do not intend to imply that any such social form is a fully discrete society, nor that it is a higher-order entity than the individuals and networks of which it consists.

Human society depends on general human capacities.[14] Humans share a number of such capacities, including capacities to learn and use language; to create, understand and use symbols; to act on reasons and explain (or conceal) those reasons; to have and act on a variety of emotional and dispositional states apart from reasons; to make and use tools; to create and challenge hierarchies; to act in, and by using, social networks; to make decisions; to be selfish or altruistic; to be violent or friendly; to perceive oneself as a self in the context of other selves; and to create, internalise and perform rituals. Many of these capacities are shared in some form or degree by our close relatives, including chimpanzees, gorillas, orang-utans and other primates. For

12 Mann, *Sources of Social Power*, vol. 1, p. 1.

13 Ibid., p. 2.

14 'All human beings have various generic capacities to acquire skills, which, though they differ in their specific forms from tribe to tribe, are nevertheless of the same general kind', Rom Harré, *Social Being* (2nd edn, Oxford, 1993), p. 3.

the same reason that we are a particular kind of evolved creature, humans also share some general interests. They include interests in food, shelter, company, continued life, the respect of peers and the absence of (threatened or actual) violence. These interests can be trumped by other, often socially constructed ones, but are typical of humans and very strong. So, an appeal to such interests, to a stranger, can often be effective. Individual humans' interests can clash at least because they sometimes differ, and because although you and I both have interests in food, for instance, our interests clash in conditions of scarcity.[15]

If this theory that human society consists in overlapping and interpenetrating networks, not discrete and mutually exclusive societies, is true, then Walzer's theory cannot get off the ground. Although we do share meaning, the possibility of doing so is dependent on society, and society is not such that it could make one set of meanings for us, and another incommensurable set for them. So, the critical and imaginative utopian practice I propose is vindicated. However, we still need to show that this network theory is true. I shall argue for it by contrasting it with three other ways of characterising human society, chosen to emphasise and support the distinctive features of my theory.

### *Against Social Totalities*

To the extent that it is not simply a careless way of talking or a traditional working assumption, the assertion of the existence of social totalities is the claim that humans are typically found in discrete, unified social 'boxes', which have boundaries, subsystems, levels or dimensions, and perhaps an internal 'evolutionary' dynamic. On this view, social change and conflict can be divided into endogenous and exogenous types, human behaviour can be explained by reference to 'social structure as a whole',[16] and there are two distinct, but analogous, problems for political philosophy: one about how individuals *within* a society should organise themselves, and another, at a 'second level', about how *distinct societies* should organise their interrelations. These problems have been thought sufficiently analogous by Kant and by Rawls, for instance, that they have attempted to answer both with the device of a hypothetical contract.[17] These claims can be empirical ones about how humans now, or always, live. But they are false. As Mann argues:

> Empirical proof can be seen in the answer to a simple question: In which society do *you* live? Answers are likely to start at two levels. One refers to national states: My society is

15 This paragraph sets out a conception of human nature which is minimalist by comparison with those discussed in Chapter 1. It is minimalist in particular because I do not suggest that it stands as a norm for humans: it is an account of (some of) the (biological and cognitive) capacities which make society possible, not an ideal to live up to.

16 Mann, *Sources of Social Power*, vol. 1, pp. 1–2.

17 Immanuel Kant, 'Perpetual Peace: A philosophical sketch' in Hans Reiss (ed.), *Political Writings*, trans. H.B. Nisbet (2nd edn, Cambridge, 1991), pp. 93–130; John Rawls, *The Law of Peoples* with *The Idea of Public Reason Revisited* (Cambridge, MA, 1999).

> "the United Kingdom," "the United States," "France," or the like. The other is broader: I am a citizen of "industrial society" or "capitalist society" or possibly "the West" or "the Western alliance." We have a basic dilemma – a national state society versus a wider "economic society." For some important purposes, the national state represents a real interaction network with a degree of cleavage at its boundaries. For other important purposes, capitalism unites all three into a wider interaction network, with cleavage at its edge. They are both "societies." Complexities proliferate the more we probe. Military alliances, churches, common language, and so forth, all add powerful, sociospatially different networks of interaction. We could only answer after developing a sophisticated understanding of the complex interconnections and powers of these various crosscutting interaction networks. The answer would certainly imply a confederal rather than a unitary society.[18]

The argument so far is that we in particular do not live in unitary and discrete societies, despite the enormous power and reach of modern states which try to divide us up into such boxes.[19] This is shown, especially, by the overlapping coexistence of two different kinds of social network – national states and capitalism – and emphasised by the range of other, sociospatially different networks in which we are also involved. Mann continues by arguing that this confederal situation is typical of human life, not just of our life. Empires, trade-and-cultural networks, world religions, all cut across one another: 'Overlapping interaction networks are the historical norm … The forms of overlap and intersection have varied considerably, but they have always been there.'[20] It is not only we who live in a confederal situation: most humans have always lived like that. The belief in social totalities badly misrepresents the current and historical experience of social humans, and should therefore be abandoned. In its place, we need to recognise the typical human situation of being involved in multiple, cross-cutting networks of interaction, with particular and different spatial and social reaches, tactics and dynamics. Humans 'are social, but not societal, animals'.[21]

General names for social totalities like culture, nation or tribe, and particular ones like 'Iroquois, Greece, Persia, or the United States'[22] distort our perception of human social organisation. They need not therefore be abandoned (they are occasionally useful), but they obscure complex and cross-cutting interrelations, and must not be hypostasised.

### *Against Cultural Evolution*

Since the nineteenth century, evolutionary rhetoric and metaphor has colonised our political and historical imaginations, partly in the form of a discourse of 'cultural evolution'. It is not a single position, but a cluster of notions and research projects

---

18 Mann, *Sources of Social Power*, vol. 1, p. 16.

19 See Chapter 3.

20 Mann, *Sources of Social Power*, vol. 1, pp. 16, 17.

21 Ibid., p. 14.

22 Wolf, *Europe and the People Without History*, p. 7.

which differ in their purposes, claims and results. Its unity may rest on little more than the rhetorical heft of the idea of evolution after Darwin, and a shared, reasonable ambition to focus on social change and its explanation. However, those involved in this cluster also tend to share a few central, contingently associated ideas and plans. Cultural evolutionary stories typically involve a recognition that human social life has changed over prehistorical and historical time, and a resulting ambition to describe and explain that change at a fairly high level of generality. They divide human social forms into a small number of ideal types,[23] and map those types onto a scale running from low to high, from primitive to civilised, from less to more evolved, or, most commonly, from simple to complex. These scales and oppositions bring (not always admitted) normative baggage with them. Marshall Sahlins, for instance, claims that 'Higher cultural forms arise from, and surpass, lower. Culture produces successively higher *levels* of organisation as new forms capable of harnessing greater amounts of energy emerge. In popular terms, this is culture's movement towards complexity, the general, progressive aspect of evolution.'[24]

Cultural evolutionary stories typically involve unilinealism, 'the view that societies (most or all) pass through the same sequence of stages of social types' over time.[25] Some of the time, they also involve metaphors of organic growth, as for instance when Eric Hobsbawm claims that the Mafia are 'a sort of embryo' of 'more highly developed movements'.[26] Particular examples of cultural evolutionary projects and interventions include the texts by Morgan, Childe, Service and Sahlins already noted; for histories and literature surveys, see for instance Timothy Earle's 'Political Domination and Social Evolution', Ted Lewellen's *Political Anthropology*, or Stephen Sanderson's *Social Evolutionism.*[27] My examples are all from anthropology, not because anthropologists are especially prone to tell such stories (they seem currently to be out of fashion in the discipline), but because these

---

23 Lewis H. Morgan, for instance, distinguished savages, barbarians and the civilised in *Ancient Society: Or, researches in the lines of human progress from savagery through barbarism to civilization* (Chicago, IL, 1877), and influenced Engels's *The Origin of the Family, Private Property and the State: In the light of the researches of Lewis H. Morgan* (London, 1972). V. Gordon Childe distinguished hunter-gatherers, farmers and the civilised, in *Social Evolution* (London, 1963); Elman Service did the same with bands, tribes, chiefdoms and states, in *Origins of the State and Civilization: The process of cultural evolution* (New York, 1975).

24 'The Segmentary Lineage: An organisation of predatory expansion', *American Anthropologist* vol. 63 (1961): 322–45, p. 324.

25 Ernest Gellner, 'Soviets against Wittfogel: Or, the anthropological preconditions of mature Marxism' in John A. Hall (ed.), *States in History* (Oxford, 1986), pp. 78–108, p. 80.

26 *Primitive Rebels: Studies in archaic forms of social movement in the 19th and 20th centuries* (3rd edn, Manchester, 1971), p. 30.

27 Earle, 'Political Domination and Social Evolution' in Tim Ingold (ed.), *Companion Encyclopedia of Anthropology* (London, 1994), pp. 940–46; Lewellen, *Political Anthropology: An Introduction* (2nd edn, Westport, CT, 1992); Sanderson, *Social Evolutionism: A critical history* (Cambridge, MA, 1990).

examples display the cultural evolutionary cluster of ideas with particular starkness. Individually, these ideas and plans are interesting and may be useful. However, we have good reasons to reject their contingent association in a research project.

First, there is no tendency for societies to grow up through different ideal types from low to high (or primitive to civilised, or simple to complex), because there are no unified, discrete societies. Therefore, societies are not born, they do not age, and they do not die. The activity, *society*, involves many changing and overlapping networks of individuals. The multiple networks which make up human social activity are not coextensive in space, in time, or in the sets of individuals they involve. Particular people create new relationships, detach themselves from old ones, move away, die, and are born and initiated. Individuals grow up, but societies do not.

Secondly, the cultural evolutionary project involves a 'disastrous tangle between the ideas of time, height, and value'.[28] Being more recent is not the same as being more valuable: it is, of course, possible that things have got better; but it is equally possible that they have got worse, and we need to be able to make that judgement without begging the question. The relationship between time and height is obscure. Time does not move up, or in any direction: it passes. Height is a strange metaphor for value, as Ursula Le Guin dramatises in *The Dispossessed.* Her central character Shevek, from the anarchist world Anarres, is en route to Urras, whose politics are more familiar to us, and has been talking to his doctor:

> Kimoe flustered easily. He had the physician's brisk self-assurance, but Shevek continually upset it. All his explanations ended up, after two or three of Shevek's questions, in floundering. Each took for granted certain relationships which the other could not even see. For instance, this curious matter of superiority and inferiority. Shevek knew that the concept of superiority, of relative height, was important to the Urrasti; they often used the word 'higher' as a synonym for 'better' in their writings, where an Anarresti would use 'more central' … It was one puzzle among hundreds.[29]

My point is not that centrality is a better metaphor than height, but that the equation of height with value would be hard to explain to someone who had not been brought up casually making it. Height is perhaps a passable synonym for status, and makes metaphorical sense in the context of a hierarchy: but it is not the same as value.

The confused association of height, time and value may, as Midgley argues, be a hangover from pre-evolutionary modes of thought:

> Before anyone thought of evolution, [a scale of value] was expressed in the idea of a Great Chain of Being – a scale of creatures reaching from the least to the most important. From inanimate matter the chain led through the simpler living things to the more complex, then on through man and the Heavenly Beings to God. It was eternal and unchanging. When, however, people began to think about evolution, they made (as commonly happens) no more changes in their ways of thinking than they were forced to. They did not scrap the

---

28 Mary Midgley, *Beast and Man: The roots of human nature* (Revised edn, London, 1995), p. 153.

29 Le Guin, *The Dispossessed*, p. 20.

> Great Chain of Being. Instead, they simply unhooked the top end from Heaven and slung it into the Future. Its axis now was time. But its associations with value did not vanish.[30]

Whatever its source, this three-stranded knot should be cut. To take one important case: states are not 'higher' than other social forms. They appeared later than some (nomad bands, chiefdoms, male outgroups) and earlier than others (trade unions, environmental pressure groups, rock bands). This order of appearance is a matter of interest, and may not be coincidental: large, widespread and powerful states probably had effects on what other forms were possible or likely in their shadows. However, that tells us nothing about their value. In general: lateness in time is not value; nor is it height; nor is height value.

Third, cultural evolutionary projects' ambitions to describe and explain change on one hand, and to produce a typology of human social forms on the other, work against each other. Change in human social forms does not happen as if a switch has been flicked, but gradually, with new forms of interaction emerging out of, and competing with, surviving older ones. So, if we focus on change in human sociability, we are focusing on the point where the boundary between two types of sociability is most blurred. Further, much social change is not change from one type to another, but within social forms which are in other ways relatively stable. So, if we focus on change from one of a small number of ideal types to another, we ignore some of the changes we had intended to investigate. For both of these reasons: it is a reasonable research project to distinguish the chiefdom, for instance, as a human social type, and to investigate whether non-tautological generalisations hold of all chiefdoms; it is also a reasonable project to investigate the nature and causes of social change; but trying to do both at once limits our ability to do either.

Fourth, unilinealism is a very strong claim about the pattern of human history, and at best unproven. Even supposing what is not the case, that we can, for instance, discover unitary and discrete Spanish and Maya societies which enclose, and are of a different type from, all of the various other networks in which the people involved in them were also involved, is it plausible that the two went through 'the same sequence of stages of social types'? The claim would perhaps be that 'the Maya society' was at a lower (more primitive, less evolved, simpler) stage already passed by 'the Spanish society', and that it was cut off before it could complete its 'natural growth'. However, even if we perversely ignore the fact that Spanish and Maya people had enormous and complex effects on one another,[31] I suggest that unilinealism requires very strong empirical evidence, not so far forthcoming, to be plausible.

Fifth, cultural evolutionary stories typically invoke, and map their typologies of social forms to, a linear scale from simple to complex. Lewellen's representative textbook, instance, offers 'a classification of early states based on their degree of complexity'.[32] However, the idea of complexity is at best ambiguous, and may well

30 Midgley, *Beast and Man*, p. 152.

31 On which see, for instance, Inga Clendinnen, *Ambivalent Conquests: Maya and Spaniard in Yucatan, 1517–1570* (2nd edn, Cambridge, 2003).

32 Lewellen, *Political Anthropology*, p. 21.

be worse than that: 'The concept of complexity includes too much which makes it a lumpen catch-all that explains everything but signifies nothing.'[33] I shall return to the question of complexity, in relation to states and their appearance in history, in Chapter 3. For the moment, I note that the unexplained introduction of a scale running from simple to complex, and its unargued application to typologies of social forms and to the passing of time, is at best problematic. I further suggest, and shall show in Chapter 3, that complexity is an ambiguous and non-distinguishing, and therefore bad, metrical concept for analysing change in human sociability, and especially the development of states.

I have made five objections to cultural evolutionary projects involving the contingent association of ambitions to describe and explain human social change at a high level of generality; typologies of social forms; a linear scale of height, civilisation, evolution or complexity; and metaphors of organic growth. These objections jointly show that the association of these ideas and plans has been a mistake, and ought to be abandoned. Such projects badly distort our perception and understanding of human social experience.

### *Against the State of Nature*

The state of nature is one motif of the social contract vocabulary, which has been used by theorists as different and historically distant as Thomas Hobbes and Robert Nozick.[34] States of nature and their analogues can be hypothetical scenarios, or (attempts at) realistic descriptions of historical or contemporary circumstances; they can refer to presocial, or apolitical, or even asocial forms of life; the individuals in them can be presented as driven only by appetite, or as rational and self-interested (because the theorist thinks humans are really like that, or because doing so allows morality or political obligation to be derived from, or justified by, minimalist amoral assumptions). Other past variations could be noted, and there seems no reason to bar future reuses and modifications of the idea.

I oppose my theory of society to the state of nature in only one of its many meanings. The state of nature is sometimes thought to be an empirically real groundstate, in which humans naturally live, up from which societies and especially states can be built like skyscrapers, and back down to which the collapse of fragile social institutions might throw us. This groundstate can be described in various ways, and made to seem more or less attractive, but it is typically thought of as simple by comparison with our complex arrangements, and associated with past and

---

33 Clive Gamble, 'Hunter-Gatherers and the Origin of States' in John A. Hall (ed.) *States in History* (Oxford, 1986), pp. 22–47, pp. 28–9.

34 Hobbes, *Leviathan*, ed. Edwin Curley (Indianapolis, IN, 1994) – originally published 1651; Nozick, *Anarchy, State, and Utopia* (Oxford, 1974). On understanding contract as a vocabulary (rather than an ideal form which successive theorists more nearly approached) see Harro Höpfl and Martin P. Thompson, 'The History of Contract as a Motif in Political Thought', *American Historical Review* vol. 84 (1979): 919–44.

contemporary 'primitive' groups.[35] Their simple, natural form of life is contrasted with our complex, artificial one, and it is assumed that we, too, could lose the latter and 'return' to the former.

I deny these claims. Almost all humans live in social networks, of various kinds, between which we can make moral and organisational comparisons. Particular networks have particular histories, and that two social forms are somewhat similar does not mean that they have the same history, nor, in the case of 'primitives', any lack of history. If there are some similarities between, for instance, aboriginal Australian and Amazonian hunting and gathering groups, that tells us very little about how they got to these somewhat similar forms. It certainly does not show that they got there in the same way, nor that either are relics of a natural groundstate. The distinction between nature and artifice does not cut at these joints. All human social networks are natural, in the sense that we could not make them, and would not make the ones we do, if we were not the particular evolved creatures we are, with the natural capacities we have. However, we do deliberately *make* social networks, although not often according to explicit plans, at least partly because that is a natural thing for us to do. We are naturally social artificers. So, for instance, a human brought up by wolves would not be a natural human, untainted by culture, but an incomplete one, deprived of the conditions of her natural development and of the exercise of some of her natural capacities, including language, conceptual reasoning and human social action. This is not because humans are higher, or more evolved, or more complex than wolves, but just because we are different (despite also having many similarities).

Similarly, Colin Turnbull's claim that the Ik, the once-nomadic, then starving, distintegrating and callous tribe he studied in northern Uganda, show us that 'Our much vaunted human values are not inherent in humanity at all, but are associated only with a particular form of survival called society, and that all, even society itself, are luxuries that can be dispensed with',[36] is false. The Ik are not without society, but trapped, partly by environmental and political factors outside their control, in a particular and disastrous social form. Humans are capable of creating and maintaining other disastrous social forms, from abusive marriages to fascist dictatorships, but this does not show that humans are 'really', 'fundamentally', or 'in the state of nature' like that, and that better ways of life are artificial, just window-dressing. It shows only that these are human social possibilities.

In general, humans are capable of a wide variety of different social forms, and we can and often must make moral and other comparisons between them, but no one form is more natural than another. Change, including the collapse of particular institutions, may take us in various directions, and may be for better, for worse, neutral or mixed. There is no single, simple social form into which we naturally fall, or which is a groundstate on which we might build more complex, artificial ones.

---

35 When it is positively described, as by Rousseau in some of his moods, the state of nature can be part of primitivist rhetoric.

36 *The Mountain People* (New York, 1972), p. 294.

### *There Are No Primitive Societies*

We should note a major consequence of accepting my theory: there are no 'primitive' societies (hence my use of scare-quotes around the term, throughout this book). Other social forms differ from, and can be compared with our own, but the forms we are sometimes inclined to call 'primitive' are not low or simple, not necessarily older or less (or more) valuable than our own, and not the natural groundstate of human life. The changes which perhaps turned some social forms like them into ones like ours were not like organic growth. Even if we are correctly identifying similarities between different 'primitive' groups, this does not mean that they have the same history (or the same or any lack of history).[37]

I want particularly to emphasise that there are no relics. According to Elman Service:

> If the aboriginal culture of the Arunta of Australia [for instance] is not a form of adaptation to a particular kind of (total) environment made long, long ago and preserved into modern times because of its isolation, then what is it? Does a people have whatever kind of culture it might dream up at any given time? Obviously not … What else can explain such a culture, then, but that there have been survivals into the present of ancient cultural forms which because of relative isolation have maintained a relatively stable adaptation. Many primitive societies have changed greatly in modern times and all ultimately will be changed, assimilated or obliterated, but that only makes the point more clear. Where an Arunta-like way of life is not yet significantly altered by modern influences it is a culture that is primitive, ancient, and preliterate. And it has a very long history, too, for the Arunta culture is paleolithic in type, although the paleolithic *era* ended when and where higher stages arose – a long time ago.[38]

On my opposite view, what explains Arunta culture (if it or any other culture is explicable) is that the Arunta are people making a living and pursuing their other interests in a particular, historically and environmentally conditioned (but not determined) way, just as we are. The claim that all Arunta-like cultures will ultimately be 'changed, assimilated or obliterated' – and how could we be sure of that? – is irrelevant to the question of whether they are relics. The derivation of the claim that the Arunta have a very long history from the assertion that their culture is paleolithic in type assumes that no group could have adopted a paleolithic lifestyle any later than the paleolithic era; but there is no reason to believe that assumption. Finally, 'higher stages' is either meaningless, or bald self-congratulation: 'hooray for us!'.

No social form stands to ours or to any other as a child does to an adult, and still less as a child does to the particular adult she will become. In any case, that child is not lower or less valuable than that or any adult. 'Primitive' is a term of contempt, or occasionally of praise, but not of understanding.

---

37 On the history of the illusion of 'primitive society' in anthropological theory and practice, see Adam Kuper, *The Invention of Primitive Society: Transformations of an illusion* (London, 1988).

38 Service, *Origins of the State and Civilization*, p. 8.

## *General Features of Human Social Networks*

Now that we have a general account and defence of a theory of society, I want to identify and discuss some important general features of human social networks.

As already noted, human social networks typically both create and assign capacities. Indeed, creating a capacity entails assigning it, because there is no state of nature, that is, no groundstate in which particular capacities are the natural property of the strongest, or the heads of households, or the heirs of Adam. In general, there are no human social situations which do not involve both the creation and the concurrent assignment of various capacities.

Secondly, human social networks often incorporate mechanisms for their own maintenance, for regulating the relationships between networks, and thereby for maintaining a particular mode of the creation and assignment of capacities. We tend to create not just social networks but *institutions*, which are formal, rule-guided and ritually performed networks, bundles of networks, or ways of representing and understanding networks. They often involve the idea of roles, including king, priest, minister and managing director, which can survive the removal of their current incumbents. Institutions are often also regarded as having (legal) personae of their own, separate from any of the individuals involved in them.[39] Institutionalisation is perhaps distinctively human: certainly, no other animals institutionalise to the extent that we do.

However, third, the tendency to institutionalise is continually challenged by another human tendency, to create new networks and capacities: 'In pursuit of their goals humans further develop these networks, outrunning the existing level of institutionalization. This may happen as a direct challenge to existing institutions, or it may happen unintentionally and "interstitially" – between their interstices and around their edges – creating new relations and institutions that have unanticipated consequences for the old.'[40]

There are tendencies both to deliberate resistance and to what Mann calls 'interstitial emergence'. In general, there is a tendency to try to create stable, unified and discrete social forms which embody particular modes of the creation and assignment of capacities, but 'underneath, human beings are tunneling ahead to achieve their goals, forming new networks [and] extending old ones.'[41] Human social forms have never been sufficiently institutionalised to prevent all resistance or to resist all interstitial emergence. Further, institutions are vulnerable to many changes which are not the result of either: one can collapse, for instance, because of environmental change, natural disaster, disease, or because it exhausts a resource on which it relies.[42]

---

39 Compare Hobbes, *Leviathan*, Chapter XVI.

40 Mann, *Sources of Social Power*, vol. 1, p. 15.

41 Ibid., p. 16.

42 See Jared Diamond, *Collapse: How societies choose to fail or survive* (London, 2005).

Fourth, human social networks are 'functionally promiscuous'.[43] Even when deliberately created for some particular purposes, they tend also to perform other actions, and to be available for use for other purposes. Having set up or discovered some network or bundle of networks, individuals often use them for new purposes, and find that they do more (and sometimes completely other) things than expected or intended.

*Society Against Societies*

I have mapped human society as a notably flat landscape: without a unifying gradient of value or evolution; without a single mode from which everything came, and to which it might return; and without impermeable boundaries. Humans, pursuing various ends and interests, create, discover, modify and destroy social organisations, which are networks of humans interacting in various ways, and creating and assigning capacities. These networks overlap and interpenetrate one another. Networks change in response to changes in, or discoveries of, interests; to the effects of other networks; and to changing environments and the opportunities and demands they create. Humans do not organise themselves into unitary and discrete social totalities, but live in confederal social situations. Human history is not best understood by cultural evolutionary stories, and there is no single, simple groundstate of human life. We can identify some quite general features of human social life as it has historically appeared. All social networks create and assign capacities (especially to create and distribute goods, manage conflict, dominate others and resist domination), display opposing tendencies to institutionalisation and interstitial emergence, and are functionally promiscuous.

My minor purpose in arguing for this theory of society is to show why it is worth refuting the accusation that anarchists are golden age primitivists. That form of primitivism must rely on a false theory which presents society as developing and deteriorating away from a simple beginning, a state of nature.[44] It is therefore a mistake, and if the accusations refuted in Chapter 1 were true, anarchism would be convicted of that mistake.

My major purpose is to refute Walzer's anti-utopian challenge to my project. Walzer's claim that our only moral and critical resources are to be found in our discrete shared meanings relies on a faulty theory of society. Since there are no discrete societies, but only cross-cutting networks, there can be no such conflicts of incommensurable meaning. The social meanings and forms of others are available to us for warning, emulation and utopian construction. I have not argued that humans never face each other across divides in understanding: that would be merely silly. I have argued that the divides do not separate us into discrete bodies of people who share meanings internally, but have no access or understanding externally. Each of

43 Mann, *Sources of Social Power*, vol. 1, p. 17.

44 Or, on one of a set of theories of society which share this value-gradient, but perhaps not a great deal else.

us has many networks in which we share meaning, and many boundaries at which we currently do not. I say *currently*, because humans clearly do have capacities to cross such boundaries: we have the capacity to create shared meaning with strangers. If we did not, it is difficult to see how the shared meanings to which Walzer appeals could have come about, since all of us frequently meet and deal with strangers, beginning with our parents. That is, the capacity which makes Walzer's shared meanings possible also makes his mutually incomprehensible bodies of meaning-sharers impossible. Humans can only share meaning because we can reach across divides in understanding. There is no 'we' and incomprehensible 'they', and the social practices of the Nuer,[45] for instance, are as available to us as to any other human.

To recap: I have argued that the possibility of shared meaning depends on society; that society is not such as could support the existence of incommensurable meanings; and further, that the very social capacity which creates shared meanings makes separate societies of *us* and *them* impossible.

### *Epistemic Colonialism*

It may be suggested that I have missed the point. Walzer is talking about *cultures*, not societies, as his appeal to shared *meaning* indicates. He is following Clifford Geertz (his colleague in the Institute of Advanced Studies at Princeton) in believing that 'man is an animal suspended in webs of significance he himself has spun' and taking 'culture to be those webs, and the analysis of it to be therefore not an experimental science in search of law but an interpretive one in search of meaning'.[46] His interpretation of shared meanings and consequent critical practice are interpretive, and he has taken to heart the idea that there is something especially difficult about interpretation *abroad*, as opposed to *at home*. This is not a counter-argument to what I have claimed, unless we are prepared to suppose that culture is independent of the society of the people who are its carriers and makers. In the absence of such a claim (which would surely be absurd), the fact that humans do not live in discrete, mutually exclusive societies means that their cultures are not discrete or mutually exclusive either.

---

45 I discuss the Nuer in Chapter 4.

46 Clifford Geertz, 'Thick Description: Toward an interpretive theory of culture' in *The Interpretation of Cultures: Selected essays* (London, 1993), pp. 3–30, p. 5. Walzer explicitly appeals to Geertz's work in *Thick and Thin*, p. xi, note 1. The claim that mutual human understanding must be interpretive rather than (what is called) naturalistic will be most familiar, to philosophers, from the work of Charles Taylor (see for instance his 'Interpretation and the Sciences of Man', in *Philosophy and the Human Sciences: Philosophical papers 2* (Cambridge, 1985), pp. 15–57). It is therefore worth noting that Geertz is not as sympathetic to Taylor's work as might, at first glance, be expected: see his 'The Strange Estrangement: Charles Taylor and the natural sciences', in *Available Light: Anthropological reflections on philosophical topics* (Princeton, 2000), pp. 143–59.

The point about culture, and about Geertz's semiotic understanding of it in particular, is none the less important. Walzer has adopted Geertz, and Geertz's work does *appear* to support particularist claims: but, I shall argue, it does not (and consequently, anthropological theory does not support the particularist theories I am using Walzer to exemplify).

Geertz is importantly a deflator of the pretensions of scientific anthropology.[47] It had been believed that one could (for instance) travel from England to the Sudan, describe the social form of the Nuer as a 'segmentary lineage', and thereby understand the Nuer themselves (this is of course a pastiche, but it will do to make the point). The understanding gained would help one to predict Nuer behaviour, to bring them under 'rational' administration as part of an empire, and to place them in a wider taxonomy of human social forms and their historical development (as a certain kind of acephalous tribe). Geertz argues that, on the contrary, understanding the Nuer or anyone else is a difficult, and never complete process of *interpretation*. Encounters with cultures are attempts at reading: 'Doing ethnography is like trying to read (in the sense of "construct a reading of") a manuscript – foreign, faded, full of elipses, incoherencies, suspicious emendations, and tendentious commentaries.'[48] Further, what one reads or interprets is always already an interpretation. There is no bedrock of uninterpreted data: the ethnographer is always 'explicating explications'.[49]

Two things have lent themselves to misinterpretation in this argument. The first is that Geertz's examples are typically, and unsurprisingly, from ethnographic fieldwork. He describes, for instance, a complex 'confusion of tongues' between Jewish, Berber and French 'frames of interpretation' in Morocco, in 1912 (as reported to him in 1968).[50] This may give rise to the thought – in my view, *has* given rise to it – that there is something especially difficult about going *abroad* and attempting to understand *them*, or in attempting to translate between Jewish, Berber and French self-understandings, but that no such difficulty applies when we are *at home*, or when Jews, Berbers or French people talk amongst themselves. The second thing which lends itself to misunderstanding is Geertz's emphasis on the incompleteness of interpretation. There is no final reading of culture, only an ongoing process of rereading, of attempting to reunderstand what is already understood. This may give rise to the thought that interpretation (when abroad) cannot be done at all, because it cannot be finished.[51]

---

47 He is part of the interpretive turn which overtook so many of the human sciences from the mid-twentieth century, and which also included, for instance, the work of Jerome Bruner in psychology. See Bruner, *Acts of Meaning* (Cambridge, MA, 1990).

48 Geertz, 'Thick Description', p. 10.

49 Ibid., p. 9.

50 Ibid., pp. 9–10.

51 We might be reminded of the David Lodge character who plans 'a series of commentaries on Jane Austen which would work through the whole canon, one novel at a time, saying absolutely everything that could possibly be said about them. The idea was to be utterly exhaustive, to examine the novels from every conveivable angle, historical, biographical, rhetorical, mythical, Freudian, Jungian, existentialist, Marxist, structuralist,

Neither of these thoughts seems to me to do justice to what Geertz says. Geertz is importantly influenced by the later Wittgenstein,[52] and his method is best understood as an application and development of Wittgenstein's approach to language. Culture, like language, is *public*, and understanding it does not consist in cracking its code, discovering its logical form or subsuming it under a concept ('segmentary lineage'). It consists in learning to go on in the right way. So, 'finding our feet' in someone's culture is a matter of 'seeking, in the widened sense of the term in which it encompasses very much more than talk, to converse with them, a matter a great deal more difficult, *and not only with strangers*, than is commonly recognized'.[53] Geertz's point is not that there is something fundamentally problematic about conversing when abroad, but that there is something mysterious about conversing *at all*. None the less, we do manage to converse: 'The famous anthropological absorption with the (to us) exotic [is] essentially a device for displacing the dulling sense of familiarity with which the mysteriousness of our own ability to relate perceptively to one another is concealed from us.'[54]

So: Geertz's point is not that, when we venture abroad, we leave behind a people and a culture which we effortlessly understand, and encounter a people and a culture which is and must remain wholly opaque to us. It is that our interpretations of one another are always tentative and ongoing, wherever we are: 'Foreignness does not start at the water's edge but at the skin's ... The wogs begin long before Calais.'[55] The anthropological exotic (apart from its intrinsic interest) is a way of bringing home to ourselves both the difficulty and the surprising *possibility* of mutual understanding. Geertz's interpretive anthropology, far from supporting the Walzerian claim that understanding and critique cannot leave home, emphasizes the fact that, unavoidably, we *continuously* cross our own boundaries, and encounter strangers.

I have already pastiched one kind of anthropology, which attempts to understand others by discovering the logical form of their culture, or by subsuming it under concepts. This kind of anthropology certainly was involved in actual colonial projects: E.E. Evans-Pritchard's pioneering work with the Nuer,[56] for instance, was involved with British colonialism. When Evans-Pritchard lived with and studied

---

Christian-allegorical, ethical, exponential, linguistic, phenomenological, archetypal, you name it; so that when each commentary was written there would be simply *nothing further to say* about the novel in question', *Changing Places* (London, 1975), p. 44.

52 See 'Passage and Accident: A life of learning', in *Available Light: Anthropological reflections on philosophical topics* (Princeton, NJ, 2000), pp. 3–20.

53 Geertz, 'Thick Description', p. 13. My emphasis.

54 Ibid., p. 14.

55 Geertz, 'The Uses of Diversity', in *Available Light: Anthropological reflections on philosophical topics* (Princeton, NJ, 2000), pp. 68–88, p. 76.

56 *The Nuer: A description of the modes of livelihood and political institutions of a Nilotic people* (Oxford, 1940); 'The Nuer of the Southern Sudan', in Meyer Fortes and E.E. Evans-Pritchard (eds), *African Political Systems* (London, 1940), pp. 272–96; *Kinship and Marriage Among the Nuer* (Oxford, 1951); *Nuer Religion* (Oxford, 1956). I discuss the Nuer further in Chapter 4.

them in the 1930s, the Nuer were a group of perhaps two or three hundred thousand people living around the Nile, in what was then the Anglo-Egyptian Sudan, in East Africa. They were having to deal rapidly with invasion by British military forces and the consequent imposition of new administrative and political institutions, including, for instance, a colonial governor who argued that the Nuer 'are slow to appreciate the blessings of European civilization and the benefits arising from an ordered administration of their country. Although this outspoken self-consciousness was bound to lead to conflicts, it must be admitted that the personal qualities of the people that caused these conflicts are of a kind that ought to be cultivated and guided rather than blamed and suppressed.'[57] Evans-Pritchard 'was profoundly aware of "the colonial encounter" and was, in fact, part of it',[58] having been commissioned by the state to investigate the Nuer. We should be wary of ascribing crudely colonial motives to him personally, but should be aware that at least part of the point of his investigations was to render the Nuer transparent to bureaucratic surveillance, and thereby to put them under state control.

So, one sort of attempt to understand others – the Nuer, in this case – is clearly historically related to one sort of colonial project. The two are also analogous, at least in that both are one-sided and probably self-interested (they involve the imposition of structures of understanding or control by one side on the other, apparently for purposes of exploitation). Perhaps the thinking which leads to positions like Walzer's is this: (attempted) understanding of other cultures was part of morally disastrous colonial projects; we should never have undertaken such projects (we should have stayed at home); critiques of this kind of understanding (such as Geertz's) are therefore critiques of 'going abroad' in understanding, and of the consequent attempt to criticize and transform local arrangements in terms of 'the blessings of European civilization'. However, as I argued above, this misunderstands Geertz's critique. We can certainly reject attempts to impose our own social arrangements on others, especially when doing so requires violence and oppression, but we are unwise to do so in terms of a rejection of the possibility of understanding other cultures. Not all transcultural understanding takes that form; if Geertz is right, no genuine understanding of humans *could* take it, for reasons analogous to Wittgenstein's reasons for denying the possibility of private language.

This last point seems to take us further than I want to go. In later chapters, I shall use information about human social forms of precisely the kind which Geertz's argument rejects, including Evans-Pritchard's research on the Nuer. However, I suggest that this information is not worthless. Whether or not we think that mutual human understanding must take the form Geertz describes, rendering local, opaque social forms transparent to bureaucratic surveillance has historically been an effective

57 Diedrich Westermann, Introduction to Ray Huffman, *Nuer Customs and Folk-Lore* (London, 1970; first published 1931), pp. v–xi, p. v.

58 Sharon E. Hutchinson, *Nuer Dilemmas: Coping with money, war, and the state* (Berkeley, CA, 1996), p. 30.

method of domination.[59] *Something*, therefore, is apparently being understood in such cases, even if it is not culture. Anthropological research of this non-Geertzian kind is useful for domination; it can therefore be useful for resistance, and for discovering human social possibility.

In subsequent chapters, I shall describe and make use of some landmarks in the human social landscape: in Chapter 3, some warnings; in Chapter 4, some elements of a possible utopia. In the rest of this chapter, I shall further investigate some of the significant capacities which humans create and deploy in social networks.

## Capacities of Domination and Resistance

I have emphasised the point that humans collaborate in social networks to create, and to assign capacities which they could not individually attain. These include productive, semiotic, ritual and communicative capacities. In particular, we create and assign capacities to dominate and to resist domination. I now want to investigate these capacities in more detail.

Domination and resistance are *cooperatively created* capacities, and not, except derivatively, capacities of individuals. Individuals dominate, or are able to resist, because they have the cooperative (not necessarily the voluntary) support of others. My argument for this point derives from Hobbes's egalitarianism of fear. For Hobbes, human equality is a brute fact about human bodies. No matter what small advantages she enjoys over other individual humans, no one is strong or vigilant enough to resist a coalition. The others can always gang up on you – and they know where you sleep. So, the dominance of one person over others is the product both of cooperation in her support, and of its absence (or lesser extent) in resistance, and not of her individual superiority. One obvious counterargument to this claim is to point out that some human bodies are clearly not equal to others, because they are damaged or genetically disordered. Some people need constant care even to stay alive, and cannot be a threat to anyone. Although true, this misses the point. Hobbes's egalitarianism is based not on a claim of equal potential for threat, but of *equal vulnerability*. The claim is not that anyone could kill you, but that anyone could be killed. A dictator dominates because she is surrounded by armies, bureaucracies and their supporting industries, not because she is herself invulnerable.[60]

Humans frequently cooperate to create capacities of domination, and just as frequently to resist domination. However, there are clearly many different ways in which they do so. In the rest of this section, I shall discuss some forms of domination and resistance, and of the particular ways in which, historically, they have been enacted.

---

59 See James C. Scott, *Seeing Like a State: How certain schemes to improve the human condition have failed* (New Haven, CT, 1998).

60 I hope to pursue this idea of an egalitarianism based on shared vulnerability elsewhere.

## *Power and Freedom*

Domination is a multifaceted feature of human life, and therefore so is resistance. Neither has a single, simple definition: both can be seen in a variety of social performances, which display family resemblances rather than expressing a single form. I shall explore these various facets of domination and resistance by drawing on philosophical analyses of two related, contested concepts: power and freedom.[61] The central ambiguity of the concept of power is that it can be attacked (or justified) as the power of one person or group over another on the one hand, but celebrated as collective action ('people power') on the other. Anarchists have often assumed that power, as such, is domination and an evil; but need to celebrate power, particularly the power of people against and in the absence of domination. I shall now consider some parts of Talcott Parsons's account of power, in order to theorise this distinction.

Parsons's account was developed as a response to elite theory in political science, and first stated in a review of C. Wright Mills's *The Power Elite*.[62] The final section of Parsons's critique of Mills begins with an analogy between power and wealth, and his later account of power elaborates that analogy into one between analyses of policial and economic 'sub-systems'. According to Parsons, 'To Mills, power is not a facility for the performance of function in and on behalf of the society as a system, but is interpreted exclusively as a facility for getting what one group, the holders of power, wants by preventing another group, the "outs", from getting what it wants.'[63] For him, this is metonymic: it confuses a 'secondary and derived'[64] aspect of power with the whole phenomenon. Certainly, there is such power, but that is not the whole story. This is where the analogy with wealth first appears:

> There is obviously a distributive aspect of wealth and it is in a sense true that the wealth of one person or group by definition cannot also be possessed by another group. Thus the *distribution* of wealth is, in the nature of the case, a focus of conflicts of interest in a society. But what of the positive functions of wealth and of the conditions of its production? It has become fully established that the wealth available for distribution can only come about through the processes of production, and that these processes require the "co-operation" or integration of a variety of different agencies … Wealth in turn is a generalized class of facilities available to units of the society – individuals and various types and levels of collectivities – for whatever uses may be important to them. But even apart from the question of where each share goes, the fact that there should be wealth to divide, and how much, cannot be taken for granted as given except within a very limited context.[65]

61 Both are often claimed, in fact, to be *essentially* contested; however, the idea of essential contestation has become so stretched and muddled since W.B. Gallie's original, careful statement of it ('Essentially Contested Concepts', *Proceedings of the Aristotelian Society* vol. 56 (1956): 167–98) that I think it best left alone here.

62 Mills, *The Power Elite* (New York, 1956); Parsons, 'The Distribution of Power in American Society', *World Politics* vol. 10 (1957): 123–43.

63 Parsons, 'The Distribution of Power in American Society', p. 139.

64 Ibid.

65 Ibid., pp. 139–40.

Parsons's point is that power is not necessarily or even normally 'zero-sum'.[66] Power, like wealth, is not subject to anything like the law of conservation of energy. It can be created and destroyed, as well as redistributed.

As stated, Parsons's analysis relies on the picture of 'a society' as a discrete unit which I have rejected. However, it need not. In Michael Mann's terms, power can be either 'distributive' or 'collective'.[67] In the first case, for A to gain power over B, B must lose power over A. We can think of there being a fixed amount of power available for distribution between two agents, just as we can think of there being a fixed amount of money, perhaps from an inheritance, similarly available. In the second case, 'persons in cooperation can enhance their joint power over third parties or over nature.'[68] In the terms I have so far adopted, capacities, including the capacity for domination, can be created by cooperation in networks; domination is distributed power. This vocabulary of 'capacity' and 'domination' has the advantage of clarity over the double use of 'power'.

Many social situations display both created capacities and domination: states, for instance, create many new capacities and greatly increase old ones, and assign vast capacities of domination to their elites.[69] However, the two are independent: during the Spanish civil war, collective creation of organisational and productive capacities kept trams, trains, factories and food-production going without supposedly-necessary domination, as well as creating and supplying militias to resist Franco's attempted coup.[70]

Domination is distributed power; but we need to say more. Specifically, we need to distinguish the main forms which that distribution takes, and then to describe some ways in which these forms are negotiated. In order to carry out the first task, I make the initial assumption that freedom and distributed power are opposites: to be free is not to be the object of such power (perhaps because one has power over others). This assumption will be complicated by further analysis of the two concepts.

According to Steven Lukes, (distributed) power is three-dimensional: it has three aspects or forms.[71] The first dimension concentrates on the observed success of an actor in getting her own way in a conflicted decision, made by or in a political institution. That actor who most often succeeds in having decisions made in line with her explicit preferences, against the explicit preferences of others, is, according

66 Parsons, 'On the Concept of Political Power', in *Sociological Theory and Modern Society* (New York, 1967), pp. 297–354, p. 337.

67 Mann, *Sources of Social Power*, vol. 1, p. 6. Mann's analysis is explicitly indebted to Parsons's.

68 Ibid.

69 See Chapter 3.

70 See Chapter 4.

71 *Power: A radical view* (London, 1974). Lukes develops this analysis by criticism of the 'one dimensional' view of Robert Dahl in *Who Governs? Democracy and power in an American city* (New Haven, CT, 1961) and of the 'two dimensional' view of Peter Bachrach and Morton Baratz in 'Two Faces of Power', *American Political Science Review* vol. 56 (1962): 947–52.

to this view, the one with the most power.[72] The actors who typically lose such conflicts are therefore, according to my initial assumption, unfree to the extent that they do so. We should note that this makes freedom a matter of degree: one could be more free in some contexts than in others, and unfree to some greater or lesser extent in general. This picture of unfreedom as being prevented from getting one's way complements the negative conception of freedom, on which to be free is not to be prevented from getting what one desires by external obstacles (bars and chains; threats of violence).[73] The second dimension adds that power has two faces. The first is success in *explicit* policy conflicts; the second, 'mobilisation of bias' to prevent some policy conflicts from *becoming* explicit. This is still matched by the negative conception of freedom, complicated by the idea that the freedom-limiting obstacle bars access to the *means* – the levers of collective power – by which one might get what one desires. Lukes's third dimension adds that 'the most effective and insidious use of power is to prevent … conflict from arising in the first place.'[74] While distributed power is exercised in getting its object to do what she does not want to do, and in preventing her access to collective means for getting what she wants, it is also exercised in shaping her wants such that no conflict with the wants of the powerful arises. This third aspect complements some positive conceptions of freedom:[75] the types of unfreedom include barriers and distortions in the self; to be free is to have capacities of self-shaping, self-control and resistance to external manipulation. Someone whose self has been shaped such that she chooses to pursue a life which is in others' interests and not her own may be unfree, even though she is not in chains, because she is not autonomous.[76]

So far, we have a fairly general distinction of types of domination and related unfreedoms (that is, of capacities to distribute power and their effects). We now

72 It is not always clear whether this is intended to make an ontological or only an epistemic claim: whether the claim is that this is what power is, and the only situation in which it exists, or only that this is a good proxy indicator for power, and the only situation in which we can reliably identify it.

73 The term is, of course, Isaiah Berlin's: 'Two Concepts of Liberty' in *Four Essays on Liberty* (Oxford, 1969), pp. 118–72.

74 Lukes, *Power*, p. 23.

75 I say only *some* positive conceptions, because I doubt that '*the* positive conception of freedom' is a useful category. Its contents appear to be defined only as 'not negative', and are widely various. The claims that freedom requires resources (so that I am not free to eat unless I can afford to buy food, as well as being free of obstacles to my eating) and that it requires the true, rational self to be in charge (so that I am not free if I act on my passions) are both 'positive' conceptions of freedom, but have little in common.

76 This formulation raises the question of whether we can identify someone's interests independently of her desires. I take it that we can in principle do so. We might relate interests to (basic) needs. Or we might appeal to counterfactuals of two types: the choice the subject would make, if she could experience both the satisfaction of her current desires, and the satisfaction of (what we claim are) her real interests, and then pick one; and the desires she would have in an ideal situation of perfect information and undistorted rationality. Clearly, this issue raises complex problems, but I do not need to consider them further here.

need to move from the general to the more particular, and consider some historically common forms of domination and resistance.

### *Forms of Domination and Resistance*

Capacities, and capacities of domination and resistance in particular, can be created and destroyed as well as assigned. There are two common ways in which they are created. The first is cooperation: by working together, humans create capacities which none could attain individually. I mean 'cooperation' to cover all cases of humans working together, and not to be limited, for instance, to the subset of voluntary collaboration. The second way of creating capacities can be called 'expertise' or 'technique'. An increase in knowledge about how things work and in skill in applying that knowledge creates new capacities and increases old ones: the development of techniques of agriculture creates capacities to live in new ways (especially ways which require leisure from gathering food) and increases our capacity to feed people (measured as the number of humans who can be supported per unit area). Technique and cooperation are analytically distinct, but often appear intertwined and codependent in real social situations. Much development of technique is and must be cooperative, and much cooperation depends on particular (typically organisational) technique.

Power can be distributed in a wide variety of ways, from equality to slavery. That is, from low to extreme levels of domination. In this section I shall consider three ways in which domination can be enacted and resisted: violence, authority and property.

First, violence and the credible threat of violence (from now on just 'violence') are effective and common ways both of enacting and of resisting domination. It has sometimes been argued, as for instance by John Hospers,[77] that states' capacities for domination are centrally or even solely maintained by violence, in the form of publicly known coercive sanctions, up to and including (the threat of) death, monopolised by state institutions. That is, that violence is a state's only means of meeting resistance to its domination. This is simplistic: as I show below, there are other ways in which states, and other organisations, can and do maintain particular forms of domination. However, it is undeniable that states do make considerable use of this way of maintaining their domination.

Secondly, it is fairly common practice among anarchists and their critics to characterise anarchism as anti-authoritarianism. On the face of it, this gloss has some force: anarchists do devote much of their time and energy to activities (from research to pamphleteering to rioting) which can easily and plausibly be described as anti-authoritarian. However, there are good reasons not to focus anarchist theory too closely on the concept of authority. They parallel my reasons for not understanding anarchism as anti-statism, in my Introduction. The arguments given there also apply here: a characterisation of anarchism as anti-authoritarianism is not distinguishing,

77 *Libertarianism: A political philosophy for tomorrow* (Los Angeles, CA, 1971).

complete or helpful. Further, we can distinguish at least two types of authority. Someone can be *an* authority *on* some*thing*, that is respected in, an expert on, or worth listening to about, some subject or domain; or *in* authority *over* some*one*, that is in an institutional position which is supposed to confer the right to command, and to impose a corresponding duty to obey, in some domain.[78] Anarchists sometimes explicitly, and very often implicitly, accept and celebrate authority of the first kind. Kropotkin, for instance, is widely remembered by anarchists with respect and affection, and his work is still read for more than nostalgic reasons (as by me). Anarchists certainly do set themselves against the second kind of authority, whether held by teachers, sergeants, priests or politicians. However, at least some of these attacks are grounded in the point that the people *in* authority are not authorities *on* the right way to live, and anarchists have typically been just as worried about domination which involves no claim of authority: a powerful bully is just as bad as an authoritative drill-sergeant. So, I suggest that authority is best brought in, as here, as derivative of domination.

By an 'authority discourse' I shall mean a shared vocabulary and habit of social action which makes use of, and is justified and motivated by, a concept of (legitimate) authority. To take one example: the shared vocabulary and habit of representative democratic politics involves a concept of authority. The idea of politicians' derivative authority is used to maintain their share of domination, and to justify and motivate their use of the distinctive capacities which are assigned to their institutional roles. This is not a necessary, but is apparently a widespread and effective, way to maintain forms of life in which some individuals dominate. It is also a widespread and effective form of resistance to such domination. Democratic politicians' authority is understood in terms of their representation of 'the people', and their domination can therefore be challenged with a claim that they have lost their authority (or legitimacy) by failing to be representative. Non-democratic elites can similarly be challenged with the claim that they do not enjoy what is claimed to be the only possible source for legitimate authority: popular consent. Democratic discourse is therefore both a way of maintaining and a way of challenging this particular form of domination, as grounded in claims about authority. Further, authority discourses in general can be a way of attempting to move towards a situation of more equal power (less domination). Claiming my authority over my own person is one way to resist a form of domination where someone else has power over, for instance, my sexual choices.

Two remarks: as I have characterised them, authority discourses involve the related concept of duty. Authority to command is understood to convey a reciprocal duty to obey. I am aware that the idea of duty is not in general restricted to this role (and describe another of its roles in relation to property, below), but do not need to consider it further here. Secondly, by focusing on the idea and discourse, rather than the fact of authority, I do not mean to imply acceptance of the philosophical anarchist

78 See, for instance, Richard E. Flathman, *The Practice of Political Authority: Authority and the authoritative* (Chicago, IL, 1980).

position that there is logically no such thing as real or legitimate authority.[79] I neither have nor need an opinion about that claim. I focus on authority discourse rather than real authority because I am interested, here, in the ways in which we can create and resist domination. Authority discourses are apparently effective for those tasks, whatever view we take of the reality of their subject, so long as they are understood by, and at least partially convincing to, the people involved in them. Whether or not authority is morally real, it is a social fact.

Third, by a 'property discourse' I shall mean a shared vocabulary and habit of social action which makes use of, and is justified and motivated by, a concept of (legitimate) property. It is worth analysing the elements of such concepts in some detail. Property-ownership is minimally a triadic relation between two (individual or collective) agents and some (tangible or intangible) good: 'A owns B against C.'[80] If I say that this is *my* copy of *Leviathan*, I am asserting a complex relationship between A = me, B = this tangible object, a book, and C = some (perhaps all) other people. The relationship asserted by property discourses is not single, and can profitably be analysed as a bundle of relations. The relations variously asserted and socially instantiated by particular property discourses, in relation to particular goods, include *claim-rights* with correlative *duties* and opposite *no-rights*, and *powers* with correlative *liabilities* and opposite *disabilities*.[81] This 'analytical vocabulary'[82] allows us to unpick particular examples of property-talk. So, for instance, if I own a farm, I have a *power* to transfer that ownership, and some other people have a corresponding *liability* to receive it. Or, if I owe you £10, you have a *claim-right* for £10 from me, I have a corresponding *duty* to give it to you; but if I do not, you have *no right* to take it from me. The vocabulary does not give any guidance on how to resolve particular disputes about property, but merely allows us to describe particular property-claims and their differences. Nor does it necessarily identify all of the possible relations we might want to include in a description of some property discourse; it does, however, identify some important and common ones.

Although this analysis was originally designed as a conceptual toolkit for lawyers and judges working in a 'mature system of law',[83] it has wider application. E. Adamson Hoebel, for instance, puts it to use in describing the property discourse

79 See Wolff, *In Defence of Anarchism*, and my Introduction.

80 A.I. Hallowell, 'The Nature and Function of Property as a Social Institution' in *Culture and Experience* (New York, 1967), pp. 236–49, p. 239.

81 See further Stephen R. Munzer, *A Theory of Property* (Cambridge, 1990), p. 19. This Hohfeld-Honoré analysis has been widely used in legal, philosophical and anthropological accounts of property. See, for instance, L.C. Becker, *Property Rights: Philosophical foundations* (London, 1977); John Christman, *The Myth of Property: Toward an egalitarian theory of ownership* (New York, 1994); E. Adamson Hoebel, 'Fundamental Legal Concepts as Applied in the Study of Primitive Law', *Yale Law Journal* vol. 51 (1942): 951–66; Jeremy Waldron, *The Right to Private Property* (Oxford, 1988).

82 Munzer, *A Theory of Property*, p. 18.

83 A.M. Honoré, 'Ownership' in A.G. Guest (ed.), *Oxford Essays in Jurisprudence* (Oxford, 1961), pp. 107–47, p. 108.

of the Yurok Indians of Northern California.[84] Whether or not a property discourse is enacted in the context of a formal legal system, and whatever legal, customary or other sanctions are used to support it, the vocabulary is useful in describing the ways in which people understand, claim and dispute the various claim-rights, privileges and so on which make it up.

So, property as a discourse and social institution can profitably be analysed into a bundle of distinct incidents which may attach to one person, be shared by a group of people, or be divided amongst several people. Modern Western property law has tended to attach most or all of the elements of ownership to one legal person, the owner of the object in question. However, there is nothing necessary or universal about that agglomeration. The different elements which are involved in property discourses can be distributed between people in many different ways, for different practical, traditional and moral reasons. So, for instance, 'in the early middle ages, land in England could not plausibly be said to be "owned" because' the various relations of power, privilege and so on 'were so divided between lord and tenant that the position of neither presented a sufficient analogy with the paradigm case of owning a thing.'[85]

Property discourses are a means of domination because, where a particular discourse is understood, mostly convincing and sanctioned in a social form, it is an effective way of assigning differential capacities to hold and use goods. In the first place, such goods can be used to influence the behaviour of others such that one gets one's own way in conflicted decisions, can bar access to decision-making processes, and can transform their wants. That is: property, and especially money, can buy distributed power. In the second place, where a property discourse allows the ownership of other people – slavery – it is directly involved in domination.[86] Property discourses can also be a means of resistance. To return to an earlier example: the workers on my farm may argue that, because the wheat crop is the product of their labour (while I sit in the farmhouse counting my money), they rather than I own it. Or, my slaves may assert their self-ownership. In both cases, I may respond by asserting a legal property discourse and by calling on the sanctions with which the state backs it up.

As with my account of authority, I do not mean to imply any view on the reality of property by concentrating on the social effectiveness of property discourses. I do, in fact, think that patterns of property-ownership often fail to reflect any moral reality, but not for conceptual or definitional reasons. The significance of property discourses, here, is that they are apparently a widespread and effective way of creating and resisting domination, whatever view we take of property's reality, or of the justice of the particular property distributions which a particular discourse supports or challenges.

84 'Fundamental Legal Concepts as Applied in the Study of Primitive Law'.

85 Honoré, 'Ownership', p. 109.

86 See Chapter 3.

All three of the ways of creating, maintaining and resisting domination are historically common and apparently effective. They also commonly appear intertwined and in concert, at least in our current arrangements. States, in particular, use all three, and support one with another.[87]

## Conclusion

I began this chapter with a problem: the utopian practice I propose was under threat from a powerful objection, represented by Michael Walzer's argument that there are no moral resources for *us* outside our own particular world of shared meanings. I have answered that objection by arguing that the possibility of shared meaning depends on society; that society is not such as could support the existence of incommensurable meanings; and further, that the very social capacity which creates shared meanings makes separate societies of *us* and *them* impossible. In making the second part of that argument, I set out and argued for a theory of society. That theory – a projection of the human landscape – answers Walzer's objection, but it also goes further. It is intended not merely as an answer, but as the context for the rest of this book. In Chapter 3, I move further from the general towards the particular, and describe some major, familiar landmarks within the human landscape. They stand as warnings for us in their exemplification of domination. In Chapter 4, I locate some perhaps less familiar landmarks and reasons for hope. In Chapter 5, I pull them together into a (schematic) anarchist utopia.

87 See Chapter 3.

# Chapter 3

# Living With Domination

I have so far dealt with several objections to the possibility of an anarchist utopia, and to the practice of anarchist utopianism. It may be suggested, however, that I have yet to face the most obvious objection to my project and claims: the facts of human life. Looking at our immediate surroundings and history, we can see that humans live, and therefore probably can *only* live, in systems of domination. States are everywhere. Slavery is common. Anarchist utopianism, therefore, is unacceptable in a very simple way: it is naïve about real human life.

This is a powerful objection, but not in the end a killer blow. It is undeniable that the world is, and often has been full of systems of domination. However, a closer examination of some of the more widespread of those systems, in the context of my account of the human landscape in the previous chapter, will show that our situation is not as bad as this objection claims.

## States

States are not the only, but are the pre-eminent dominating institutions in our current world (despite challenges by, and partial integration with multinational corporations and international organisations). I argued in my Introduction that anarchism should not be characterised as anti-statism; but it is undeniable that anarchists are against and interested in states, and also undeniable that they should be. Here, I consider two anarchist accounts of the state, before going on to analyse two important kinds of state: pristine and modern states. First, however, I describe states in general.

The question, What is the state?, invites the response, Which one? Derbyshire and Derbyshire[1] list nearly two hundred currently existing states, and even if we ignore past states and limit ourselves only to those, are we asking about the Republic of the Ivory Coast, or the Kingdom of Thailand, or the Federation of Malaysia, or the United States of America? Post-colonial states or superpowers? 'Modern states come in a variety of shapes and sizes, and they arrived by different routes.'[2] Any list assumes that we can separate states from the nations, or forms of production, or other networks in which they are embedded, or with which they compete. Are armed forces part of the state? Are corporations based in its territory? We might come to

---

1 J. Denis Derbyshire and Ian Derbyshire, *Political Systems of the World* (New York, 1996).

2 James Anderson, 'The Modernity of Modern States' in Anderson (ed.), *The Rise of the Modern State* (Brighton, 1986), pp. 1–20, p. 1.

agree with A.J.P. Taylor that 'one of the great blunders of modern political thinking is to invent an abstract entity called the State.'[3]

State is 'undeniably a messy concept',[4] and names a large and contested set of ideas, institutions, organisational tactics and social networks with a complicated history of invention, change, interaction and collapse. In one sense, a history of the state would be a history of humanity: 'most questions about the origins of the state could be answered very simply: discover the origin of *Homo Sapiens Sapiens*.'[5] In another sense, which I shall pursue here, the states we find around us now are no more than, and often very much less than, seven hundred years old. They appeared in the latest moments of a human history which stretches back perhaps one hundred thousand years.[6] Although Clive Gamble is right that the capacities which make states possible for us are generic human capacities, I shall argue that what is particularly noticeable about those capacities is just how infrequently they have been used.

I take my beginning definition from Michael Mann: 'The state is a differentiated set of institutions and personnel embodying centrality, in the sense that political relations radiate outward to cover a territorially demarcated area, over which it claims a monopoly of binding and permanent rule-making, backed up by physical violence.'[7] States operate in a geographically defined area, a territory, where they (fairly successfully) claim a monopoly in the control of much (potentially all) human activity; and, typically, in an international arena made up of other sovereign states. The territory is organised around an administrative centre containing or representing an elite with distinctive capacities for domination. That elite consists of a network (or several networks) of power-holders including, for instance, kings, parliamentarians, aristocrats, bureaucrats, the wealthy, and military and religious leaders. Elite networks are typically hierarchically organised, and claim permanent authority over the citizens or subjects of 'the country', usually for their defined roles rather than for the particular individuals who happen currently to inhabit them. They have and exercise distributed power in all three of the dimensions explored in Chapter 2: they frequently get their way in conflicted decisions, they manage access to the arenas in which conflicts are resolved, and they modify the desires of the governed to limit conflict. All of the individuals involved in interaction with, and governed by a state cooperate in creating its social form and capacities (including the elite's capacity for domination).

---

3 'The Failure of the Habsburg Monarchy' in *Europe: Grandeur and decline* (Harmondsworth, 1967), pp. 127–32, p. 131.

4 Michael Mann, 'The Autonomous Power of the State: Its origins, mechanisms and results' in John A. Hall (ed.), *States in History* (Oxford, 1986), pp. 109–36, p. 112.

5 Clive Gamble, 'Hunter-Gatherers and the Origin of States', p. 22.

6 On the debate over the age of modern humans, see Richard Leakey, *The Origin of Humankind: Unearthing our family tree* (London, 1995), Chapter 5. Estimates range from 40,000 to 200,000 years.

7 Mann, *Sources of Social Power*, vol. 1, p. 37. Mann gives a near-identical definition in 'The Autonomous Power of the State'.

States are highly institutionalised bundles of networks which direct the creation of vast extra capacity (especially for domination, production and organisation), and which have successful, but not completely successful, unitary pretensions. These pretensions are of two kinds, and tend to be unsuccessful in two ways. First, states attempt to create unified and discrete societies in defined territories, which contain their subjects and physically or administratively exclude others, and which have precise cleavages at their boundaries. But humans – nomads, traders, refugees, internationalists, the members of diasporas – keep forming new networks across such boundaries. Secondly, states attempt to turn themselves into single organisations, but are, in fact, internally differentiated: 'States have multiple institutions, charged with multiple tasks, mobilizing constituencies both through their territories and geopolitically.'[8] States typically involve unstable compromises between different institutions, all attempting to gain primacy and to unify on their own terms. However, despite these two kinds of failure, states have been more successful than any other social form in making their subjects and territories tend towards an unreachable unity and discreteness.

State capacities are available, and have been used, for an enormous variety of purposes: codification and control of behaviour; redistribution of resources; organisation of warfare; imposition or encouragement of some, and suppression of other kinds of social network; promulgation of some, and suppression of other kinds of speech and claims; maintenance or transformation of social hierarchies; organisation of knowledge-gathering, exploration and colonisation; and the simplification of lives and networks through tactics intended to make opaque local practices legible to supervisory discipline. All of these purposes have also been carried out by non-state networks and institutions, despite state attempts to monopolise them.

In general, there seem to be no limits set by the structure of states on the limits to which their immense capacities can be put. States are available to be used by any individual or network which can get hold of their reins, because of the functional promiscuity which is characteristic of states as of all human networks and institutions. Left-wing anarchists can, in fact, approve of some of the uses to which state capacities have been put: redistributing wealth, welfare and socialised health systems, and limiting the influence of aristocracies and wealthy capitalists. Most anarchists would argue that even these achievements are poisoned by their use of state tactics and forms, including authority and property discourses, violence, hierarchy and attempted national unification, but it should not be denied that there are worse uses for states. To note some obvious examples: state capacities are available, and have been used, for the personal benefit of dictators and their cliques, for violent repression, to start and prosecute wars, and for genocide. The holocaust required, amongst other preconditions, the bureaucratic, productive and coercive capacities of a state.[9]

---

8 Mann, *Sources of Social Power*, vol. 2, p. 75.

9 On Nazi infiltration, use and transformation of the state, see for instance Michael Burleigh, *The Third Reich: A new history* (London, 2001), particularly Part Two. On the

As these examples imply, the final point to be made about states in general is their immense capacity for violence; I shall pursue this point further, below. First, I shall consider how and why some anarchists have separated states from non-states, before filling out my general characterisation of states for two of their particular kinds: pristine and modern states.

*Two Distinctions of State From Non-state*

Anarchists have often made and argued for a distinction between states and other forms of social activity (both concurrent with and prior to states' existence), and have criticised others for conflating them. Kropotkin, for instance, notes that 'There is the German school that likes to confuse the *State* with *Society*. This confusion is to be met even among the best German thinkers and many French ones, who cannot conceive society without State concentration; and thence arises the habitual reproach cast on Anarchists of wanting to "destroy society" and of "preaching the return of perpetual war of each against all".'[10] The point of this distinction between state and society is that 'the State is but one of the forms taken by society in the course of history',[11] and that humans are capable of organising themselves in other ways. Kropotkin goes on to define the state as involving a governing power, territorial concentration, and 'a concentration of many or even all of the functions of the life of society in the hands of a few'.[12] His distinction is useful for at least two purposes. It makes the argumentative point that anarchists want to remove the state (amongst other things), not social organisation and cooperation, and therefore that the common equation of anarchy with chaos cannot stand (without further argument to show that the state is the only way to avoid chaos). Secondly, it makes the historical point that current states are only one, recent human social form amongst many other possibilities.

Another separation of state from non-state:

> This latest form of the state, based on the pseudo-sovereignty of a sham popular will, supposedly expressed by pseudo-representatives of the people in sham popular assemblies, combines the two main conditions necessary for [capitalists'] success: state centralization, and the actual subordination of the sovereign people to the intellectual minority that governs them, supposedly representing them but invariably exploiting them.[13]

Bakunin intends both to attack the false identification of the interests of the capitalists and governors with the interests of the dominated people, and to assert a continuity of

---

bureaucratic detail of extermination, Lucy S. Dawidowicz, *The War Against the Jews, 1933–1945* (Toronto, 1976).

10 *The State: Its historic role*, ed. and trans. G.W. [probably George Woodcock] (London, 1943), p. 10.

11 Ibid.

12 Ibid.

13 Michael Bakunin, *Statism and Anarchy*, ed. and trans. M.S. Shatz (Cambridge, 1990), p. 13.

function between democratic and non-democratic states. 'Sham popular assemblies' do not, on this account, change the fundamental character of the state, which Bakunin goes on to describe as the organised exploitation of 'the people's labour' maintained by 'constant coercion and compulsion',[14] and as necessarily expansive and aggressive.

These characterisations of the state, and distinctions of it from society or the people, share a common purpose. Both insist that states, far from being universal or inescapable, are local, particular and only part of the human story. I shall now go on to analyse some of that particularity, by describing two kinds of states and their histories. First, pristine states.

### *Pristine States*

A 'pristine' or 'primary' state is defined as one which got started without influence from other states. They are extremely unusual: there have probably been only six pristine states in the history of humanity. The exact count depends, in particular, on the controversial inclusion of the Minoan state on Crete; the generally accepted members of the set are, in Eurasia, the Sumerian, Egyptian, Indus Valley and Yellow River states, and, in America, the Mesoamerican and Peruvian states.[15] Every other state (again ignoring the contested Minoan case) formed at least partly under influences from other states, including but not limited to conquest, colonisation, secession, importation of skilled bureaucrats, and deliberate mirroring intended to share in the perceived advantages of statehood, or to fight an invading state effectively.

What I have to say about pristine states is necessarily tentative. With just six examples, we can say something about how these particular states *in fact* got started, but cannot support many firm claims about how pristine states *must* get started. Worse, the available evidence is fragmentary and often difficult to interpret. Worse still, although we can make some generalisations, the six pristine states differ from one another in a number of ways. They appeared in differing environments, for instance: Mesopotamia and Egypt are 'basically great arid river valleys with little of the ecological variability of the New World regions',[16] and the New World lacked the large domesticable animals of the old.[17]

---

14 Ibid.

15 Mann, *Sources of Social Power*, vol. 1, p. 74. For a map of these states' distribution, see Lewellen, *Political Anthropology*, p. 49. Debate about this list of pristine states has often been of two kinds: for and against diffusionist theories which argue that the transition to a state happened only once, probably in the Middle East, and that the form then spread to the other supposed pristine states; and for and against monocausal theories which argue that transitions to states had one shared (type of) cause across all of these cases. I can remain neutral about these questions here.

16 Service, *Origins of the State and Civilization*, p. 203.

17 For discussion of the significance of environmental differences, see for instance Jared Diamond, *Guns, Germs and Steel: A short history of everybody for the last 13,000 years* (London, 1998).

The background to the appearance of pristine states is not a gradual climb through lower or simpler stages towards the pinnacle of statehood. Humans had complex and various social arrangements before they had states, and went through a long history of cycles of the creation and collapse of various social organisations and distributions of power. People 'would freely give collective, representative authority, to chiefs, elders, and bigmen for purposes ranging from judicial regulation to warfare to feast organisation', but those figures 'could not convert that into permanent, coercive power'.[18] Not only did the conditions of such conversion (discussed below) not usually obtain, but people 'devoted a considerable part of their cultural and organisational capacities'[19] to making sure that stable institutionalised domination could not be created, or was rapidly destroyed. People without states, on the archaeological and ethnographic evidence, live complicated lives; make their livings in many different ways (as hunters and gatherers, herders, farmers, or various combinations of these modes); know a great deal about their environments and each other; interact in highly mediated and complex ways across very large distances; and very rarely create states.

There are two major, necessary but not sufficient, conditions for the creation of a pristine state. The first is that 'the population not only had to be large (about 10,000 to 30,000 people), but it had to be "circumscribed".'[20] Circumscription means that people who would prefer not to submit to an incipient state are either unable to leave, or think the costs of doing so too high. This may be because of a lack of empty fertile land to move to; because of their investment in the land, often over generations, by planting, building and irrigation; or because they lack the technologies and skills necessary to make a living elsewhere. That is, for these or other reasons, they will not or cannot use one major tactic by which people have typically resisted state-formation: moving away. The second necessary condition is that some technologies, including writing, accounting and techniques for long-term food storage, had to exist. Once a state had got going, these technologies were further developed, particularly by the bureaucratic, aristocratic or priestly classes (which may not have been distinct) made possible by unequal distribution of resources.[21]

These conditions did not guarantee the creation of a state, which, it must appear from the small number of times it actually happened, was extremely difficult. On such rare occasions, the typical features of the state were: ceremonial and administrative centralisation; institutionalised unequal distribution of power and of

18 Mann, *Sources of Social Power*, vol. 1, p. 63.

19 Ibid., p. 39.

20 Marvin Harris, *Our Kind: Who we are, where we came from, where we are going* (New York, 1989), p. 388.

21 It has sometimes been argued that there is a third condition: the existence of a food surplus over subsistence level, allowing a community to support political and ritual specialists who do not produce their own sustenance. This claim has been attacked on the ground that 'subsistence level' is not and cannot be independently defined (see Marvin Harris, 'The Economy Has No Surplus?', *American Anthropologist* vol. 61 (1959): 185–99). Again, I can remain neutral about this issue.

the capacity to control the assignment and use of resources; the maintenance of classes of aristocrats, bureaucrats, priests and soldiers; the organisation of war and conquest in search of new territory, slaves, tribute or sacrificial victims; conscription of labour for large public works (like irrigation) and monumental projects (like pyramids); the codification of law; the creation and administration of central stores of goods for redistribution; and, finally, the ability to maintain itself past the deaths of significant individuals, by the creation of roles (king, priest, champion) separate from, and able to survive the death of, the people who happen currently to inhabit them. These features may or may not have appeared simultaneously, and they may individually have developed slowly or suddenly. Pristine states typically maintained their institutional structures, and their ways of creating and assigning capacities, by calling on authority discourses involving ritual and mythical elements which related the political to the cosmic order, and which often attributed divine attributes and ancestors to power-holders.

It is not clear to what extent the capacity to dominate involved in this strange new social form was taken, and to what extent given:

> One school of thought concerned with the origin of the state rejects the idea that ruling classes gained control over commoners as a result of a violent conspiracy carried out by the chiefs and their militia. In contrast, they see commoners submitting peacefully out of gratitude for the services that ruling classes provided. These services included emergency rations in times of famine, protection against enemy attacks, and construction and management of agricultural infrastructures such as dams and irrigation and drainage canals. Also, people believed that the rituals carried out by chiefs and priests were essential for everyone's survival.[22]

Harris plausibly suggests that 'both voluntaristic submission and violent repression were present';[23] we can add that there were probably different mixtures in different cases. Administrative centralisation would be (or seem to be) a good idea for the organisation of, in particular, the irrigation agriculture which was so important for the Eurasian river-valley civilisations, and such centralisation would then be pre-adapted for the other features of pristine states, or for the coups of would-be kings. But simultaneously, once a ruling mafia organisation had settled itself, it could come to be used and valued by commoners for purposes the rulers never intended.

In summary: humans can organise, and have organised themselves in a wide variety of ways, and for most of the time there have been humans, there have not been states. People can create and assign capacities, and in particular can distribute power, in various ways and for various purposes, but for most of human history 'authority was freely conferred, but recoverable; [distributed] power, permanent and coercive, was unattainable',[24] not least because people often deliberately resisted or moved away from attempts to institutionalise domination. However, on a few occasions, in

---

22 Harris, *Our Kind*, p. 383.

23 Ibid., p. 384.

24 Mann, *Sources of Social Power*, p. 39.

somewhat unusual circumstances, a new social form appeared: a pristine state. This centralised, administrative, expropriating institution made use of several tactics and technologies, especially for war, the creation and maintenance of class divisions, the codification of behaviour, and the organisation of collective projects. In general, it allowed the creation of increased capacity and new capacities, and assigned those capacities in a distinctive, unequal way.[25]

What morals and interest should we derive from this account of pristine states and their separation from the vast majority of human history? It reiterates and gives evidence for Kropotkin's point, noted above, that the state is just one of many possible human social forms. More, it is not a commonly created one. States have appeared only rarely without influence from other pre-existing states. The account implies some suggestions as to how to avoid state-formation in the currently, but not necessarily or normally unusual situation of being without one. It also suggests a question: given that pristine states are so hard to start, why are they currently ubiquitous? An answer to that question, which I approach below, should provide some useful information on how states spread, and therefore on how we might prevent their doing so.

However, I want to concentrate on two main morals. The first we should derive is that the most obvious characteristic of pristine states was their violence. Non-state groups do carry out limited and often formalised wars, and individuals obviously hurt one another, but only states maintain an army, carry out long campaigns, or hold onto and exploit conquered territory. While this does not show that (pristine) states are *necessarily* violent, violence does seem, as a matter of fact, to be one of their typical characteristics. War is historically a practice of states, not of humans in general.

The second and final main moral to draw is that the appearance of a pristine state is not an increase in complexity. In many ways, pristine states *simplify* their territories and the interactions of the people involved in them. According to Kent Flannery, states may typically be associated with deliberately simplified ecosystems.[26] More importantly, in place of interactions between mutually known individuals with complex kinships, friendships and other relationships, pristine states put, or try to put, stereotyped interactions between roles: king, priest, farmer, slave. In place of an often immense web of trade and gift-giving negotiated by individuals and overlapping groups: a single, central store of goods administered by power-holders. In place of a lifestyle often involving a wide range of skills and activities: craft specialisation, the division of labour, and the narrowing of individuals' activity and

25 What I have said here is deliberately an account, not an attempt at explanation, of the appearance of pristine states in human history. For recent reviews of explanatory theories of that appearance, see for instance Lewellen, *Political Anthropology*, Chapter 3, or Brian M. Fagan, *World Prehistory: A brief introduction* (New York, 1999), Chapter 8.

26 'The Cultural Evolution of Civilizations', *Annual Review of Ecology and Systematics*, vol. 3 (1972): 399–426, p. 399, note 1.

knowledge (this last did not begin with, but was increased and formalised by pristine and other early states).

The last point will become important in later chapters: although division of labour is now widespread, and is a tactic available in the absence of states, it is not a human universal. Humans have not always organised their production by assigning (ever-smaller) sub-tasks within some larger project to individuals who perform only that task. I take up the point about complexity again when I discuss modern states, in the next section.

The pristine states I have discussed did not turn into modern states: all six collapsed long before modern states appeared. In between, many other human social forms, including universalist religions and their heresies, empires, communes, guild-cities and monasteries, appeared, were transformed or absorbed, and collapsed. Some are still extant. I move from considering pristine to modern states not in order to write a history of states in general, but to describe two types of state which are important for our purposes.

### *Modern States*

Modern states are not the result of any general tendency, but a historically unique occurrence, and so, to describe them, we must understand their unique background and development. They appeared quite gradually, in Europe, from the early fourteenth century. It took them several hundred years to develop their repertoire of organisation, technical, social and ideological capacities, and to spread across the world.[27] I shall now sketch their background, development, nature and spread.

By definition, individual pristine states appeared in a stateless context. We should immediately note that modern states did not: they appeared and developed in a European and eventually a world state system, in competition and consort with one another. The system we now find ourselves in consists of modern states with sovereign legal personalities in relation to one another, not of 'the' modern state.

In order to simplify a complex story, I divide my account into four sections: the background and rise of absolutism; surveillance; nationalism; the spread of modern states.[28] Although these sections, with the exception of the last, do roughly follow the temporal order of appearance of the major features of modern states, I am more interested in analysing them than in reviewing their precise histories. I divide the spread of modern states from the rest of the story, not because it happened afterwards – it did not – but in order to see the methods of that spread clearly.

---

27 I adopt this long perspective, including absolutist states as modern, in order to indicate continuities between then and now. For other purposes, absolutist states are often regarded as mere ancestors of modern states: see, for instance, James Anderson (ed.), *The Rise of the Modern State* (Brighton, 1986).

28 The division is based on Martin Van Creveld, *The Rise and Decline of the State* (Cambridge, 1999). I draw extensively on Van Creveld for the general shape of my account of modern states.

Again in order to simplify a complex story, and to focus on the points which are important for our purposes, I deliberately exclude consideration of two other important developments over roughly the same period as the development of modern states: the economic transformation of western Europe and then the rest of the world; and the development of scientific, technical and historical knowledge, together with institutions which maintain and produce more of it. I do not suppose that these developments were independent of the rise of modern states, or of each other. However, their interdependence is extremely complex, and unlikely to be resolved into the causal primacy of any one of the three; and further, to consider them would be to tend towards writing a general history of our last thousand years, which, quite apart from its length, would obscure the points I want to make.

A final exclusion: I do not treat liberal democracy as typical of modern states, for the simple empirical reason that it is not. Derbyshire and Derbyshire's markers for identifying a liberal democracy are evidence of constitutional government; evidence of free elections for assemblies and executives; the active presence of more than one political party; evidence of checks and balances between the three elements of government: executive, legislative, and judicial; evidence of an independent judiciary; evidence of the protection of personal liberties through constitutional or other legal guarantees; and evidence of stability in liberal democratic government (defined as the system having been in place for at least the decade up to 1996).[29] Only slightly more than a third – 73 out of 192 – of the states they describe meet even these quite weak criteria. So, liberal democracy is one form, but not typical, of modern states.

*The background and rise of absolutism* The background to the gradual development of modern states is the social form usually known as feudalism. The name is problematic, for three reasons. Feudalism was neither static nor unitary, but an unstable compromise changing and eventually collapsing under a variety of pressures. Worse, the term itself is ambiguous: 'feudalism' can mean not only 'a lot of different things',[30] but, as the same author goes on to argue, may be so multivalent as to mean nothing useful. Worse still, the idea of feudalism may, as Elizabeth Brown has argued, be an artefact of nineteenth-century historiography, an ideal type without application to concrete history.[31] I continue to use the term for convenience, and as better than clumsy alternatives like 'the social form which prevailed in Europe before the rise of absolutism', while bearing these caveats in mind, and without intending to imply either that feudalism was monolithic, or that the term covers everything important about European life in this period.

---

29 *Political Systems of the World*, pp. 24–5.

30 Susan Reynolds, *Fiefs and Vassals: The medieval evidence reinterpreted* (Oxford, 1994), p. 1.

31 'The Tyranny of a Construct: Feudalism and Historians of Medieval Europe', *American Historical Review* vol. 79 (1974): 1063–88.

Feudalism was 'the outcome of the violent dissolution of older societies',[32] and characterised by fragmentation and by various attempts at (re)unification. In a narrow sense, feudalism involves the exchange of allegiance for the grant of land, with conditions on its use and linked duties of service and protection on both sides of the bargain. In an even narrower one, it applies only to such a relation between nobles.[33] More broadly, it is characterised by 'a subject peasantry; widespread use of the service tenement (i.e. the fief) instead of a salary, which was out of the question; the supremacy of a class of specialised warriors; ties of obedience and protection which bind man to man ... [and] fragmentation of authority'.[34] The features I especially want to emphasise are that feudalism involved a deep fragmentation of power and of the incidents of property, and a proliferation of overlapping and competing dominating institutions. The major players in this competition were the Church, the Holy Roman Empire, the nobility, the self-governing towns, and the monarchies which laid the groundwork for modern states.

Absolutist states appeared out of a long struggle between these players, which some of the monarchies eventually won. So, for instance, the Church was strong at the start of the period, having a near-monopoly on literacy, estates all over Europe, and the sophisticated financial, judicial and administrative apparatus required to manage them. However, by the end of it, the Church had been weakened by papal schism, humanist scholarship and the Reformation, all encouraged or utilised by the monarchies to consolidate their own power.[35] The victory of the monarchs may have depended in part, as Martin Van Creveld argues, on the multiplicity of power-holders, who could be played off against one another, Church against Empire and towns against nobles. That victory was incomplete: although nobles and towns lost their political independence, the former retained their privileges and monopoly on government positions, and the latter's merchants and manufacturers were 'able to flourish as never before'.[36] However, some monarchs did manage to unify many of the feudal fragments and networks in particular territories into single, hierarchical structures focused on a sovereign. The social form which resulted is usually called absolutism (perhaps with similar caveats as for feudalism).

Absolutism had four vital features. First, territoriality. Although feudal power-holders did claim and operate in bounded physical spaces, their powers and reach did not typically coincide with those spaces, both because others also had claims within them, and because they had equally important claims and links outside them or unrelated to physical boundaries (in particular, bonds of service and formal kinship). The absolutist states importantly linked both their internal hierarchies and their external powers to territory. Rather than a map of (formally) distinct territories, feudal Europe was a web of overlapping familial, communal, fealty and authority

32 Maurice Bloch, *Feudal Society*, trans. L.A. Manyon (London, 1961), p. 443.

33 Reynolds, *Fiefs and Vassals*, p. 2.

34 Bloch, *Feudal Society*, p. 446.

35 Van Creveld, *The Rise and Decline of the State*, pp. 62–75.

36 Ibid., p. 119.

relations. As Hendrick Spruyt puts the point, the vital transformation from feudalism to absolutism was the development and realisation of the 'principle of territorial exclusivity', involving 'internal hierarchy' and 'external autonomy' in relation to other sovereign states.[37] The second vital feature was the sedentarisation of the monarch and centralisation of the administrative apparatus, increasingly in elaborate palaces with large staffs, as opposed to the near-nomadism of earlier monarchs. The third was the increasing isolation of the monarch from commoners and from traditional tasks. Kings were less and less easy to approach personally, and more and more required to socialise and marry only within a very limited group. They stopped being active war-leaders: where earlier monarchs had led their armies personally, absolute monarchs retired to their palaces and left the fighting to others. This isolation was accompanied by an increasing heroisation of the monarch, often involving comparisons with pagan exemplars like Hercules and superstitions about the ability to cure disease. Finally, absolutist states developed a symbolic theatre of power: elaborate court ritual, etiquette, costumes, triumphs and celebrations.[38] These features, the power-distribution at their heart, and the new capacities of domination they created, were supported by violence, by discourses of authority and property, and by ritual.

Territoriality is perhaps the most significant feature of absolutist states, and an important feature of modern ones. During the feudal period, an individual became considerable by forging or maintaining multiple, overlapping networks of fealty, duty and power. In the modern state, these networks are effaced by one loyalty, to the state. An individual normally belongs to only one state. She is either physically and administratively inside it, or outside it. States make considerable efforts to sedentarise 'people who move around'[39] like nomads, refugees, slash-and-burn agriculturalists and gypsies, who are hard to fit into this scheme. More, becoming stateless – a refugee or asylum-seeker – is now a disastrous fate, and to be without a territorial state is to be 'primitive', without history, a non-person.

Although they involved the first appearance of features characteristic of modern states, absolute monarchies were not yet our states. In particular, they lacked the vast apparatus of management and control of more recent states. That missing feature is considered in my next section. Absolute states contained the germ of their own transformation: 'Other things being equal, the more absolute any monarch the greater his dependence on impersonal bureaucratic, military, and legal mechanisms to transmit his will and impose it on society at large. In the end, those mechanisms

37 *The Sovereign State and its Competitors: An analysis of systems change* (Princeton, 1994), p. 3.

38 For a vivid description of such theatre, see Frances Yates, *The Rosicrucian Enlightenment* (St. Albans, 1975), Chapter 1. On rituals of power in a variety of contexts, see for instance the studies in Frans Theuws and Janet L. Nelson (eds), *Rituals of Power: From late antiquity to the early middle ages* (Leiden, 2000) and David Cannadine and Simon Price (eds), *Rituals of Royalty: Power and ceremonial in traditional societies* (Cambridge, 1987).

39 Scott, *Seeing Like a State*, p. 1.

showed themselves capable of functioning without him and were even destined to take power away from him.'[40] I focus on this transformation and its results next.

*Surveillance* The term 'surveillance' covers both information-gathering and supervisory discipline, which are central features of modern states.[41] Surveillance involves the creation and empowerment of bureaucratic institutions, which allow and are further empowered by the formalisation of law, the creation of legal tender, and the monopolisation of internal and external violence. I shall sketch these four features in that order.

First, bureaucracies are institutions made up of salaried administrators filling a hierarchy of professional roles, which survive the removal or promotion of their current incumbents, ideally on impersonal criteria of competence; which have clearly defined functions; and which are enacted according to prescribed rules.[42] They create and assign extra capacity and many new capacities, especially capacities to record, systematise and control people and their practices. Having appeared, they gradually created internal functional distinctions into treasuries, foreign ministries and so on, at the same time as the monarch's personal property and household were gradually distinguished from the territory and administration of the state. Bureaucracies took over many of the activities of absolute monarchs, and created many of the distinctive features of modern states.[43]

'Bureaucracy both presupposes the existence of information – the indispensable grist to the administrator's mill – and enables more of it to be generated.'[44] The new bureaucracies created and used a variety of techniques and capacities for the creation, storage and application of information, in order to facilitate control and taxation. In particular, they made use of cartography, both for describing the resources and defences of the state's territory, and for defining boundaries with other states; of statistics, particularly from population censuses; and of standardisation in names, measures, customs of land tenure, and ways of recording births, deaths and transfers of property. 'In each case, officials took exceptionally complex, illegible, and local social practices ... and created a standard grid whereby it could be centrally recorded and monitored.'[45] More, these maps, literal and figurative, were intended to remake as well as to record: 'A state cadastral map created to designate taxable property-holders does not merely describe a system of land tenure; it creates such a

40 Van Creveld, *The Rise and Decline of the State*, p. 125.

41 Christopher Dandeker, *Surveillance, Power and Modernity: Bureaucracy and discipline from 1700 to the present day* (Cambridge, 1990), pp. 37-8.

42 This definition is based on David Beetham, *Bureaucracy* (Milton Keynes, 1987), p. 3 and on Mann, *Sources of Social Power*, vol. 2, p. 444, and ultimately, through both, on the work of Max Weber.

43 For a detailed account of one such development, see G.R. Elton, *The Tudor Revolution in Government: Administrative changes in the reign of Henry VIII* (Cambridge, 1953); on the process in general, Mann, *Sources of Social Power*, vol. 2, Chapter 13.

44 Van Creveld, *The Rise and Decline of the State*, p. 143.

45 Scott, *Seeing Like a State*, p. 2.

system through its ability to give its categories the force of law.'[46] These bureaucratic 'attempts at legibility'[47] were tactics of rule and means of creating and distributing capacities to dominate, and their development and spread allow modern states their extraordinary reach into the details of the lives of their subjects.[48]

Over the history of modern states, there has been a great increase in their technical and social capacities of surveillance. Early bureaucratic states attempted to make their subjects and territories legible, but there were still many areas which were outside states' reach and oversight, because of technical difficulties or lack of interest. More recent states have tended towards conquering these difficulties, and have increasingly left nothing unreadable: sexual behaviour, private assembly and knowledge are now all at least theoretically matters of interest to, and legible by states. In twentieth-century totalitarianisms an attempt was made to read and control all of these in practice (a trend satirically extended by George Orwell in *Nineteen Eighty-Four*).

Secondly, law can in general be defined as 'the body of rules, *whether formally enacted or customary*, which a particular State or community recognises as governing the actions of its members and which it may enforce by imposing penalties'.[49] Probably, no human community has ever lacked law in this wide sense. However, many human communities have certainly lacked what we might think of as paradigmatic law, which is defined, written down and procedurally enforced, by states which fairly successfully claim a monopoly on doing so in their territories. There are of course many different kinds of law, including for instance business, comparative, constitutional, criminal, family, international, military, procedural, tax, tort, sumptuary and immigration law, and they have their own specific histories and interactions. However, the central change which the surveillance state brought about was to transform law from customary to formal, and to monopolise its definition and enforcement. This process is not and probably cannot be complete. Humans continue to create, maintain and modify rules and sanctions outside state control; and, further, the promise of an effective monopoly on social control may never have been realistic:

> In crime control, as in other spheres, the limitations of the state's capacity to govern social life in all its details have become ever more apparent, particularly in the late modern era.

46 Ibid., p. 3.

47 Ibid., p. 2.

48 On one example of the development of taxation structures, see Michael J. Braddick, *The Nerves of State: Taxation and the financing of the English state, 1558–1714* (Manchester, 1996); on some examples of the developing uses of cartography, the studies in David Buisseret (ed.), *Monarchs, Ministers, and Maps: The emergence of cartography as a tool of government in early modern Europe* (Chicago, 1992); on the developing use of statistics in various countries, the studies in J. Koren (ed.), *The History of Statistics: Their development and progress in many countries* (New York, 1918); on these developments in general, Charles Tilly (ed.), *The Formation of National States in Western Europe* (Princeton, 1975).

49 *Oxford English Dictionary*, my emphasis.

> So, having arrogated to itself control functions and responsibilities that once belonged to the institutions of civil society, the late modern state is now faced with its own inability to deliver the expected levels of control over crime and criminal conduct.[50]

Nonetheless, modern states' control of social activity, through the techniques of formal law and its enforcement, is deep and effective even if necessarily incomplete.

Third, 'Unlike their successors, premodern rulers and communities did not themselves *create* value by fiat; instead, all they could do was confirm, by adding their seal, that *existing* valuable commodities … did in fact conform to a certain standard of purity, weight, etc.'[51] Modern states, in order both to increase their capacity to dominate, and to claim the immense resources required to support themselves, had not only to increase taxation to previously impossible and unimagined levels, but also to redefine the meaning of money by inventing 'legal tender'. That is, tokens issued or licensed by states which legally must be accepted in payment of debts. Once this confidence trick has succeeded, states' control of the economy, and of much else, is greatly increased. Modern states literally do have a licence to print money.

Fourth, over the course of development of modern states, war has been transformed from a 'vocation of the upper classes',[52] to an activity of temporary, entrepreneurial bands of mercenaries, and then further, to its modern conduct by professional armed forces, recognised by the enemy as servants of a state doing their duty, and formally entitled to consideration if captured or wounded. This transformation created not only the armed forces themselves, with a culture, tradition and organisation of their own, and distinguished by wearing uniform, but two other excluded categories: the state which conducts the war, distinct from those who fight and die in it; and the civilian population.[53]

Permanent armed forces both require elaborate bureaucracies to manage their hierarchy, pay, training and supply, and are tools of bureaucratic surveillance. They are used to monopolise internal violence, crush rebellions and control subject populations, through the development of networks of roads, garrisons, forts and ordnance survey maps, as much as to fight external wars. Functional distinctions within these institutions were gradually created: police, including secret police, became distinct from armies, navies and eventually air forces, and prisons were built and staffed.

With these transformations, the institutional structure of modern states was largely in place. Their apparatus of control of space, sociability and violence, and many of their means of creating and assigning capacities, were in place, but in order for our states to come into being, one further element was needed.

---

50 David Garland, *The Culture of Control: Crime and social order in contemporary society* (Oxford, 2001), p. 110.

51 Van Creveld, *The Rise and Decline of the State*, p. 225.

52 Ibid., p. 155.

53 On the development of modern armed forces in its wider context, see Michael Howard, *War in European History* (Oxford, 1976).

*Nationalism* Nationalism is a successful 'form of politics'[54] which appeared in the late eighteenth century, and by the twentieth had become 'easily the most powerful political phenomenon in the contemporary world'.[55] A political movement is nationalist when it seeks or exercises state power, and justifies such action with 'nationalist arguments', which are built on three basic assertions:

(a) There exists a nation with an explicit and peculiar character.
(b) The interests and values of this nation take priority over all other interests and values.
(c) The nation must be as independent as possible. This usually requires at least the attainment of sovereignty.[56]

The last of these is, perhaps, the most important, since it encapsulates the doctrine that state territorial boundaries ought to be coterminous with often imaginary linguistic, cultural and ethnic boundaries. That is, that 'the only legitimate type of government is national self-government',[57] where the 'self' is understood as national character.

This definition of nationalism is not the only one available. I adopt this short and political perspective because, first, although some elements of nationalism can be discovered long before the late eighteenth century, they did not appear together. For instance: while part of the powering doctrine of the Hussite revolution in Bohemia, in the fifteenth century, was 'linguistic nationalism',[58] it was not linked to a demand for a linguistically unitary *state.* The Hussites demanded a vernacular liturgy, and the reservation of judicial and academic positions for native Czech-speakers, but wanted a reformed church, or in some cases a universal 'primitive' church in place of the papacy, not a Czech state. Secondly, I am considering nationalism in the context of modern states, and it did not become a mass political project, and therefore significant in that context, until the recent date I have set for its beginning. Nationalism as a mass form of politics appears in consort and competition with modern states, and is best understood in that context: 'The key to an understanding of nationalism lies in the character of the modern state, which nationalism both opposes and claims as its own.'[59]

---

54 John Breuilly, *Nationalism and the State* (2nd edn, Chicago, IL/Manchester, 1994), p. 2.

55 John Gray, 'Notes Towards a Definition of the Political Thought of Tlön' in *Enlightenment's Wake: Politics and culture at the close of the modern age* (London, 1995), pp. 11–17, p. 13.

56 Breuilly, *Nationalism and the State*, p. 2.

57 Elie Kedourie, *Nationalism* (London, 1960), p. 9.

58 Malcolm D. Lambert, *Medieval Heresy: Popular movements from Bogomil to Hus* (London, 1977), p. 319.

59 Breuilly, *Nationalism and the State*, p. 15. For further discussion of this and other perspectives on nationalism, see Ibid., Appendix. The same short perspective is taken, for instance, by E.J. Hobsbawm in *Nations and Nationalism Since 1780: Programme, myth, reality* (Cambridge, 1990), and by Ernest Gellner in *Nations and Nationalism* (Oxford, 1983).

The territorial boundaries which are justified or attacked by nationalist movements often pre-exist those movements, having appeared several centuries earlier with absolutist states. These administrative cleavages may even have helped to form nationalist consciousness, by creating a fracture in communication: communicative possibilities were greater inside these boundaries than across them, which created a sense of something shared inside the boundary which excluded those outside.[60] However, nationalist movements often attack existing states. Opposition nationalism takes three major forms: reform nationalism, which 'accepts existing state territory as approximately coterminous with national territory' but disputes 'the non-national basis of state legitimacy and sovereignty'; unification nationalism, which 'regards the existing states as occupying fragments of the national territory', and separatist nationalism, which 'regards the existing state as an imperial power'.[61]

Nationalist movements very often oppose the particular states in which they find themselves, and attempt to take them over in order to transform them. Nationalism is often a central force in, especially, secession and decolonisation movements, and is, in general, an effective form of political opposition. Since its appearance, states have either been split, absorbed or ousted, or have tamed nationalism:

> Rising to the challenge, the state, embracing nationalism, deliberately sought to turn the situation to its own advantage and began to sing its own praises by every means at its disposal. Gone were the days when such things as national food, national costume, and national habits could be left to the care of mere patriotic societies; by means of its education system … the state sought to harness not only them but also "culture" in the form of history, painting, sculpture, literature, drama, and music. All these ceased to be either a matter for lone individuals or part of the common human enterprise. Instead they became compartmentalized into English, French, German, or Russian as the case might be; often coming under the auspices of some ministry of culture (which might or might not be the same as the ministry of education), they were subsidized and studied primarily as a means of glorifying the national heritage.[62]

Grandiose ritual spectaculars – 'Independence Day, National Day, Armed Forces Day, Jubilee Day, Flag Day, Heroes' Day, Memorial Day, Victory Day, Great Trek Day'[63] – became part of states' repertoire of tactics for self-maintenance.

After the First World War, the world was reorganised according to nationalist principles: 'The "peoples" entitled to exercise the right to [national] self-determination, according to the Paris Peace accord of 1919, were ethnic groups which had become nationally mobilized, and numerous states were carved out of the ruins of the Russian, German, Austro-Hungarian, and Ottoman empires along

60 Karl W. Deutsch, *Nationalism and Social Communication: An inquiry into the foundations of nationality* (Cambridge, MA, 1953).

61 John Breuilly, 'The State' in Alexander J. Motyl (ed.), *Encylopedia of Nationalism* (2 vols, San Diego, CA, 2001), vol. 1, pp. 769–92, p. 771.

62 Van Creveld, *The Rise and Decline of the State*, p. 201.

63 Ibid., p. 202.

broadly ethnic lines.'[64] States which could not or would not turn nationalism to their advantage were soon replaced with ones which did. The post-war settlement gave 'sixty million people a state of their own, but it turned another twenty-five million into minorities'[65] inside nation-states characterised by an (imagined) exclusive identity to which they were aliens.

Nation-states and nationalist challenges to states are now ubiquitous, and 'nation-ness is the most universally legitimate value in the political life of our time.'[66] The success of nationalism has had two consequences, one major and one minor. The minor consequence is that its doctrine of national self-government has become a presupposition of diplomacy and of political thought: 'The existence of nations is a tacit presupposition of most current discourse in political theory.'[67] Its major and disastrous consequence is that it makes possible, and to some extent causes the mobilisation of whole populations and economies for total war, which 'involves all citizens and mobilizes most of them … is waged with armaments which require a diversion of the entire economy to produce them, and which are used in unimaginable quantities … produces untold destruction and utterly dominates and transforms the life of the countries involved in it',[68] as well as being involved in numerous smaller but equally terrible civil wars and ethnic cleansings. The twentieth century was the era of nation-states, and one of the most violent in human history: during it, something like 187 million people were 'killed or allowed to die by human decision'.[69]

Nationalism is both a way of creating capacities, by motivating and channelling cooperation, and a way of maintaining or challenging particular assignments of those capacities. It is also an example of the general fact about human sociability already noted, that there is a persistent tendency both to resist particular institutions, and towards the interstitial emergence of new networks. States did not create nationalism, but had to deal with it.

*The spread of modern states* Modern states began in Europe, and for the first century of their existence 'occupied only between 2 and 3 percent of the earth's surface'.[70] They are now ubiquitous: nearly all of the earth's land area is the territory of nation-states, and what little that is not, such as Antarctica, is managed, together with the oceans, by collaborating nation-states. The spread of states differed in detail

---

64 Margaret Moore, 'Introduction: The self-determination principle and the ethics of secession' in Moore (ed.), *National Self-Determination and Secession* (Oxford, 1998), pp. 1–13, p. 3.

65 Mark Mazower, *Dark Continent: Europe's twentieth century* (London, 1998), p. 41.

66 Benedict Anderson, *Imagined Communities: Reflections on the origin and spread of nationalism* (London, 1983), p. 12.

67 Margaret Canovan, *Nationhood and Political Theory* (Cheltenham, 1996), p. 13.

68 Eric Hobsbawm, *Age of Extremes: The short twentieth century 1914–1991* (London, 1995), p. 44.

69 Ibid., p. 12. The estimate is Zbigniew Brzezinski's.

70 Van Creveld, *The Rise and Decline of the State*, p. 263.

in each case according to local conditions, decisions, mistakes and chance, but can broadly be divided into four forms. Modern states spread by deliberate mirroring, by colonisation of sparsely populated spaces, by colonisation of densely populated spaces, and by commercial contact.[71] I use the spread of modern states into Russia, North America, South America and India, respectively, as exemplary cases of these forms. I do not suppose that any of these cases were really as simple or monocausal as my accounts may suggest: I intend only to provide illustrative sketches.

Before considering the spread of states in more detail, we should note that in no case did modern states expand into entirely empty spaces. In the rare cases where there were no human inhabitants, states still encountered and made immense changes to native ecosystems, typically in order to exploit their resources. In no case did states meet isolated 'savages' in a 'state of nature': 'European expansion everywhere encountered human societies characterised by long and complex histories.'[72]

First, then, deliberate mirroring: the Russian monarchy initially failed to consolidate itself into an absolutist state, when several western European monarchies succeeded. But Peter the Great deliberately mirrored those Western states in his reforms, turning a powerful independent nobility into part of a hierarchy whose titles were granted by him, becoming de facto head of the Russian church, and reforming and greatly enlarging taxation and the armed forces. In many cases these reforms were carried out 'at the hands of western experts, both civilian and military, specifically imported for the purpose'.[73]

In North America (and Australia), the British and other states expanded into vast and resource-rich, but very sparsely populated spaces. These new territories were initially administered as extensions of the colonising states, but later became sovereign modern states. Typically, this form of expansion has involved the near-extermination (not necessarily deliberate) of the native populations, and the assimilation of the survivors into the expanding state culture. In the specific case of North America, it involved the population and exploitation of the territory by huge numbers of mostly African slaves.[74]

In South America, by contrast, the Spanish, Portuguese and other states expanded into a densely populated, resource-rich space. Again, the territory was initially administered as an extension of the colonising state, but has become a complex

71 This division again follows Van Creveld: ibid., Chapter 5.

72 Wolf, *Europe and the People Without History*, p. x.

73 Van Creveld, p. 281; see also ibid., pp. 264–81; for a detailed account of Peter's life and reforms, see Evgenii V. Anisimov, *The Reforms of Peter the Great: Progress through coercion in Russia*, trans. John T. Alexander (New York, 1993).

74 Van Creveld, *The Rise and Decline of the State*, pp. 281–97; on North America, Alan Taylor, *American Colonies: The settlement of North America to 1800* (London, 2002); on Australia, Robert Hughes, *The Fatal Shore: A history of the transportation of convicts to Austrailia, 1787–1868* (London, 1987); on slavery, the second section of this chapter.

system of often military-run, sovereign modern states. In this form of spread, the native population was typically enslaved rather than exterminated.[75]

Finally, in India, the British and other states expanded by commercial contact backed by state power. Initially, trade was carried out by organisations like the East India Company, which technically were not organs of their home states. But in practice the personnel of states and companies were often interchangeable; they collaborated in particular by lending each other military personnel and equipment; and the companies used many state forms and tactics, especially including modern armed forces and bureaucratic techniques of reading and control. Companies traded with local power-holders, and therefore had an incentive to encourage or create social forms structured for their advantage, and dominating institutions sympathetic to them. Their help to such institutions typically involved the loan or supporting use of their military and bureaucratic expertise, for the creation of state-like surveillance, taxation and armies. In many cases, this process was accompanied by deliberate mirroring by local power-holders of the companies' techniques for creating and assigning capacities of domination and for extraction of revenue, which were so obviously effective, often to resist the company or company-backed rivals. So, in trying to structure the social space they operated in to their commercial advantage, the companies helped to spread state forms and tactics.[76]

The result of these processes, separately or in combination and modified by local circumstances, was our social world. Nation-states structure the lives of all humans, create huge capacities to attain goods and to dominate people, and assign those capacities extremely unequally. Complex social networks of state power-holders exercise their power over the entire earth. States are not the only powers or structures in world, but they are large and important ones.

*Modern states: summary and morals* In 1200, there were no nation-states: now, they are everywhere. The world and its human population are structured and controlled by a system of centralised, territorial institutions, making use of elaborate and highly effective techniques of surveillance, and taming or being challenged by nationalism. In general, the appearance of modern nation-states was the development and use of a collection of effective techniques for organising human social networks, creating an immense range and scale of capacities, and unequally assigning it in favour of bureaucratic elites. As with pristine states, I have given an account, not an

75 Van Creveld, *The Rise and Decline of the State*, pp. 298–314; on Mexico, Hugh Thomas, *The Conquest of Mexico* (London, 1994); on the anthropologies developed to explain, and in some cases to justify colonisers' encounters with, and treatment of native populations, Anthony Pagden, *The Fall of Natural Man: The American Indian and the origins of comparative ethnology* (Revised edn, Cambridge, 1986).

76 Van Creveld, *The Rise and Decline of the State*, pp. 315–32; on India, Lawrence James, *Raj: The making and unmaking of British India* (London, 1997).

explanation, of the development and nature of modern states.[77] Now, what morals and interest should we draw from my account of modern states?

I want to make three minor points and one major point here. The first minor point is that this account, like my account of pristine states, reiterates, expands on and gives further evidence for Kropotkin's point that this is just one of many humanly possible forms of social organisation. We have not always organised ourselves in this way, did not until recently, and such organisation is therefore not necessary for us. Secondly, modern states are differentiated. That is, they consist of several different structures and techniques, including a centre, a territory, a bureaucracy (or even several competing or collaborating bureaucracies), law, armed forces, nationalism and an apparatus for its control. These elements are not necessarily linked: they are currently found together, but need not be. It is not obvious, for instance, that law requires territoriality. Third, and again as for pristine states, we have noted modern states' immense capacity for violence. Nothing I have said shows that they must be violent, but it is clear that they have as a matter of fact been so. Probably, no other kind of institution or social form in human history has had the capacity to mobilise whole populations for war, for years at a time; probably, no other has killed, or been responsible for the deaths of, so many people.

The major point is to do with complexity. I argued above that the appearance of a pristine state was not necessarily an increase in the complexity, indeed was in some ways a simplification, of human social life. The point needs further discussion in relation to modern states. There are senses of 'complex' in which the appearance of modern states was, or accompanied, an increase in complexity. For instance, we might choose to follow Randall McGuire in defining complexity as involving two variables: heterogeneity and inequality.[78] Heterogeneity describes 'the frequency of individuals among social parameters' of two kinds: nominal, 'such as sex, kinship and occupation', which 'define roles and are categorical groupings that have distinct boundaries and lack inherent rank ordering'; and graduated, 'such as age, power and wealth' which 'define status and are inherently rank ordered and continuous'.[79] Inequality describes 'the extent of differential access to material and social resources, such as wealth and power', and 'measures how much difference there is between comparable levels of access'.[80] The point of this definition, for McGuire, is to help answer the question 'What changes separate Pleistocene hunter-gatherers from the

77 For attempts at explanation, see for instance Charles Tilly, *Coercion, Capital, and European States, AD990–1992* (Cambridge, MA, 1992) or Spruyt, *The Sovereign State and its Competitors*; for a review of explanatory theories of the modern state, see Roland Axtmann, 'The Formation of the Modern State: The debate in the social sciences' in Mary Fulbrook (ed.), *National Histories and European Histories* (Boulder, CO, 1993), pp. 21–45.

78 'Breaking Down Cultural Complexity: Inequality and heterogeneity', *Advances in Archaeological Method and Theory* vol. 6 (1983): 91–142.

79 Ibid., p. 101.

80 Ibid., p. 102; Peter M. Blau gives a nearly identical two-variable definition of complexity in *Inequality and Heterogeneity: A primitive theory of social structure* (New York/London, 1977).

modern industrial world system?',[81] and his answer is that the central change is an increase in heterogeneity and inequality, which he proposes to call 'complexity'. This is reasonable for his purposes. But here our question is whether or not the appearance of modern states was an increase in complexity, and we need not deny that it was an increase in heterogeneity and inequality. So, this definition is question-begging for our purposes.

McGuire's definition of 'complexity' does not catch all we might mean by the term. For example: in his novel *Big Planet*, Jack Vance imagines Kirstendale, which appears on its surface to be a somewhat feudal city of aristocrats and their servants. Its secret is that everyone plays both kinds of role: a porter in the morning, a duke in the afternoon, and 'every man a millionaire'[82] some of the time. In an ordinary sense of 'complex', this social form is more complex than the feudal one it appears to be, a change from the latter to a Kirstendale-like form would be an increase in complexity, and the lives of the Kirsters are more complex than the lives of people who are only and always porters. But McGuire's definition of complexity cannot catch this difference. Because the social roles remain the same, while being played by different people at different times, there is no difference between the ordinary feudal and the Kirster heterogeneity or inequality.

Further, there are three important senses in which modern states create or are accompanied by a *simplification* of human life. Bureaucracies typically simplify complex local social forms for purposes of legibility. Modern states have partially effaced complex and overlapping webs of association with simpler, exclusive, hierarchical ones. And finally, while our networks of interaction in modern states often involve a larger number of people than networks in other known social forms, they do so by making use of technologies which simplify our interactions, often by making many people (and objects) interchangeable. In a strange town, I do not have to form any complex relationship in order to get food and a bed for the night, just so long as I have the simplifying tool: money. In a strange landscape, I can read the road signs. And these simplifying technologies, of course, were created or are maintained by modern states.

On the grounds of the multivalence of 'complexity', and the fact that in some ordinary senses of the term, the appearance of modern states involves a simplification of human social life, I suggest that it is not helpful or particularly meaningful to regard the appearance of states as an increase in complexity. Only confusion is added to McGuire's useful point about heterogeneity and inequality by involving the term 'complexity'. We should therefore abandon the scale of simple to complex in comparing states with other social forms.

81 McGuire, 'Breaking Down Cultural Complexity', p. 101.

82 Jack Vance, *Big Planet* (Sevenoaks, 1977), p. 77.

### States: Summary and Conclusions

I have characterised states in general as one particular social form among the many possible for humans. They are centralised, territorial, differentiated institutions, which create or increase, and assign, an immense range of capacities. In the common human situation of being without and uninfluenced by states, we very rarely create them, and when we do, the transformation is not an unambiguous increase in complexity. Our modern states are a recent, historically unique development, which adds further techniques and forms, including bureaucracies, armies and nationalism, to the basic pattern of the state. Again, their appearance is not best thought of as an increase in complexity, both because 'complex' is multivalent and because there are senses of the term in which that appearance is a simplification of human life.

Because of their current ubiquity, it is easy to find the existence and spread of states unsurprising. However, anyone who wants seriously to argue that states, and especially our current state-infested arrangements, were very likely, must deal with three strong counterarguments: pristine states have appeared only very rarely; the development of modern states involved a series of apparently adventitious victories and inventions; and for most of the time there have been humans, there have not been states. This does not entirely preclude an argument that (modern) states were not actually as unlikely as I have made them appear: it does make such argument difficult.

I have analysed states by considering their historical development in the context of the human landscape. As I have emphasised throughout this section, states are just one of many ways humans can organise, and have organised themselves. Further, the alternative to having a state is not chaos. There are multiple and differently ordered alternatives to the state social form (I consider two of them in more detail in Chapter 4).

As I argued in my Introduction, anarchism cannot be characterised merely as anti-statism. But anarchists certainly are against states, as one disastrous and currently ubiquitous social form, among other possibilities. In my next section, I consider another non-state social form against which anarchists should and do set themselves.

## Slavery

On the historical evidence, any complete list of the basic capacities of humans would have to include the capacities to enslave and to be enslaved. According to Peter Kolchin, 'Throughout most of human history, slavery and other forms of coerced labour were ubiquitous.'[83] According to Orlando Patterson,

> There is nothing notably peculiar about the institution of slavery. It has existed from before the dawn of human history right down to the twentieth century … There is no

83 *American Slavery 1619–1877* (London, 1993), p. xi.

> region on earth that has not at some time harboured the institution. Probably there is no group of people whose ancestors were not at one time slaves or slaveholders.[84]

However, the world-spanning form slavery took between the fifteenth and nineteenth centuries is distinctive in a number of ways, and I concentrate on it here. I follow common practice in calling it 'Atlantic slavery' or 'the Atlantic system'. Before considering it further, I shall characterise slavery in general.

### *A General Characterisation of Slavery*

Slavery is extreme, institutionalised domination of slaves by masters. Centrally, it is created and maintained by violence and the threat of violence: people are violently enslaved, and then held in subservience by the use and threat of corporal and ultimately capital punishment. However, slavery also involves other modes of creating and maintaining domination. It involves authority discourses, grounded in various ways, including the use of ideas of an authority derived from having spared the slave's life in battle, or from natural superiority, or from an unpaid debt (all of which can be stretched far into metaphor or formal fiction). It involves property discourses. A slave is the object of many of the incidents of property, including being something someone has an exclusive right to use and a right to sell to some others.

A slave is also an object in another sense: masters attempt to make slaves non-persons, in four related ways. First, slaves are natally and culturally alienated:

> Not only was the slave denied all claims on, and obligations to, his parents and living blood relations but, by extension, all such claims and obligations on his more remote ancestors and on his descendants. He was truly a genealogical isolate. Formally isolated in his social relations with those who lived, he also was culturally isolated from the social heritage of his ancestors … Slaves differed from other human beings in that they were not allowed freely to integrate the experience of their ancestors into their lives, to inform their understanding of social reality with the inherited meanings of their natural forebears, or to anchor the living present in any conscious community of memory.[85]

Slave families are typically broken up, or always afraid of being broken up, by their masters. The escaped American slave and abolitionist campaigner Frederick Douglass, for instance, records that 'My mother and I were separated when I was but an infant – before I knew her as my mother', that it was 'common custom, in the part of Maryland from which I ran away, to part children from their mothers at a very early age', and that 'I was not allowed to be present during her illness, at her death, or burial.'[86]

---

84 *Slavery and Social Death: A comparative study* (Cambridge, MA, 1982), p. vii.

85 Ibid., p. 5.

86 *Narrative of the Life of Frederick Douglass, an American Slave, Written by Himself*, ed. H.A. Baker (New York, 1982), pp. 48–9. I use Douglass illustratively as an especially articulate slave-voice; for many other voices and testimonies, see for instance John W. Blassingame (ed.), *Slave Testimony: Two centuries of letters, speeches, interviews, and*

Secondly, masters attempt to limit slaves to having a social personality only through them. Slaves are dishonoured and nameless. In Atlantic slavery specifically, according to Robin Blackburn, 'Planters gave slaves names normally used for dogs, horses, donkeys or cows ("Jumper", "Gamesome", "Ready", "Juno", "Caesar", "Fido", and so forth). Alternatively, the adult slave would be known by a diminutive and would often lack any family name.'[87] In general, a slave has 'no name of his own to defend. He can only defend his master's worth and his master's name.'[88]

Third, masters attempt to stop slaves joining and forming new social networks of their own, for whatever purpose. Douglass records that when he and other slaves set up a Sunday school, mostly so that he could teach the others to read, 'Messrs. Wright Fairbanks and Garrison West … in connection with others, rushed in upon us with sticks and stones, and broke up our virtuous little Sabbath school, at St. Michael's – all calling themselves Christians!'[89] In some cases this prevention is rhetorically justified, or really motivated by a (rational) fear of conspiracy to revolt or to escape. But it is also a more general part of the maintenance of slavery: if slaves form social networks of their own, in their own interests, they become less socially and psychologically dependent on their masters, and therefore less enslaved.

Fourth, masters attempt to keep slaves as tools created for their purposes, instead of people who create themselves for their own purposes. In a slave, the skill of reading and the consequent ability to gain knowledge, for instance, is dangerous. Douglass, with the help of his mistress Sophia Auld, and despite her later, corrupted attempts to stop him, learned to read. Both he and his owners recognised the liberating power of education. According to Sophia's husband Hugh: 'Learning would *spoil* the best nigger in the world … If you teach that nigger … how to read, there would be no keeping him. It would forever unfit him to be a slave.'[90] And, according to Douglass himself, 'From that moment, I understood the pathway from slavery to freedom': 'Education and slavery were incompatible with each other.'[91]

These four ways of trying to make slaves into animals or objects instead of people all lead towards Patterson's definition of slavery: a slave is 'a socially dead person'.[92] She is metaphorically dead because alienated from both familial and community networks, prevented from having a social personality except through her master,

---

*autobiographies* (Baton Rouge, LA, 1977) and Henry Louis Gates (ed.), *The Classic Slave Narratives* (New York, 1987).

87 *The Making of New World Slavery: From the baroque to the modern 1492–1800* (London, 1997), p. 325.

88 Patterson, *Slavery and Social Death*, pp. 10–11.

89 Douglass, *Narrative*, p. 120.

90 Ibid., p. 78. 'Some of the language in this book may disturb readers; it disturbs me. Whenever "nigger" appears in the sources, it has been retained … The word is offensive, but I believe that its omission would only anesthatize subject matter infinitely more offensive.' – Eugene D. Genovese, *Roll, Jordan, Roll: The world the slaves made* (New York, 1974), p. xvii.

91 Douglass, *Narrative*, pp. 78, 82.

92 Patterson, *Slavery and Social Death*, p. 5.

prevented from forming new social networks, and prevented from recreating herself as anything other than a tool of others' purposes and interests.

None of these attempts to make slaves non-persons could succeed completely, because, first, of the technical difficulty of continuous surveillance and control. Secondly, because even the extreme and supposedly permanent social divisions between slave and master are to some extent permeable. David Brion Davis, for instance, notes the case of the slave April Ellison, who 'won his freedom after learning how to build and repair cotton gins. After changing his first name to William, buying the freedom of his wife and daughter, and winning a legal suit against a white man who had failed to pay a debt, Ellison became a wealthy planter and owner of sixty-three slaves, a statistic that placed him by 1860 among the upper 3 percent of the slave holders in South Carolina.'[93] Third, because resistance of various kinds is a permanent feature of slavery, of which masters are always, correctly afraid. I consider some of the forms this permanent resistance took against Atlantic slavery in particular, below. Before that, I shall sketch the Atlantic system and consider its distinctiveness.

### *A Brief History of the Atlantic System*

The spread of state social forms into North and South America, described above, was not the only spread of networks and forms, or the only social activity, going on there. At the same time as states were spreading, the Atlantic system was being created. These two changes were related, but not identical.

The immediate sources of the Atlantic slave trade are in the Portuguese and Spanish trade with, and exploitation of West Africa, especially in search of gold and spices; and in their increasing colonisation of Atlantic island-groups including the Canaries and Azores, beginning in the fifteenth century. The import of fairly small numbers of African slaves to these islands, to South America, and especially to the Caribbean, began in the early sixteenth century. African slaves were first brought to North America in the early seventeenth century.[94]

Atlantic slavery reached its peak in the eighteenth century, and involved two interlinked networks and institutions, apart from slavery itself: the triangular trade and the plantation mode of production. Trade items including rum, firearms and cotton goods would be shipped from a European port, for instance Liverpool, to the African west coast. These would be exchanged for slaves procured from a deep African hinterland, mostly by other black Africans, at factories along the coast. These slaves were then taken to the islands or the American continent (the 'middle passage') and sold, usually to be workers on plantations. The products of those

93 'Introduction: The problem of slavery' in Seymour Drescher and Stanley L. Engerman (eds), *A Historical Guide to World Slavery* (New York, 1998), pp. ix–xviii, pp. ix–x.

94 Blackburn, *The Making of New World Slavery*, Chapter 2; Wolf, *Europe and the People Without History*, pp. 196–7.

plantations, including tobacco, coffee, rice, cotton and, especially, sugar, would then be shipped to Europe.[95]

By 1860, there were approximately four-and-a-half million slaves in North America alone. Altogether, perhaps eleven or twelve million black people were transported.[96] 'It is thought that 20 to 40 percent of the slaves died while being transported to the [African] coast, another 3 to 10 percent died while waiting on the coast, and about 12 to 16 percent of those boarded on ships died during the voyage',[97] mostly from disease. The slave mortality rate for the middle passage, which is probably the most accurate of these estimates, is approximately six times higher than the mortality rate for free immigrants to the Americas.

The Atlantic slave trade was immensely profitable, and a major condition of the industrial revolution and the development of capitalism, especially in Britain.[98] It ceased in the nineteenth century: why it did so is a matter of controversy, focused in particular on the relative weight of moral and political campaigns, shifting ideas of progress, and changing economic, social and geopolitical factors.[99]

---

95 David Eltis, 'Slave Trade: Trans-Atlantic trade' in Seymour Drescher and Stanley L. Engerman (eds), *A Historical Guide to World Slavery* (New York, 1998), pp. 370–75; James A. Rawley, *The Transatlantic Slave Trade: A history* (New York, 1981). Barry Unsworth gives a powerful fictional account of the triangular trade in *Sacred Hunger* (London, 1992).

96 The first estimate is from Rawley, *The Transatlantic Slave Trade*, and the second from Eltis, 'Slave Trade: Trans-Atlantic trade'. A widely-accepted earlier estimate of fifteen million now seems to have been ill-grounded. For further estimates and consideration of the difficulty of making them accurately, see Philip D. Curtin, *The Atlantic Slave Trade: A census* (Madison, WI, 1969).

97 Raymond L. Cohn, 'Mortality in Transport', in Seymour Drescher and Stanley L. Engerman (eds), *A Historical Guide to World Slavery* (New York, 1998), pp. 290–92.

98 Blackburn, *The Making of New World Slavery*, Chapter 12; Joseph E. Inikori, 'Capitalism and Slavery', in Seymour Drescher and Stanley L. Engerman (eds), *A Historical Guide to World Slavery* (New York, 1998), pp. 107–10; Barbara Lewis Solow and Stanley L. Engerman (eds), *British Capitalism and Caribbean Slavery: The legacy of Eric Williams* (Cambridge, 2004); Wolf, *Europe and the People Without History*, pp. 199–200.

99 Robin Blackburn, *The Overthrow of Colonial Slavery 1776–1848* (London, 1988), Chapter 13; David Brion Davis, *Slavery and Human Progress* (New York, 1984); David Eltis et al. (eds), *The Abolition of the Atlantic Slave Trade* (Madison, WI, 1981); Stanley L. Engerman, 'Historiography: An overview', in Seymour Drescher and Stanley L. Engerman (eds), *A Historical Guide to World Slavery* (New York, 1998), pp. 222–7; Richard H. Steckel, 'Economics', in Drescher and Engerman (eds), *A Historical Guide to World Slavery*, pp. 179–84. I do not intend to suggest that slavery disappeared with the end of the Atlantic system: it has only taken on a new form. Kevin Bales's 'best estimate of the number of slaves in the world today is 27 million' – *Disposable People: New slavery in the global economy* (Berkeley, CA, 1999), p. 8.

### *The Distinctiveness of Atlantic Slavery*

The Atlantic system of slave procurement, transportation and exploitation partook of the general character of slavery, as described above, and had many continuities with other forms of slavery. To note one example: as in many other forms, the central implement of punishment and physical threat in Atlantic slavery was the whip. However, Atlantic slavery was also distinctive, in four important ways.

First, slaves in this form were very largely used only for a limited range of menial tasks. Other forms of slavery have been more diverse:

> To those accustomed to thinking of slaves as agricultural laborers and house servants, it may be startling to learn that slaves have also served as warriors, government officials, wives, concubines, tutors, eunuchs, and victims of ritual sacrifice. In many pre-modern societies there were high-status slaves who exercised considerable authority; such elite slaves ranged from stewards who managed vast agricultural estates in China and early-modern Russia to high government officials in Rome and the Ottoman Empire. Throughout much of Asia, Africa, and Latin America, slaves served in the armed forces, at times – especially in the Islamic world – achieving high rank and wielding considerable power.[100]

Atlantic slaves, in contrast, were almost entirely used as agricultural workers on the plantation, 'a productive unit ideally suited for the regimentation of agricultural labor and hence the large-scale cultivation of staple crops'.[101] The profitability of the Atlantic system, and therefore part of the demand for slaves, depended on the demand in the old world for these staples from the new.

Secondly, Atlantic slavery involved a racial discourse dividing white European masters from black African slaves. Institutions of slavery have typically required some division of *us* from *them*, grounded in varied ways, including differences of religion, of 'level' of culture, of origin, and of mythical lineage. Atlantic slavers created and used a complex, political discourse of race to distinguish (potential) slaves from (potential) masters. Atlantic slavery 'was predicated on new, unequal relationships between Europe and Africa and between white and black'.[102] With few exceptions, slaves were black Africans and their descendants, and masters were white Europeans and their descendants.

Third, Atlantic slavery was 'intensely commercial'.[103] Slavery was largely powered by desire for *profit*, and not, for instance, for status, or for the maintenance of traditional social hierarchies. Slavers used and developed new techniques of bookkeeping, long-distance exchange, insurance and business planning.

Finally, and as I have already suggested with some statistics, above, the Atlantic system was distinctive in its sheer size and global effects. Atlantic transport of slaves

---

100 Kolchin, *American Slavery*, p. 4.

101 Ibid.

102 Ibid., p. 6.

103 Blackburn, *The Making of New World Slavery*, p. 3.

populated the new world and transformed the old. Not only the developing capitalist nation-states of Europe, and not only America, were changed by the trade: 'The demand for African slaves reshaped the political economy of the entire [African] continent.'[104]

*Slavery and Civil Society*

The Atlantic system appeared in the context of (developing) modern states, and the spread of its institutions was simultaneous with the spread of theirs, but it was neither created nor wholly maintained by states. 'Modern states bore their share of responsibility for the cruelties of the Atlantic slave traffic', and 'the process of colonisation itself was to a greater or lesser extent state-sponsored',[105] but the Atlantic system was created and maintained by commercial organisations and networks of slave-owners, not by states. The vast infrastructure required to procure and distribute slaves, the plantation mode of production, and the racial justification of slavery, were 'invented by European traders and settlers with little prompting from state functionaries'.[106] Indeed, it appears that 'slavery was inversely proportional to the exercise of metropolitan authority'[107] by colonising states.

Anarchists should draw the moral that states are not the only institutions worth criticising and resisting. Even if I am wrong that historical anarchism cannot be characterised merely as anti-statism, we have good reason, here, to extend anarchist consideration beyond states. The creation, maintenance and actions of states are not the only social activities with forms and consequences anarchists should resist: 'the spontaneous dynamic of civil society is also pregnant with disaster and mayhem.'[108]

*Resistance*

The 'bitter central fact'[109] about Atlantic slavery is that it lasted so long. However, despite masters' general success in maintaining the slave system, they faced continuous resistance from their slaves.

A number of different taxonomies of that resistance have been developed. Eugene Genovese, influenced by Marxism and especially by the pioneering work of C.L.R. James, distinguishes two major forms of slave resistance:

> Until the Age of Revolution the slave revolts did not challenge the world capitalist system within which slavery itself was embedded. Rather, they sought escape and autonomy – a local, precapitalist social restoration. When they did become revolutionary and

104 Wolf, *Europe and the People Without History*, p. 230.

105 Blackburn, *The Making of New World Slavery*, pp. 6, 7.

106 Ibid., p. 12.

107 Blackburn, *The Overthrow of Colonial Slavery*, p. 17.

108 Blackburn, *The Making of New World Slavery*, p. 6.

109 R.S. Dunn, Review of Michael Craton, *Testing the Chains*, *Journal of Interdisciplinary History* vol. 15 (1984): 173–5, p. 175.

> raise the banner of abolition, they did so within the context of the bourgeois-democratic revolutionary wave, with bourgeois-democratic slogans and demands and with a commitment to bourgeois property relations.[110]

This distinction between restorative and revolutionary resistance is useful for some purposes; other, more fine-boned distinctions are useful for others. In *Testing the Chains*, Michael Craton distinguishes between 'revolts of the Maroon type, those led by unassimilated Africans, and the late slave rebellions led by Creole (colony-born) members of the slave elite',[111] in the Caribbean. In later work, Craton has described seven 'forms of slave resistance and planter response'.[112] They are: 1) general uprising, or plots for it, responded to by the formation of planter militias, by draconian laws, and by conscious attempts to instil fear in the slave population. Examples of this first form include rebellions in Jamaica in 1760, 1776, 1795 and 1831–32; Barbados in 1816; Antigua in 1736; and, most successfully, Haiti in 1791–1804. 2) Mass running away to form colonies of Maroons (the term is from American Spanish *cimarrón*, wild, applied especially to runaway cattle). Responses included attempts at extermination, but also negotiation and non-aggression pacts. Examples include Barbados in the 1650s, Antigua, Martinique and Guadeloupe up to the 1730s, and even 'New Providence in the Bahamas as late as 1823'.[113] 3) 'Petit marronage', that is short-term, short-distance running away by individuals and very small groups. This especially seems to have been a continuous feature of Atlantic slavery, and a continuous problem for slave-owners, throughout the lifespan of the system. 4) Poisoning, industrial sabotage, feigning stupidity, and malingering. 5) Subtle social sabotage including exaggerated deference, disguised satire, and the deliberate fostering of divisions between masters. 6) Internalised rejection including abortion, suicide, intra-slave violence and madness. And finally 7) resistance through the maintenance or recreation of African culture: African language and writing, craft skills, religion, music, traditional family life and ways of making a living.

I do not intend (and am not qualified) to arbitrate between these different taxonomies. I am not, in any case, convinced that arbitration is necessary: they are intended for different purposes, and may be able to coexist. I note them for two purposes of my own. I want to emphasise the permanence and variety of resistance, by the slaves themselves, to the Atlantic system.[114] Further, I want to note the social creativity of resistance. In Maroon colonies throughout the Caribbean, runaway slaves created and maintained viable social forms and networks, even under extreme

---

110 *From Rebellion to Revolution: Afro-American slave revolts in the making of the modern world* (Baton Rouge, LA, 1979), p. xxi–ii.

111 *Testing the Chains: Resistance to slavery in the British West Indies* (Ithaca, NY, 1982), p. 13.

112 'Forms of Resistance to Slavery' in Franklin W. Knight (ed.), *General History of the Caribbean* vol. 3: *The Slave Societies of the Caribbean* (London, 1997), pp. 222–70, p. 224.

113 Ibid., p. 230.

114 For more examples of that permanence, see for instance the chronology of slave resistance in the Caribbean in Craton, *Testing the Chains*, pp. 335–9.

pressure and attempted extermination by white colonists and planters. Maroon groups did not merely reproduce African social forms: 'Maroons were socially opportunistic and eclectic. Practices derived from any available culture area – African, European, plantation slave culture, occasionally even Amerindian – were incorporated.'[115] The Black Caribs, for instance,

> … traced their origins to a cargo of African slaves wrecked on the … island of Bequia around 1690 who were harboured by the 'Yellow Caribs' there who were in control of St. Vincent. Within a few decades – and not, it seems, without some internal disruption – the black refugees, reinforced by runaway slaves from nearby islands, had become the dominant element in an increasingly miscegenated warrior community that fearsomely combined African and Amerindian weapons and tactics of resistance.[116]

So: resistance was permanent, varied and socially creative. Even the extreme institutionalised domination, and techniques for its maintenance, of the Atlantic system, were not sufficient to prevent the expression of the general human tendencies to resist and to form new social networks.

### *Slavery: A Summary*

The potential for slavery is always with us. Slavery in general is an extreme, institutionalised form of domination, created and maintained by violence, and by authority and property discourses. It attempts to make slaves socially dead in a variety of ways. Between the fifteenth and nineteenth centuries it took a distinctive, global form: the Atlantic system. This used enormous numbers of mostly black African slaves, understood by a new racial discourse as one object of the triangular trade, to operate the plantation system of production. It was one condition of the transformation of the world towards our current arrangements. That is, it created considerable extra capacity and new capacities, and assigned them in favour of a white elite and against black Africans, including those who remained in Africa. It developed over the same period as did modern states, but was largely not created by them, and this has consequences for anarchist thought. Despite its effectiveness and longevity, the Atlantic system could not prevent the expression of the general human tendencies to resist and to form new social networks.

## Subjects and Slaves

States and slavery are both similar and different. Slavery is common, but states are a recent and peculiar innovation in human sociability (the term 'peculiar institution' might better be applied to the latter). The institutions of the two, the ways in which

115 Silvia W. de Groot et al., 'Maroon Communities in the Circum-Caribbean', in Franklin W. Knight (ed.), *General History of the Caribbean* vol. 3: *The Slave Societies of the Caribbean* (London, 1997), pp. 169–93, p. 188.

116 Craton, 'Forms of Resistance to Slavery', p. 237.

they use violence and discourses of authority and property, and the lives those involved in them lead, are all different. State institutions are more functionally promiscuous than slavery's (or, at least, than Atlantic slavery's), and have been available for better purposes. However, the two are in general alike and comparable in being organisations of humans in confederal networks, creating and assigning productive and dominating capacities and their benefits. Specifically, modern states and Atlantic slavery are alike in creating huge and unprecedented capacity for elites to dominate others. They are also historically connected: the world in which modern states operate, the wealth of some and the poverty of others, are conditioned by the Atlantic system. Indeed, Atlantic slavery's effects may be even deeper than that:

> Its development was associated with several of those processes which have been held to define modernity: the growth of instrumental rationality, the rise of national sentiment and the nation-state, racialized perceptions of identity, the spread of market relations and wage labour, the development of administrative bureaucracies and modern tax systems, the growing sophistication of commerce and communication, the birth of consumer societies, the publication of newspapers and the beginnings of press advertising, 'action at a distance' and an individualist sensibility.[117]

Whether or not this strong claim is true, modern states and Atlantic slavery are distinctive forms of human sociability which powerfully and variously condition our current world, and which are similar at least in their institutionalisation of domination.

Comparisons with slavery have long been available for moral and polemical purposes, and have often deployed the notion of 'wage slavery', which appears to have two sources. In pro-slavery polemic from the American South, the term was used to make a *tu quoque* attack on Northern anti-slavery campaigners, on the grounds that the condition of the 'free' workers they employed was at least as bad as that of Southern slaves. It was also used in socialist polemic by people like Bronterre O'Brien, from the 1830s onwards, about the condition of the British proletariat.[118] In the second case, the comparison works in the same way as Kropotkin's comparison between modern division of labour and the Indian caste system: it attempts to extend disapproval by comparison between an accepted and a supposedly unacceptable social form. The notion of wage slavery has since been used in many different ways, including its use by Marx, for instance, to emphasise the continuity, despite historical transformation, of exploitative class-relations. I now want to pursue an alternative, but structurally similar, comparison between slaves and the subjects of states.

To what extent are slaves and subjects alike? The institutions and tactics by which states and slavery dominate are somewhat different, although both use violence and discourses of authority and property. Some subjects' lives are less controlled, at least in some spheres, than are some slaves'. However, states certainly can have

117 Blackburn, *The Making of New World Slavery*, p. 4.

118 See Marcus Cunliffe, *Chattel Slavery and Wage Slavery: The Anglo-American context, 1830–1860* (Athens, GA, 1979), Chapter 1.

and exercise as much power over their subjects as slavery has over slaves. Modern states, in particular, have the techniques and technology to exercise considerably *more* power than any past system of slavery. It may be thought that the difference is that we would rather be subjects than slaves, but this is too quick: subjects of which state? Being a subject of a liberal democratic state is obviously preferable to being a slave, but as already noted, liberal democracy is an atypical form of the modern state. Some other states are at least as bad as slavery. It would be both false and offensive to the memory of slaves to acclaim myself, a subject of a wealthy liberal democracy, as sharing their suffering. However, it would be equally false, and offensive to the memory of the victims of the Cambodian state under Pol Pot, the Ugandan state under Idi Amin, or the Soviet state under Stalin, to claim that they were better off for being subjects instead of slaves. The shared experiences of domination and violence, and of resistance, makes some subjects comparable with slaves.

I have already quoted William Godwin's repetition of the 'old observation that the history of mankind is little else than a record of crimes'.[119] In this chapter, I have added to that gloomy genre. Humans' general capacities and social creativity have recently been used to build and maintain two extremely effective systems of domination and violence, with pleasant consequences for some of us, in wealthy liberal states, but terrible consequences for many others. Anarchists might be inclined to despair. However, there are reasons for hope: although it is clear that these disastrous possibilities are within the human social range, so too are some better ones. In my next chapter, I display some of them.

---

119 Godwin, *Enquiry Concerning Political Justice*, p. 83. See Chapter 1.

## Chapter 4

# Living Without Domination

States are one recent and historically uncommon way in which humans have organised themselves. For most of the time there have been humans, there have not been states:

> For 30,000 years … life went on without kings, queens, prime ministers, presidents, parliaments, congresses, cabinets, governors, mayors, police officers, sheriffs, marshals, generals, lawyers, bailiffs, judges, district attorneys, court clerks, patrol cars, paddy wagons, jails, and penitentiaries. How did our ancestors manage to leave home without them?[1]

Marvin Harris suggests that 'small populations provide part of the answer' to his question.[2] However, in his attempts to explain war and sexism, he also appeals to the fact that these small populations in bands and villages interacted across their borders, especially in trade, exogamous marriage and competition for food resources. As I argued in Chapter 2, there are no discrete social totalities, only confederal networks, and so the small populations of bands and villages cannot fully explain how they organised themselves without states. Their problems were of the same type as ours: how to live together and manage conflict resolution, despite the differences and clashes between people's interests.

The general answer to Harris's question is that our ancestors managed in many different ways. They did to a considerable extent succeed in living together in relatively ordered ways, and to limit and resolve violent conflict. Stateless life has not in general been chaotic or a permanent war, any more than life in and under states has been (and perhaps less so). But the tactics used by people in non-state arrangements, and the ways in which they live together, are various. This is unsurprising: 'non-state' means nothing more than 'not using one particular, historically unusual set of institutions and tactics for living together'. Non-state people vary in their types of social network, means of creating and assigning capacities, mode of subsistence, equality (especially gender equality), and level and type of violence. On the latter two: the !Kung of the Kalahari desert, for instance, have highly (although not perfectly) egalitarian gender relations, and are generally (although not perfectly) peaceful.[3] The Yanomami, who live on the border between Brazil and Venezuela, are

1 Harris, *Our Kind*, p. 344.
2 Ibid.
3 Ibid, pp. 279–81, p. 288.

by contrast both sexist and violent, both amongst themselves and in their relations with their neighbours.[4]

In the first section of this chapter I focus on one non-state social form, that of the Nuer in the southern Sudan, in order to exemplify some of the capacities and tactics humans have for living together and resolving conflict, without states or other forms of institutionalised domination. I consider an acephalous social form both because it provides a comparison with other ways of living and managing conflict, and because it exemplifies the wide range of human sociability and possibility of alternatives to our current arrangements. I consider it also because stateless people have been an enduring subject of interest for anarchists: I have already noted Kropotkin's interest in 'savages'; further examples of this anarchist concern, in various styles and as part of various projects, include Harold Barclay's *People Without Government*, Pierre Clastres's *Society Against the State*, Michael Taylor's *Community, Anarchy and Liberty*, and parts of Colin Ward's *Anarchy in Action.*[5] My practice here is thus an extension of the tradition, as is my particular choice of example.

## The Nuer

I focus on the Nuer for two further reasons. First, Evans-Pritchard's classic studies both stand as a paradigm of one kind of anthropological investigation, and instigated a prolonged engagement with the Nuer:

> The enduring disciplinary fame of 'the Nuer' of southern Sudan derives directly from the intellectual virtuosity of their original ethnographer, Sir Edward E. Evans-Pritchard (1902–73) … Nearly all the great disciplinary debates that have emerged in recent decades have drawn at one time or another on the Nuer ethnographic corpus of Evans-Pritchard. Indeed, with the possible exception of the 'Trobriand Islanders' made famous by Malinowski, 'the Nuer' have been more widely cited, discussed, analyzed, and theorised about than any other 'imagined community' within the anthropological discourse.[6]

That there is therefore a great deal of material on the Nuer does not unambiguously mean that we know a great deal about them: Hutchinson goes on to argue that 'the cumulative effect of decades of secondary reanalyses of Evans-Pritchard's materials' has been both to foster an illusion that the Nuer are 'somehow above history and

4 Ibid, pp. 290–91. There may, as Harris argues, be general causal relations between these different features, such that, for instance, groups of people making their living by plough-based agriculture tend to be both more sexist and more violent than those who rely on rice-paddies (ibid., pp. 328–31). I do not need to consider this debate for my purposes.

5 Barclay, *People Without Government: An anthropology of anarchism* (London, 1982); Clastres, *Society Against the State*, trans. Robert Hurley and Abe Stein (Oxford, 1977); Taylor, *Community, Anarchy and Liberty* (Cambridge, 1982); Ward, *Anarchy in Action* (2nd edn, London, 1973), Chapter 4.

6 Hutchinson, *Nuer Dilemmas*, p. 21.

beyond change',[7] and to perpetuate several false images of their social form. However, that there is such a mass of material at least means that we are likely to have correctives to one-sided and ideologically motivated accounts, which we might lack in the case of less studied people and social forms.

My second reason for focusing on the Nuer is that they are not especially far towards the peaceful end of the variation I have noted in non-state social forms. As described by Evans-Pritchard and others, individual Nuer are fairly quick to use, and to retaliate with violence. My argument is not just that some people are wonderfully peaceful, and that we would do well to emulate them. It is that even where people are not much given to being peaceable, the non-state tactics for conflict resolution I discover are still effective. The relatively violent Nuer life is therefore a good exemplary social form to use to make the argument. I do not want to give the impression that non-state conflict resolution depends on the unusual mildness of the people involved in it: even among fairly violent people like the Nuer, non-state conflict resolution works. This is a distinction of my use from other anarchist uses of this example: where the tradition has typically used an account of the Nuer social form to display the possibility of peace in the absence of the state, I use one to display the possibility of conflict resolution in the face of ongoing violence.

### *A Sketch of the Nuer Social Form*

Since Evans-Pritchard's work in the 1930s, the Nuer's way of life has been transformed, and partly destroyed by government interference, trade, disease, and two Sudanese civil wars. I do not attempt to give anything like a full account of the complexities of Nuer life here, but consider only enough of the material about them to provide an empirical example of effective conflict-resolution without institutionalised domination.

The Nuer live (or lived) on savannah, which is parched and dry from December to June, and flooded from June to December. They husband cattle, hunt, fish, collect wild fruit and roots, and cultivate millet and maize. During the wet season, they live in villages of between fifty and several hundred people, on high ground, separated from other villages by between five and twenty miles of flooded grassland; during the dry season, in camps concentrated around permanent water-sources. Camps and villages involve some, but not all of the same individuals living together: 'People who form separate village communities in the rains may unite in a common camp in the drought. Likewise, people from the same village may join different camps.'[8] The Nuer live in a general situation of scarcity. Famine is not uncommon, and there are few natural resources – no iron or good stone, and very few trees – for toolmaking.

7 Ibid. For brief consideration of, and references for the multiple reinterpretations of Evans-Pritchard's material, see ibid., pp. 31–2; for some examples of that reinterpretation, the studies in T.O. Beidelman (ed.), *The Translation of Culture: Essays to E.E. Evans-Pritchard* (London, 1971).

8 Evans-Pritchard, 'The Nuer of the Southern Sudan', p. 275.

Cattle and their husbandry have been particularly important to the Nuer: 'According to Evans-Pritchard … the Nuer of the early 1930s were almost totally absorbed in the care, exchange, and sacrifice of their beloved cattle.'[9] Humans and cattle were involved in an 'intimate symbiosis of survival'.[10] Cattle were not only the central metaphor for value, but were both 'the principle means by which people created and affirmed enduring bonds amongst themselves as well as between themselves and divinity'[11] through a symbolic equation of cattle with people, and 'an incessant topic of conversation among Nuer men and women'.[12] On her first field trip to the Sudan in 1979, Hutchinson found that this topic had largely been replaced in conversation by 'national political issues, cabinet shake-ups, regional troop movements, and the Jonglei Canal scheme'.[13]

The significance of cattle has been transformed since the 1930s by Nuer involvement in state politics and monetary exchange, but not wholly lost. Hutchinson argues that, throughout the 1980s and early '90s, Nuer were 'actively grappling' with the relationship between cattle and money, and developing a 'unique system of hybrid wealth categories … in order to facilitate movements of cattle and money between "market" and "non-market" spheres of exchange while simultaneously affirming the existence of an axiological boundary between these spheres'.[14] Money has not passed the Nuer by, but neither has it effaced their earlier modes of exchange and understandings of value.[15]

The Nuer in the 1930s had no government, no long-standing inequalities of power, no police or tax collectors, and no leaders:

> The ordered anarchy in which they live accords well with their character, for it is impossible to live among Nuer and conceive of rulers ruling over them. The Nuer is a product of a hard and egalitarian upbringing, is deeply democratic, and is easily roused to violence. His turbulent spirit finds any restraint irksome and no man recognizes a superior. Wealth makes no difference. A man with many cattle is envied, but not treated differently from a man with few cattle. Birth makes no difference. A man may not be a member of the dominant clan of his tribe, he may even be of Dinka descent, but were another to allude to the fact he would run a grave risk of being clubbed. That every Nuer considers himself as good as his neighbour is evident in their every movement. They strut about like lords of the earth, which, indeed, they consider themselves to be. There is no master and no servant in their society, but only equals who regard themselves as God's noblest creation … Among themselves even the suspicion of an order riles a man and he either does not carry it out or he carries it out in a casual and dilatory manner that is more insulting than a refusal. When a Nuer wants his fellows to do something he asks it as a favour to a kinsman, saying, 'Son of my mother, do so-and-so', or he includes himself in the

9 Hutchinson, *Nuer Dilemmas*, p. 59.
10 Ibid.
11 Ibid.
12 Ibid., p. 33.
13 Ibid.
14 Ibid., p. 50
15 See further ibid., Chapter 2.

> command and says: 'Let us depart', 'Let the people return home', and so forth. In his daily relations to his fellows a man shows respect to his elders, to his 'fathers', and to certain persons of ritual status, within the circuit of his reference, so long as they do not infringe on his independence, but he will not submit to any authority which clashes with his own interests and he does not consider himself bound to obey any one. I was once discussing the [neighbouring] Shilluk with a Nuer who had visited their country, and he remarked, 'They have one big chief, but we have not. This chief can send for a man and demand a cow or he can cut a man's throat. Whoever saw a Nuer do such a thing? What Nuer ever came when some one sent for him or paid any one a cow?'[16]

Evans-Pritchard's repeated use of 'man', 'he' and 'his' in this passage is not accidental: he spent most of his time with male, and in his terms 'aristocratic' Nuer, and his account may therefore be distortedly viricentric. Hutchinson makes it clear that being female allowed her access to interactions and social spaces which were closed to Evans-Pritchard; she is also very funny about the difficulties raised by her being 'an awkward cross between a woman and a girl'[17] since she was married, but had no children. I shall briefly consider Nuer gender relations in a moment, but before doing so, I want to note two related points.

At least for some Nuer, sociability is egalitarian, anti-authoritarian, and potentially violent, and this form of life is not the result of the mere absence of alternative, inegalitarian tactics. In general, there is no simple state of nature on which more complex systems can be built; in particular, the Nuer's 'turbulent spirit' is a distinctive way of maintaining a (relatively) equal distribution of power. The Nuer are well aware of the possibility and danger of chiefs, and have tactics to resist incipient domination, including their attitudes to authority and orders. Such tactics are widespread. Marvin Harris records a parallel example in the experience of Richard Lee:

> To please the !Kung, [Lee] decided to buy a large ox and have it slaughtered as a present. After several days searching Bantu agricultural villages looking for the largest and fattest ox in the region, he acquired what appeared to be a perfect specimen. But his friends took him aside and assured him that he had been duped into buying an absolutely worthless animal. 'Of course, we will eat it,' they said, 'but it won't fill us up – we will eat and go home to bed with stomachs rumbling.' But when Lee's ox was slaughtered, it turned out to be covered with a thick layer of fat. Later, his friends explained why they had said his gift was valueless, even though they knew better than he what lay under the animal's skin: 'Yes, when a young man kills much meat he comes to think of himself as a chief or a big man, and he thinks of the rest of us as his servants or inferiors. We can't accept this, we refuse one who boasts, for someday his pride will make him kill somebody. So we always speak of his meat as worthless. This way we cool his heart and make him gentle.'[18]

---

16 Evans-Pritchard, *The Nuer*, pp. 181–2.

17 Hutchinson, *Nuer Dilemmas*, p. 46.

18 Harris, *Our Kind*, pp. 345–6.

I am not making the obviously false claim that such egalitarian tactics are always successful. My point is that egalitarian people are typically aware of the possibility of other arrangements, and they have tactics explicitly intended and used to maintain their situation. Now, back to gender equality.

Nuer distinguish between men and women, especially as fathers and mothers; descent is reckoned on the male line; and males hold positions of responsibility and ritual status which are not usually open to women – although it is open to a woman who is unable to conceive children 'to become a social man, gather cattle, and marry a wife to produce children for her'.[19] Men and women have different roles in relation to husbandry and cultivation, to food preparation, to children, and to violence. However, it is not clear to me to what extent these differences in roles translate into gender differences in power. Hutchinson traces the changing roles, metaphorical understandings, and reciprocal autonomies of Nuer men and women since the 1930s with considerable subtlety.[20] Her account cannot be taken as unambiguously supporting either the claim that women are systematically oppressed in Nuer social forms, or that they are not. Rather, she argues that the metaphors of blood, cattle and food, and the culturally legitimated demands and spheres of autonomy of men and women, of husbands and wives, and of fathers and mothers, have changed in complex and interrelated ways. I therefore leave the issue of gender equality as an admitted gap in my sketch of the Nuer. We certainly have no reason to claim that the Nuer's otherwise egalitarian social form requires or gives rise to gender inequality, and that minimal, negative point is sufficient for our purposes here.

Across these differences and complexities, Nuer social and political life significantly involves two interlinked but distinct forms of interaction: tribes and their subsections on one hand, and kinship networks on the other. 'There is no common political organisation or central administration',[21] but Nuer none the less relate to one another as members of various sorts of group, not just as individuals.

Tribes are the largest groups in which 'there is machinery for settling disputes and a moral obligation to conclude them sooner or later',[22] but their boundaries are not the limits of social and political interaction: 'People move freely all over Nuer-land and are unmolested if they have not incurred blood-guilt. They marry and, to a small extent, trade across tribal boundaries, and pay visits to kinsmen living outside their own tribe. Many social relations, which are not specifically political, link members of different tribes.'[23] Further, members of different tribes encounter one another in dry-season camps concentrated around scarce sources of water.

Tribes are subdivided into what Evans-Pritchard calls primary, secondary and tertiary segments. These three levels are concentric, so an individual might be a member, for instance, of the Cuak tertiary segment of the Nyapir secondary segment

19 Hutchinson, *Nuer Dilemmas*, p. 61.

20 Ibid., Chapter 4.

21 Evans-Pritchard, 'The Nuer of the Southern Sudan', p. 279.

22 Ibid., p. 278.

23 Ibid., p. 279.

of the Jenyang primary segment of the Lak tribe.[24] An important characteristic of segmentary organisation is that how an individual characterises her membership is relative to the level of segment from which she is *excluded* in a particular context: 'A member of $Z^2$ tertiary division of tribe B sees himself as a member of $Z^2$ community is relation to $Z^1$, but he regards himself as a member of $Y^2$ and not of $Z^2$ in relation to $Y^1$. Likewise, he regards himself as a member of Y, and not of $Y^2$, in relation to X. He regards himself as a member of tribe B, and not of its primary section Y, in relation to tribe A.'[25]

So, again, my Cuak is a Cuak in relation to the Kar and Thiang tertiary sections; a Nyapir, together with the Kar and Thiang, in relation to the Kudwop secondary section; a Jenyang, with the Kudwop, in relation to the Kwacbur primary section; and a Lak, with the Kwacbur, in relation to the Gawaar, Gaajak and other tribes. In situations of violent conflict, and of blood-feud after a murder in particular, this Cuak will join with other Cuaks against the Kar, when a Kar has killed a Cuak, but will join with other Nyapir, including the Kar, against the Kudwop when a Kudwop has killed a Nyapir:

> Thus, on a structural plane, there is always a contradiction in the definition of a political group, for a man is a member of it in virtue of his non-membership of other groups of the same type which he stands outside of, and he is likewise not a member of the same community in virtue of his membership of a segment of it which stands in opposition to its other segments … The outstanding structural characteristic of Nuer political groups is their relativity. A tribal segment is a political group in relation to other segments of the same kind, and they jointly form a tribe only in relation to other Nuer tribes and to adjacent foreign tribes which form part of their political system, and without these relations very little meaning can be attached to the concepts of 'tribe' and 'tribal segment'.[26]

Tribal and segmentary groups 'are always changing in one direction or another'.[27] That is, the Nuer social form has tendencies both towards fission and towards fusion: 'Although any group tends to split into opposed parts, these parts tend to fuse in relation to other groups … fission and fusion are two aspects of the same segmentary principle and the Nuer tribe and its divisions are to be understood as a relation between these two contradictory, yet complementary, tendencies.'[28]

The Nuer's other, interlinked but distinct form of interaction is the kinship system, which cuts across tribes and tribal segments. A clan is a segmented set of lineages comprising everyone descended, through the male line, from the founder of that line. It is worth noting that 'the male line' is not constituted by physical fatherhood, but by heirs legitimated by the payment of bride-cattle: 'Without access to cattle, a man could not legally acquire heirs – no matter how many children he

24 See the diagram in Evans-Pritchard, *The Nuer*, p. 141.

25 Evans-Pritchard, 'The Nuer of the Southern Sudan', p. 281.

26 Ibid., pp. 281–2.

27 Ibid., p. 284.

28 Ibid.

sired';[29] further, 'If a man died without heirs, his relatives were able – indeed obliged – to collect cattle and marry a "ghost wife" … in the name of the deceased to bear children for him.'[30] As with tribal structure, lineage membership is relative: 'Two lineages which are equal and opposite are composite in relation to a third, so that a man is a member of a lineage in relation to a certain group and not a member of it in relation to a different group.'[31]

Kinship is supremely important to the Nuer. They have a variety of obligations to their kin, especially the duty to avenge a death, and a complex system of prohibitions of incest, even between kin we would not regard as close. Kinship crosscuts tribal membership – 'the same clans are found in different tribes'[32] – but lineage and clan relations also provide a general idiom for social obligations and interaction, as well as a rich source of gossip. Kin and tribal affiliations can clash, in particular by giving rise to conflicting duties. For instance, after a murder, 'It is not clear what would happen if close agnates of the slayer were living in the village of the slain, in which case they would have loyalties to both sides.'[33]

Kinship can be fictional: Evans-Pritchard records that, ill and leaving the Nuer, he asked the people he had been living with to help carry his belongings to the river. They refused. When asked why, a young Nuer boy replied: 'You told them to carry your belongings to the river. That is why they refused. If you had asked them, saying, "My mother's sons, assist me", they would not have refused.'[34] Of course, nobody supposed that Evans-Pritchard was actually close kin, but kinship was still the right idiom for a request for help as for other interactions: 'Rights, privileges, and obligations are determined by kinship. Either a man is a kinsman, actually or by fiction, or he is a person to whom you have no reciprocal obligations.'[35] Like other features of Nuer sociability, kinship and the social idiom it provides have been changed, but like others, not wholly effaced, by involvement with states, money and war.

The Nuer whom Evans-Pritchard encountered were quick to use violence, both individually and collectively: 'A Nuer will at once fight if he considers that he has been insulted, and they are very sensitive and easily take offence … From their earliest years children are encouraged by their elders to settle all disputes by fighting';[36] 'Feuds frequently break out between sections of the same tribe and they are often of long duration',[37] and 'from the earliest times', but not continuously, 'the Nuer have been fighting [their neighbours] the Dinka and have been generally on the

29 Hutchinson, *Nuer Dilemmas*, p. 61.

30 Ibid.

31 Evans-Pritchard, 'The Nuer of the Southern Sudan', pp. 285–6.

32 Ibid., p. 279.

33 Kathleen Gough, 'Nuer Kinship: A re-examination', in T.O. Beidelman (ed.), *The Translation of Culture: Essays to E.E. Evans-Pritchard* (London, 1971), pp. 79–121, p. 86.

34 Evans-Pritchard, *The Nuer*, p. 182.

35 Ibid., p. 183.

36 Ibid., p. 151.

37 Evans-Pritchard, 'The Nuer of the Southern Sudan', p. 283.

offensive' in raids for cattle or captives.[38] Hutchinson to some extent confirms this impression, recording for instance that many Nuer mothers 'consciously sought to inculcate the virtues of courage, self-assertion, and independence in their children',[39] and praised them for asserting themselves violently and for knowing how to fight.

However, despite this general, culturally approved tendency to initiate violence and to use it in revenge, the Nuer have (or had) systems of conflict-resolution which do not involve domination or hierarchy, and which relatively successfully prevent or limit violence. In the first place, although once a fight has begun between people of the same village, neither party can with honour give way, what generally happens is that 'people pull them away from each other, loudly protesting, and then stand between them'.[40] In the second, kinship obligations and tribe or segment membership provide a system both of deterrence, because it is generally known that the kin or tribal associates of a murder victim will seek vengeance, and of limitation of involvement, because 'the scope of direct vengeance is limited to small kinship groups and their efforts to exact it are not incessant.'[41] The duty of vengeance is felt and acted on only by a limited number of people. In the third place, and most importantly here, there is a system of arbitration and arrangement of compensation, which I shall now sketch.

### *Leopard-skin Chiefs*

The term 'chief' is misleading about this system of arbitration, because leopard-skin chiefs do not have any general authority. The Nuer regard them as 'agents through which disputes of a certain kind can be settled and defilement of a certain kind can be effaced, and I have often heard remarks such as this: "We took hold of them and gave them leopard skins and made them our chiefs to do the talking at sacrifices for homicide".'[42] Chiefs are ritual and social functionaries with specific roles, and those roles do not translate into any more general authority or to being the beneficiary of unequally distributed power: 'The chiefs I have seen were treated in everyday life like other men and there is no means of telling that a man is a chief by observing people's behaviour to him.'[43] Nor is a chief representative of any political grouping: 'he in no way represents or symbolizes the unity and exclusiveness of political groups.'[44] Nor does he gain material benefits from his position. Indeed, being a chief is often costly, since their ritual activities involve giving or sacrificing cattle. Chiefs perform a mediative role in disputes: they persuade parties in conflict to talk rather than fight; they offer but are unable to enforce a resolution; they build coalitions to

38 Ibid., p. 280.

39 Hutchinson, *Nuer Dilemmas*, p. 168.

40 Evans-Pritchard, *The Nuer*, p. 151.

41 Ibid., p. 159.

42 Ibid., p. 170.

43 Ibid., p. 176.

44 Ibid.

support a return to peace, and they arrange and preside over compensation, usually in the form of a traditionally specified number of cattle. A chief 'is simply a mediator in a specific social situation and his mediation is only successful because community ties are acknowledged by both parties and because they wish to avoid, for the time being at any rate, further hostilities … He is the machinery which enables groups to bring about a normal state of affairs when they desire to achieve this end.'[45]

Mediation is not always successful, and in general is less successful the more distant the parties to the dispute are in kinship or tribal relations. At the limit, no possibility of compensation, or therefore of mediation, is recognised in disputes between tribes (although this statement may be less informative than it appears, since Evans-Pritchard partly *defines* tribal boundaries as the limit of the possibility of mediation).[46]

### *Primitivism, Again*

I have sketched some of the features of Nuer sociability over the period from the 1930s, when E. E. Evans-Pritchard lived with them, to the 1980s and '90s, when Sharon Hutchinson did. I have not covered anything like the full complexity of Nuer life: I have not, for instance, said much about gender relations, except to leave their equality or lack of it as an admitted absence in my account. I have gestured towards, but said little about, the changes that the Nuer's encounter with state power, money and warfare have brought about. And I have said nothing at all about Nuer religious practices, or about the repeated phenomenon of religious revivals led by prophets.[47]

However, even what little I have said should be enough to show that the Nuer are not 'primitive' in one of the senses of that term: they live complex lives in a complex and fluid social form. In the case of the Nuer, and I suggest in general, Ernest Gellner's claim that 'what defines a segmentary society is not that [segmentary organisation] occurs, but that this is very nearly all that occurs'[48] is manifestly false.

Whether or not the Nuer are 'primitives' (ignoring for the moment my argument in Chapter 2 that there are no 'primitive' societies), my argument here is not primitivism.

I have not used the Nuer to display some uncorrupted human nature. They are, as sketched above, as richly and distinctively acculturated as anyone else. And, even if they did display fundamental human nature, we could not regard it as wholly good: as I have emphasised, the Nuer are fairly violent.

---

45 Ibid., pp. 174–5.

46 Ibid., Chapter 4; Evans-Pritchard, 'The Nuer of the Southern Sudan', Section V; Peter J. Greuel, 'The Leopard-Skin Chief: An examination of political power among the Nuer', *American Anthropologist* vol. 73 (1971): 1115–20.

47 On which see T.O. Beidelman, 'Nuer Priests and Prophets: Charisma, authority and power among the Nuer' in Beidelman (ed.), *The Translation of Culture: Essays to E.E. Evans-Pritchard* (London, 1971), pp. 375–415; Evans-Pritchard, *Nuer Religion*; Hutchinson, *Nuer Dilemmas*, Chapter 7.

48 *Saints of the Atlas* (London, 1969), p. 42.

I have not presented the Nuer social form as a relic of some golden age: according to my sketch, the Nuer, like the rest of us, are people making a living and pursuing their other interests in a historically and environmentally conditioned, but not determined way. And, for as long as Western anthropologists have known anything about them, the Nuer have been greatly affected by their ongoing encounter with nation-states.

I am not recommending return to a Nuer-like social form, for at least two reasons. First, it has some fairly unappealing features: I am not recommending abandoning the complex and industrially based technology we enjoy, and which the Nuer used to lack (at least in part because they also lacked the raw materials to make or support it); nor am I praising the Nuer's propensity for violence. Secondly, the idea of a 'return' to this way of living is obscure: for whom would it be a return?

As with Godwin and Kropotkin in Chapter 1, the question is, What am I doing argumentatively with this material?, and its answer is not that I am performing a primitivist argument. I am using the example of the Nuer to display some human capacities for living together, and especially for conflict-resolution. The range of human social possibility includes systems of egalitarian social networks, without institutionalised domination, in which violence is limited and conflict can be resolved.

### *Morals*

I have given one example of humans living together and resolving conflict, without institutionalised domination, and despite culturally sanctioned tendencies towards individual and collective violence. The Nuer create the productive and other capacities they need in order to satisfy their interests, which they share with most other humans, in food, shelter, company, continued life, the respect of peers, and the absence, or at least the limitation and resolution, of violent conflict. They further create capacities for complex social interaction, ritual performance, storytelling, and investigation of the world around them. However, they resist the creation of capacities to dominate of the kind that some other humans, including us, live with. They mutually organise conflict-resolution by assigning the task of mediation to ritual and coalition-forming specialists known as leopard-skin chiefs, and thereby succeed, for the most part, in living in 'ordered anarchy'. They have also been socially creative and plastic in their responses to, and appropriation of some elements of, other social forms.

The Nuer are not the only example of successful life in the absence of domination. Other examples of the effectiveness of similar strategies of mediation can be found.[49] In general, mediation without institutionalised domination is a common way of resolving conflict. Mediation 'is a kind of non-governmental system of dispute settlement which one finds widely dispersed throughout the world … [and] that it

49 See, for instance, Barclay, *People Without Government*, and John Middleton and David Tate (eds), *Tribes Without Rulers: Studies in African segmentary systems* (London, 1958).

is so common and widespread may indicate that it has proven a most successful mechanism for maintaining peace.'[50] Other tactics are also available: see, for instance, Ernest Gellner's description of trial by collective oath among Berber tribes.[51]

Humans can live together and create and assign capacities in a wide variety of ways. The range of human social possibility includes states and slavery, but it also includes forms of life which do not involve institutionalised domination, in which peace is relatively successfully maintained by tactics including mediation. It is often thought that if we do not assign capacities to dominate to institutions which maintain peace or stability, we will be unable to live in any way except a chaotic war of all against all. But this claim is empirically false: humans are capable of creating, maintaining and living in ordered, egalitarian and relatively peaceful social forms. However, it may be argued that these forms are only possible in low-technology, unindustrial situations like that of the Nuer. I shall now refute this objection, by considering another example of anarchic possibility.

## Anarchic Organisation in the Spanish Civil War

The Spanish civil war is a classic anarchist example and locus of debate: no anarchist or historian of anarchism since has been able to ignore it, or the problems and arguments it raises.[52] As with my discussion of the Nuer above, my engagement with this example is thus an extension of the anarchist tradition. However, I do not intend to intervene in, still less resolve, all of the disagreements among anarchists or others about the civil war. I do not, for instance, consider the ongoing debate about the propriety of the involvement of anarchist trade unionists in the Spanish republican government.[53] Nor do I involve myself in the bitter argument about atrocities committed by both sides.[54] I intend to invoke only enough information and make only as much argument as is necessary for my particular purposes. However, before sketching the civil war and the anarchist social experiments it provoked or allowed, I need to refute an influential false image of Spanish anarchism.

---

50 Barclay, *People Without Government*, pp. 47-8.

51 'How to Live in Anarchy' in *Contemporary Thought and Politics* (London, 1974), pp. 87–94.

52 Examples of this engagement include Murray Bookchin, *The Spanish Anarchists: The heroic years 1868–1936* (Edinburgh, 1998); Guérin, *Anarchism*, Chapter 3; Clifford Harper, *Anarchy: A graphic guide* (London, 1987), Chapters 6 and 7; Joll, *The Anarchists*, Chapter 9; Marshall, *Demanding the Impossible*, Chapter 29; Vernon Richards, *Lessons of the Spanish Revolution* (3rd edn, London, 1983); Alexandre Skirda, *Facing the Enemy: A history of anarchist organization from Proudhon to May 1968*, trans. Paul Sharkey (Edinburgh, 2002), Chapter 17; Woodcock, *Anarchism*, Chapter 12.

53 On which see, for instance, Guérin, *Anarchism*, pp. 128–30.

54 See, for instance, Peter Preston, *A Concise History of the Spanish Civil War* (London, 1996), pp. 88–91.

*Primitive Rebels?*

There is an image of specifically Spanish anarchism, sometimes illegitimately extended to other anarchisms, which pictures it as a 'primitive' social movement. This is potentially another kind of accusation of primitivism: if Spanish anarchists were 'primitive', and other anarchists admire and seek to emulate them, then anarchists are primitivists. I shall argue that this accusation falls at the first hurdle: Spanish anarchism was not a 'primitive' social movement.

Spanish anarchists have often been compared to medieval millennialists. Hugh Thomas, for instance, describes the 'regime' in Castro del Río, in the early part of the Spanish civil war, as 'comparable to that of the anabaptists of Münster of 1530, all private exchange of goods being banned, the village bar closed, the inhabitants realising the long-desired abolition of coffee'.[55] Similar analogies are made by James Joll, by Gerald Brenan and, most importantly here, by Eric Hobsbawm.[56] Where the analogy between anarchists and millennialists is made as a descriptive conceit, or as an attempt at illumination by comparison, it is unproblematic. It is of obvious historical and human interest to note the similarities in activity and aspiration between such widely separated phenomena. Ascetic ideals of purification exercised both fifteenth-century peasant chiliasts and twentieth-century peasant anarchists, and both expected radical change, even reversal, of the order of the world. They are not alone: many radicals have hoped or expected that the world would be turned upside down.

That said, we need also to recognise the striking differences between anarchists and millennialists. The latter characteristically expect that the transformation of the world is to be 'miraculous, in the sense that it is to be accomplished by, or with the help of, supernatural agencies'.[57] They regard the role of the righteous group as being 'to gather together, to prepare itself, to watch the signs of the coming doom, to listen to the prophets who predict the coming of the great day, and perhaps to undertake certain ritual measures against the moment of decision and change, or to purify themselves, shedding the dross of the bad world of the present so as to be able to enter the new world in shining purity'.[58] The Spanish anarchists, in contrast and

---

55 *The Spanish Civil War* (3rd edn, London, 1990). p. 306. It is perhaps worth noting that Thomas's book has long been 'the standard work on the Spanish Civil War' (editorial note in Raymond Carr (ed.), *The Republic and the Civil War in Spain* (London, 1971), p. 257), but that he, and it, have been attacked by anarchists on both historical and political grounds: see, for instance, Vernon Richards, Foreword to Gaston Laval, *Collectives in the Spanish Revolution* (London, 1975), pp. 7–15. I do not need to involve myself in this debate.

56 Joll, *The Anarchists*; Brenan, *The Spanish Labyrinth*; Hobsbawm, *Primitive Rebels.* For a careful history of the millennial analogy, as applied to nineteenth-century Andalusian anarchists in particular, see Temma Kaplan, *Anarchists of Andalusia 1868-1903* (Princeton, NJ, 1977), Chapter 8.

57 Norman Cohn, *The Pursuit of the Millennium: Revolutionary millenarians and mystical anarchists of the middle ages* (revised edn, London, 1970), p. 13.

58 Hobsbawm, *Primitive Rebels*, p. 58.

like other revolutionary groups, regarded their role as being to bring about the great transformation themselves, particularly through egalitarian organisation, struggle, and the general strike. Further, while we can compare the social and economic circumstances of the southern Spanish peasantry and the medieval peasants who were often the core of millennial movements, we need to recognise that Spanish anarchism was also an urban phenomenon, especially in (comparatively) wealthy, industrialised Barcelona. Indeed, Daniel Guérin is particularly concerned to show Spanish anarchism as a tense 'symbiosis' between two tendencies: one rural, southern, Kropotkinite and nostalgic for a mythologised traditional 'free commune'; the other industrial, northern, syndicalist, Bakuninite and 'more realistic, more concerned with the present than with the golden age'.[59]

The analogy between millennialism and Spanish anarchism is often intended not just to be descriptive, but to form the basis of a genealogy. If the ideologies and activities of the two are similar, it might be that millennialism is an ancestor of anarchism. This historical hypothesis, and the research intended to test it, are also unproblematic. However, more than analogy will be needed to support any such genealogical claim: specific evidence of the transformation of millennial into anarchist groups, activity and ideology is required. We will need to recognise that, although anarchism may have roots in millennial movements, it has other roots too. Spanish anarchism began most obviously in, first, the Proudhonian political theory of Francisco Pi y Margall, and secondly, the arrival of Giuseppe Fanelli, a disciple of Bakunin, in Madrid in 1868.[60] Before the civil war, it has a 60-year history of debate, polemic, and often-clandestine organisation.[61] The history of Spanish anarchism is a part of the history of nineteenth-century European socialism and Spanish politics, at least as much as it is part of the suggested transformation of millennialism.

The detail of these specifically historical debates is outside both the scope of this section and my expertise.[62] My points are, first, that while there are analogies to be drawn between millennial and Spanish anarchist movements, and while it is possible that anarchism is partly descended from millennialism, this is far from being the whole story; and, secondly, that neither of these historical claims, even if true, in themselves support the characterisation of Spanish anarchism as 'primitive', nor therefore of anarchists enthused by it as primitivists.

More than analogy or genealogy is needed to characterise Spanish anarchism as 'primitive'. The argument requires some structure in which millennial and revolutionary movements can be placed on a progressive scale from simple, undeveloped, 'primitive' or embryonic, to complex, developed, modern or fully grown. Gerald Brenan implies such a structure in his influential suggestion that

---

59 Guérin, *Anarchism*, pp. 119–20. Primitivist rhetoric has here colonised even Guérin's thinking.

60 Bookchin, *The Spanish Anarchists*, Chapter 1.

61 On which see Nettlau, *A Short History of Anarchism*, Chapter 13.

62 For a critical review of the debate, see George Esenwein, *Anarchist Ideology and the Working-Class Movement in Spain, 1868–1898* (Berkeley, CA, 1989).

Spanish anarchism was a millennial heresy of the kind which took place in the rest of Europe in the late Middle Ages, but which was delayed in Spain by the power of the Church and its Inquisition. For this claim to be meaningful, we need to assume that millennial heresy is somehow a necessary stage in the 'growth' of a discrete society. This biological metaphor – speaking of societies as if they were distinct creatures, and needed to endure millennialism as humans need to endure puberty – allows Brenan to present Spanish society between the late Middle Ages and the nineteenth century as neotenous, and Spanish anarchism as a phase that Spain had to endure to gain adulthood or modernity.

Brenan's progressive scale is largely implicit, and his picture of Spanish anarchism as delayed heresy is more metaphor than metaphysics. However, he directly inspired Eric Hobsbawm's 'primitive rebels' thesis, in which the historical metaphysic is explicit and polemical.[63] I shall now consider this account of Spanish anarchism as 'primitive' in detail.

*Primitive Rebels* is a series of studies rather than a continuous narrative, but its discussions of mafia in Sicily, Lazzarettists in Spain and others are contextualised and linked by a metaphysic of progression. The three major types of 'primitive rebellion' which Hobsbawm recognises – social banditry, mafias, and millenarian movements – are part of what he calls 'a chain of historical evolution'.[64] All three are 'archaic' or 'primitive',[65] but unlike 'what are normally thought of as "primitive" societies', they 'all have considerable historical evolution behind them, for they belong to a world which has long known the State … class differentiation and exploitation … and even cities.'[66] Hobsbawm's historical metaphysic has three stages: true primitiveness, where society is governed by 'kinship or tribal solidarity … whether or not combined with territorial links';[67] modern society; and, between them, the transitional stage which is his subject. The people involved in this last pre-modern stage are '*pre-political* people who have not yet found, or only begun to find, a specific language in which to express their aspirations about the world', and 'their movements are thus in many respects blind and groping, by the standards of modern ones.'[68] In asserting this metaphysic, Hobsbawm makes frequent use of the same biological metaphors as Brenan: mafia, for instance, are 'a sort of embryo' of 'more highly developed movements'.[69]

It should now be clear that Hobsbawm's account of Spanish anarchists and other 'primitive' movements is a cultural evolutionary story of the kind I criticised in Chapter 2. There, I characterised such stories as involving the association of five ideas or research plans: an ambition to describe and explain human social change

---

63 For Hobsbawm's debt to Brenan, see *Primitive Rebels*, p. 74.

64 Ibid., p. 4.

65 Ibid., p. 1 and passim.

66 Ibid., p. 3.

67 Ibid.

68 Ibid.

69 Ibid., p. 30.

at a high level of generality; a typology of human social forms; a linear scale of height, civilisation, evolution or complexity; unilinealism; and metaphors of organic growth. Although Hobsbawm's story is confined to revolutionary movements in western and southern Europe, rather than encompassing the whole of human social life, it similarly displays an ambition to describe and explain their development at a fairly high level of generality; a typology of revolutionary forms; a linear scale of evolution from simple to complex, and metaphors of organic growth (it is unclear to what extent Hobsbawm is a unilinealist). It appears, then, that my reasons for not adopting such stories or plans could apply to Hobsbawm's account. I shall consider this possibility further in a moment, but first, I shall say something about how Hobsbawm places Spanish anarchism in his narrative.

The Spanish anarchists find their place in Hobsbawm's story as millennialists. For Hobsbawm, millennialism, 'of all the primitive social movements … is the one least handicapped by its primitiveness',[70] because it is on the cusp of 'modernity'. Millennialists share with modern revolutionary movements the desire, not merely to correct particular injustices, but to overthrow and replace the whole present world. The differences are only that unlike millennialists, modern movements 'have – implicitly or explicitly – certain fairly definite ideas on how the old society is to be replaced by the new, the most crucial of which concerns what we may call the "transfer of power"';[71] and that millennialists lack a precise language in which to express their claims and grievances. The Spanish anarchists 'show millenarianism wholly divorced from traditional religious forms',[72] but still lack such definite ideas and precise expression. These are to be provided by modern and especially socialist revolutionary movements, and the anarchists are therefore, only just, 'primitive'.

In order for anarchists to be located in this way, at least one of the two claims made above must be true: the Spanish anarchists lacked definite ideas about the transfer of power, or appropriate language in which to express their aspirations. However, first, it is not true that the Spanish anarchists lacked definite ideas about the transfer of power. They were involved in a lively debate, through publication and conference, throughout the sixty years before the civil war, precisely about revolutionary tactics. These debates have been exhaustively recorded by Max Nettlau in his *Short History of Anarchism*, and many of the pamphlets and periodicals in which they were carried out are still extant. There was enough eventual consensus about tactics that, as I discuss below, the transfer of power was accomplished in similar ways all over the Republican sector of Spain in the early part of the civil war. The first argument for characterising Spanish anarchists as 'primitive' fails.

Hobsbawm's second argument is that the anarchists lacked the proper vocabulary to express their aspirations. The claim is that millennial Spanish anarchists shared the aspirations of modern socialist revolutionary movements, but, lacking the proper mode of expression, cloaked themselves in mystical and pseudo-religious language

70 Ibid., p. 57.

71 Ibid., p. 58.

72 Ibid., p. 65.

instead. Millennialists can 'readily exchange the primitive costume in which they dress their aspirations for the modern costume of socialist and communist politics',[73] but the Spanish anarchists failed to find the right wardrobe. Hobsbawm is not the only commentator to make such claims about costume. Josef Macek, for instance, writes of the Hussite heresy that 'The dim vision of a classless society, disguised in biblical vestments, which arose before the eyes of the Taborite brothers and sisters in 1420, reflected the yearnings of the serfs and the poor.'[74] Some Spanish anarchists did use religious language, although with more self-consciousness than Hobsbawm implies: 'Anarchist writers and orators … were not averse to using religious imagery and developing a prophetic rhetorical style, often employing the apostolic message as a guide or a point of contrast. At times in conversation the name of God might be invoked, but only to symbolise a common though incomprehensible creation and a shared heritage that calls for unity and equality among men.'[75]

This does not show that they wanted to say something else; still less that they would have said what a 'modern socialist' would say, had they possessed the vocabulary. Indeed, it is difficult to imagine what kind of evidence could be provided to support a claim that any historical actor was trying, and failing, to say something other than what she actually said. The second argument for characterising Spanish anarchism as 'primitive' is at best unsupported.

Hobsbawm's account of Spanish anarchism misrepresents it, and should therefore be rejected. However, to return to the issue of cultural evolutionary stories, do we also have reason to reject his progressive scale as a whole? The answer to that question turns on a further one about Hobsbawm's purposes.

Hobsbawm's purpose in asserting his historical metaphysic may simply be to do with the fact that *Primitive Rebels* introduced a new topic into historical conversation. As Hobsbawm characterises it, historical work on revolutionary movements before *Primitive Rebels* had concentrated on 'ancient and medieval' and modern 'labour and socialist'[76] revolutionaries. His subjects had been regarded by 'older historians' as 'marginal or unimportant phenomena'.[77] So, the metaphysic may be intended to contextualise those subjects in relation to more well-known and 'respectable' issues. It may further be a way of justifying taking an interest in such apparently marginal figures, analogously to James Joll's justification of his interest in anarchism on the grounds that 'The study of failure can often be as instructive and rewarding as the study of success.'[78]

However, I suggest that there is a further, implicit purpose in Hobsbawm's characterisation of anarchism as 'primitive'. Hobsbawm ends his consideration of Spanish anarchism with the claim that 'The history of anarchism, almost alone

73 Ibid., p. 64.

74 *The Hussite Movement in Bohemia* (London, 1965), p. 34.

75 Jerome R. Mintz, *The Anarchists of Casas Viejas* (Chicago, IL, 1982), p. 4.

76 Hobsbawm, *Primitive Rebels*, pp. 1–2.

77 Ibid., p. 2.

78 Joll, *The Anarchists*, p. viii.

among modern social movements, is one of unrelieved failure; and unless some unforeseen historical changes occur, it is likely to go down in the books with the Anabaptists and the rest of the prophets who, though not unarmed, did not know what to do with their arms, and were defeated for ever.'[79] He uses the same analysis to support his later judgement that 'The revival of interest in anarchism today seems … unexpected, surprising, and – if I am to speak frankly – unjustified.'[80] In both cases, Hobsbawm feels free to extend (dubious) conclusions about Spanish peasant anarchism to anarchism in general. Marx and Engels used their idea of utopian socialism to legitimate their, and their theories', hegemony in socialist politics; Josef Macek's claims about the Hussites were an appropriation of a Czech cultural myth as support for communist power in mid-twentieth-century Czechoslovakia. Hobsbawm similarly makes a political move: by characterising anarchism as blind, groping, misclothed and 'primitive', and by presenting modern parliamentary and Marxist socialism as the culmination of earlier, obsolete movements, he polemically supports his own politics. We therefore have good reason to reject, or at least to be suspicious of, the whole metaphysical structure.

Hobsbawm perhaps misrepresents the complexity and historical fragmentation of revolutions and revolutionary movements[81] for political reasons; he certainly misrepresents Spanish anarchism and therefore anarchism in general. The labels 'primitive' and 'millennialist' 'stamp anarchist goals as unrealistic and unattainable',[82] but they are inaccurate. The primitive rebels thesis should be rejected. Now that this influential image of Spanish anarchism is out of the way, we can go on to the civil war itself.

## *A Sketch of the Spanish Civil War*

The background of Spain's civil war is the long struggle and vacillation between 'the forces of reform and reaction which had dominated Spanish history since 1808'[83] in the persons of republicans, liberals, communists, monarchists, the army, and pro- and anti-clericals. It is grounded in this instability and in the culture of political violence which went with it. The specifically anarchist background partakes of this culture and history, and further fuses several other influences, from both within and outside Spain: the Spanish tradition and myth of village democracy and collective self-management in the *patria chica*; in many regions, and especially in Catalonia, a tradition of localist resistance to the centralising tendencies of Castille; a tradition of peasant anti-clericalism; from outside Spain, the influences of Proudhon, Kropotkin,

79 Hobsbawm, *Primitive Rebels*, p. 92.

80 Hobsbawm, 'Reflections on Anarchism' in *Revolutionaries* (London, 1999), pp. 97–108, p. 100.

81 See, for instance, Noel Parker, *Revolutions and History: An essay in interpretation* (Cambridge, 1999).

82 Mintz, *The Anarchists of Casas Viejas*, p. 5.

83 Preston, *A Concise History of the Spanish Civil War*, p. 10.

and especially Bakunin, whose doctrines were spread by apostolic anarchists travelling rural Spain from the late 1860s onwards, leaving behind them groups of vegetarians, teetotallers and anarchist revolutionaries; a sixty-year history of trade union and conspiratorial organisation and polemical publication; and, after 1917, the glorious inspiration of the Russian revolution, even if the image of it was unrealistic.

In February 1936, the latest of many vacillations of power produced a left-wing 'Popular Front' government supported by anarchists, socialists and communists. In July, an attempted right-wing military coup under General Franco and others sparked popular resistance. That resistance was organised not by the republican government, but by anarchist and communist organisations (the CNT, FAI, UGT, PSUC, POUM[84] and others). Spain was divided into republican or loyalist or socialist or revolutionary, against nationalist or Christian or fascist sectors (in each case, the description depends on who is asked). The first was concentrated in the east, around Catalonia, and in the south, around Andalusia. The second, in the west and north. The civil war was initially fought at their boundaries, for instance at the front moving back and forth near Saragossa in Aragon, before the nationalists won in the east and then the south.[85]

The war can usefully be divided, following George Woodcock, into two general periods. First, from 1936 to early 1937, was a 'dynamic period'.[86] During this period the CNT and FAI were among the most active and influential organisations in Spain. They thought and organised in terms of general strikes, insurrection and street-fighting, workers' self-management, and the collectivisation of land and industry. In alliance with other socialist unions and parties, they resisted the Generals' uprising in many areas, and their successes gave rise to a brief flourishing of free communal organisation. Factories and services were collectivised. The eye-witnesses George Orwell and Franz Borkenau both testify, for instance, to the success of worker-managed industry in Barcelona,[87] while farming land was taken over by village communes. (I consider these organisational successes further, below.)

The second phase of the war was inaugurated by the street-fighting between Republican government troops and CNT and POUM militias in Barcelona, in May 1937. The CNT and other libertarian movements thereafter 'declined both in influence

84 CNT: Confederación Nacional del Trabajo; anarcho-syndicalist. FAI: Federación Anarquista Ibérica; militant anarchist. UGT: Unión General de Trabajadores; socialist. PSUC: Partit Socialista Unificat de Catalunya; Comintern-affiliated communist; POUM: Partido Obrero de Unificación Marxista; dissident or Trotskyite communist. See Ronald Fraser, *Blood of Spain: The experience of civil war, 1936–1939* (London, 1981), pp. 11–12.

85 Bookchin, *The Spanish Anarchists*; Preston, *A Concise History of the Spanish Civil War*; Thomas, *The Spanish Civil War*. Maps can be found in Fraser, *Blood of Spain*, pp. 16–23.

86 Woodcock, *Anarchism*, p. 365.

87 *Homage to Catalonia*, in Peter Davidson (ed.), *Orwell in Spain: The full text of* Homage to Catalonia *with associated articles, reviews and letters from* The Complete Works of George Orwell (London, 2001), pp. 28–215; *The Spanish Cockpit* (London, 1986).

and drive as centralization in military and administrative affairs successfully brought the loyalist regions of Spain under the control of the republican government'.[88] The situation changed from popular resistance to a military attempt to seize power, to a modern total war, and the anarchists were ill-fitted for it. The republican government, under the influence of the Comintern-affiliated PSUC and with the material support of Stalin's USSR, centralised and militarised the anti-nationalist effort. Militia and radical leaders were arrested and in some cases, for instance that of Andrés Nin, murdered. The 'People's Army', regularised with a hierarchy of officers and differential rates of pay, and armed by the USSR, took over the conduct of the war from the rag-tag egalitarian militias.[89] And lost. Polemically: '1936: the "People in Arms" won the revolution. 1939: the "People's Army" lost the war.'[90]

The nationalists, in the meantime, were getting military support from Italy and from Nazi Germany, particularly in the form of the 'Condor Legion': some 16,000 men over the course of the war, with tanks, anti-aircraft guns and fighter-bomber aircraft.[91]

The anarchists in the Spanish civil war achieved more than any other anarchist movement, certainly in the twentieth century, perhaps ever. None the less, they failed. The civil war killed perhaps 500,000 people, and Spain ended it with a reactionary or fascist dictatorship which lasted until Franco's death in 1975. Perhaps that outcome can be blamed on the republican government and its Soviet allies, but the anarchists did not prevent it, and their social innovations and successes were short-lived.[92] The Spanish anarchists, in the judgement of both Woodcock and Guérin, were failures at war; their success, even if a fleeting one, was in their creative egalitarian organisation.

### *Anarchic Organisation*

'The military insurrection of July 1936 not only destroyed the political edifice of the Second Republic but also, in most of the areas where it proved possible to maintain opposition to the rebellion, led to the re-ordering of an entire society.'[93] Anarchic and other egalitarian organisation in Spain was improvised, socially eclectic and various:

---

88 Woodcock, *Anarchism*, p. 365.

89 Robert J. Alexander, *The Anarchists in the Spanish Civil War* (2 vols, London, 1999), vol. 1, Chapter 9.

90 Richards, *Lessons of the Spanish Revolution*, back cover.

91 Thomas, *The Spanish Civil War*, Appendix 7.

92 For further consideration of how far the communists were to blame for the nationalist victory, see Alexander, *The Anarchists in the Spanish Civil War*; Burnett Bolloten, *The Grand Camouflage: The Spanish civil war and revolution, 1936–39* (London, 1968); Emma Goldman, *Vision on Fire: Emma Goldman on the Spanish revolution* ed. David Porter (New Paltz, NY, 1983), Section Five.

93 Graham Kelsey, 'Anarchism in Aragon During the Second Republic: The emergence of a mass movement' in Martin Blinkhorn (ed.), *Spain in Conflict 1931–1939: Democracy and its enemies* (London, 1986), pp. 60–82, p. 60.

each one of these experiments 'would deserve a book to itself'.[94] For convenience, I artificially divide this range into military, urban and rural organisation, but do not intend to suggest that any of these three categories was monolithic.

The anarchic and social-revolutionary currents of Spain's civil war have been downplayed, and in some cases completely ignored, by non-anarchist historians and commentators. The reasons for this absence are various, but include at least that several of the major players in the conflict had their own reasons for not recognising the social experiments in the republican zone as anarchic or revolutionary. The republican government hoped for help from western powers, and did not want to frighten them off with the ideas of anarchy or revolution. Stalin, and therefore the Comintern-affiliated communists in the government, wanted to draw those western powers into Spain and into conflict with Nazi Germany, and thereby shift Hitler's attention away from the east. They therefore shared the republicans' desire to present the civil war as a liberal regime threatened by a military coup, rather than as a revolution. Much of the local and international support for Franco's rebels was Catholic, and they therefore had reason to present themselves as crusaders against godless Soviet communism, in line with the contemporary Church's attacks on 'Russia and Moscow and Communism with all their blasphemous and anti-democratic tyranny'.[95] Robert Alexander further suggests that 'had the Rebels drawn an accurate picture of the taking over of factories and other enterprises by their workers, and of the land by the peasants, this would certainly have had the effect of sowing discontent behind their own lines.'[96] After their victory, the rebels continued to present themselves as crusaders against communism, and went to great lengths to manipulate and control the historical record, to maintain that presentation.[97] It may further be the case, as Noam Chomsky has argued, that liberal and Bolshevik-communist intellectuals share an elitist ideology which leads to a characteristic 'antagonism to mass movements and to social change that escapes the control of privileged elites',[98] and therefore to a tendency to marginalise and to downplay the importance of such movements.

*Military organisation* The egalitarian militias were failures in war. However, that does not mean that we know why they were, nor that we can attribute their failure to their organisational form, nor that we can therefore dismiss them. It was, after all, a regular, hierarchical army that eventually lost to Franco's nationalists. Anarchist involvement in the actual fighting of the civil war is perhaps the element of Spanish

94 Skirda, *Facing the Enemy*, p. 161.

95 The Catholic polemicist Edward Lodge Curran, quoted in Alexander, *The Anarchists in the Spanish Civil War*, vol. 1, p. xxiv.

96 Alexander, *The Anarchists in the Spanish Civil War*, vol. 1, p. xxiv.

97 Peter Preston, 'War of Words: The Spanish civil war and the historians' in Preston (ed.), *Revolution and War in Spain 1931–1939* (London, 1984), pp. 1–13.

98 'Objectivity and Liberal Scholarship' in James Peck (ed.), *The Chomsky Reader* (London, 1988), pp. 83–120, pp. 84–5.

anarchism most downplayed by historians. None the less, and thanks to the work of Robert Alexander and others, we can say something about it.

After the initial, improvised and partly successful response to the Generals' uprising, militias were rapidly organised, not by the government but by the General Council of Anti-Fascist Militia, 'in which the anarchists were the overwhelmingly dominant element',[99] and by various left-wing parties and trade unions including the CNT, UGT, PSUC and POUM. The first was the famous Durutti column, raised in Barcelona on 24 July 1936. Organised by different groups as they were, the militias varied considerably in their constitution, organisation, size, and amount and quality of equipment; but in general, the vast majority of the recruits were militarily inexperienced, and militia columns often took one of two forms – anarchist or communist.

According to Burnett Bolloten, who was no fan of anarchism, the anarchist militias were egalitarian, non-hierarchical and democratic. They had

> … no military titles, badges, or distinctions in the way of food, clothing, and quarters … The basic unit was the group, composed generally of ten men; each group elected a delegate, whose functions were somewhat akin to those of a non-commissioned officer of the lowest rank, but without the equivalent authority. Ten groups formed a century which also elected its own delegate, and any number of centuries made up a *columna*, or 'column,' at whose head stood a committee of war. This committee was likewise elective and was divided into various sections in accordance with the needs of the column. The gradation into group and century delegates and a committee of war did not imply the existence of any permanent staff with special privileges since all delegates could be removed as soon as they failed to reflect the wishes of the men who had elected them. 'The first impression one gets,' ran a CNT-FAI account, 'is the total absence of hierarchy … There is no one giving orders by authority.' Nevertheless, duties had to be assigned, and in such a way as to avoid friction. In the Anarchist Iron Column, for example, lots were drawn by the militiamen to decide on who should stand guard at night and who in the early morning.[100]

That is, the anarchist militias were social networks without institutionalised domination. The communist militias, in contrast, adopted a semi-military, hierarchical organisation based on party discipline and Bolshevik tactics. As a result, they 'attracted many of the regular [army] officers who remained loyal to the Republic, many of whom were appalled at what they conceived (by no means entirely correctly) as indiscipline bordering on chaos in many of the militia units'.[101]

Accounts of anarchist militias have tended to emphasise their 'indiscipline'. It is true that the apparent need for military discipline, if they were effectively to fight the nationalist army, raised a problem for, and tensions within, the anarchist movement:

---

99 Alexander, *The Anarchists in the Spanish Civil War*, vol. 1, p. 158.

100 Bolloten, *The Grand Camouflage*, pp. 216–17; Orwell largely confirms this description.

101 Alexander, *The Anarchists in the Spanish Civil War*, vol. 1, p. 152.

> If this problem beset all the militia units, whatever their ideology, it was only in those formed by the Libertarian movement that its solution encountered a philosophical impediment, for the liberty of the individual is the very core of Anarchism and nothing is so antipodal to its nature as submission to authority. 'Discipline is obedience to authority; Anarchism recognizes no authority,' said *La Revista Blanca*, the leading anarchist journal, in an issue published before the civil war [22 June 1934].[102]

However, it is not true, as has sometimes been claimed, that this problem was insoluble in anarchist terms. In the first place, many anarchists decided that the compromise acceptance of some military discipline and hierarchy was a necessary sacrifice, and rapidly put it into practice, although they often retained general assemblies of soldiers existing in parallel to the orthodox military hierarchy, at least for a time.[103]

In the second place, and more importantly here, anarchist militias solved the problem by re-understanding *discipline*: 'The anarchists had a different concept of discipline than that of the Communists or professional military officers.'[104] If by discipline is meant military courtesy and rigid hierarchy – saluting, uniforms, deep divisions between officers and ordinary soldiers, differential rates of pay, orders obeyed without question – then the anarchists certainly lacked it. However, 'if by discipline is meant a willingness to go into battle when told to do so, or when volunteers were asked for, the anarchist troops had discipline as good as or better than that of any other elements in the Republican army.'[105] If by discipline is meant the ability to coordinate military actions, the anarchist and other egalitarian militias were disciplined. According to George Orwell:

> A newly raised draft of militia was an undisciplined mob not because the officers called the privates 'Comrade' but because raw troops are *always* an undisciplined mob. In practice the democratic 'revolutionary' type of discipline is more reliable than might be expected. In a workers' army discipline is theoretically voluntary. It is based on class-loyalty, whereas the discipline of a bourgeois conscript army is based ultimately on fear … In the militias the bullying and abuse that go on in an ordinary army would never have been tolerated for a moment. The normal military punishments existed, but they were only invoked for very serious offences. When a man refused to obey an order you did not immediately get him punished; you first appealed to him in the name of comradeship. Cynical people with no experience of handling men will say instantly that this would never 'work', but as a matter of fact it does 'work' in the long run. The discipline of even the worst drafts of militia visibly improved as time went on … 'Revolutionary' discipline depends on political consciousness – on an understanding of *why* orders must be obeyed; it takes time to diffuse this, but it also takes time to drill a man into an automaton on the barrack-square.[106]

---

102 Bolloten, *The Grand Camouflage*, p. 216.

103 Alexander, *The Anarchists in the Spanish Civil War*, vol. 1, pp. 150–51, p. 169.

104 Ibid., pp. 167–8.

105 Ibid., p. 169, paraphrasing Ricardo Sanz, commander of the Durutti column after Durutti's death.

106 *Homage to Catalonia*, pp. 50–51.

'Discipline' might name either of two modes of organising military cooperation: the orthodox military or the anarchist mode. The second proved itself sufficiently effective in the practice of war that the charge of 'indiscipline' is either false, or an irrelevant comment on the anarchist militias' lack of military courtesy.

The second major problem for the anarchists, which they failed to solve, was their rivalry with the communists, who increasingly and with the backing of the USSR took over the republican military effort and government. Despite this failure, the anarchist militias were effective fighting forces, especially in the early part of the war:

> It is clear that on all of the fronts of the Spanish Civil War, anarchist troops made up a substantial proportion of those fighting in the Republican forces. In the Catalan-Aragónese, Levante-Teruel, and Asturias areas they constituted the majority of the soldiers fighting against the Rebels; elsewhere they were not numerically as significant but nonetheless constituted an important part of the Republican forces. As a general rule, they fought tenaciously and well and, on some fronts, held out when most other elements were ready to give up. In some areas, CNT leaders such as Ricardo Sanz, Cipriano Mera, and José González Malo played key roles in organizing and leading important elements of the Republican army.[107]

There is no evidence that anarchist militias were in general less effective than others in prosecuting the war; there is evidence that they were highly effective in some cases. None the less, we must judge that the anarchists were failures at war, for exactly the same reason that we must judge the communists and the other republican forces as failures: their side lost. This does not mean that we can ignore the success and effectiveness, even though in this case temporary, of egalitarian fighting forces.

*Urban organisation* In the very early part of the civil war, many owners of industrial and commercial enterprises in Barcelona and the rest of Catalonia abandoned them, either out of sympathy for Franco's side, or out of fear of the revolutionary workers. The administrative gap this left was rapidly filled by improvised egalitarian arrangements of the workers themselves, drawing on trade union organisation. Because they were mostly organised spontaneously and locally by the workers in particular factories and shops, which varied greatly in size and form,[108] these arrangements were various. However, we can make some generalisations.

Typically, a general assembly of the workers in a particular enterprise elected a Comité de Control or Comité de Empressa, consisting of five to ten people, and theoretically including representatives of both the UGT and CNT (but in practice, especially in the early stages of the war, often CNT-dominated). This Comité contained delegates for different departments of the firm, and elected a managing director (who in some cases was the returned or sympathetic former owner). The

107 Alexander, *The Anarchists in the Spanish Civil War*, vol. 1, p. 248.

108 Sam Dolgoff (ed), *The Anarchist Collectives: Workers' self-management in the Spanish revolution 1936–1939* (New York, 1974), p. 85.

director and Comité ran the enterprise day to day, but major decisions were brought before the general assembly.[109]

Collectives of this type successfully ran enterprises including municipal transport, telephone services, railways, gas, water, electricity, textile factories, the munitions industry, even hairdressing.[110] In Barcelona, workers' collectives distributed food supplies, set up communal dining halls, and organised themselves into a Food Workers' Industrial Union, which included bakers, butchers and dairy workers:[111] 'Every shop and café had an inscription saying that it had been collectivised; even the bootblacks had been collectivised and their boxes painted red and black.'[112] In Catalonia, health services were collectivised and made available free to all.[113] In general, urban workers' collectives successfully provided food, clothing, shelter, public services and war materials.

The collectives faced problems caused by the economic situation in Spain, by the civil war, by their own organisational failings, and by their supposed allies. Like much of the West, Spain was still feeling the effects of the great depression, and had high unemployment and inflation, which made the organisation of a war economy difficult. As the war went on, the nationalist blockade made raw materials increasingly hard to source; physical plant was damaged or destroyed by bombing; and workers went to the front, leaving many enterprises understaffed. Because of their spontaneous and improvised nature, and the unpreparedness of the CNT's organisation, it was often difficult for individual enterprises to federalise and coordinate their activities. Many contemporary writers complain of the problem of 'factory patriotism'. Victor Alba, for instance, noted that 'we have occasion to see how in some workers' sectors, to collectivize a factory or an industry consists only of appropriating it without consideration of the needs of the war and of the general organization of production, nor of whether the raw materials they possess are needed by other branches of production.'[114] Both the Republican government and the increasingly influential Comintern-affiliated communists were strongly opposed

109 Alexander, *The Anarchists in the Spanish Civil War*, vol. 1, pp. 467–9.

110 Borkenau, *The Spanish Cockpit*, Chapter Two; Augustin Souchy, 'Collectivizations in Catalonia: Extracts from *Nacht Über Spanien*', in Sam Dolgoff (ed.), *The Anarchist Collectives: Workers' self-management in the Spanish revolution 1936–1939* (New York, 1974), pp. 86–98.

111 Augustin Souchy, 'Workers' Self-Management in Industry: Extracts from *Collectivisations: L'Oeuvre Constructive de la révolution Espagnole*', in Sam Dolgoff (ed.), *The Anarchist Collectives: Workers' self-management in the Spanish revolution 1936–1939* (New York: Free Life Editions, 1974), pp. 78–84.

112 Orwell, *Homage to Catalonia*, p. 32.

113 Gaston Leval, 'The Socialization of Health Services: Extract from *Né Franco Né Stalin*', in Sam Dolgoff (ed.), *The Anarchist Collectives: Workers' self-management in the Spanish revolution 1936–1939* (New York, 1974), pp. 99–101.

114 Quoted in Alexander, *The Anarchists in the Spanish Civil War*, vol. 1, pp. 474.

to local, from-the-ground-up anarchic reorganisation of enterprises by their workers, and attempted 'to undermine and destroy the collectives'.[115]

Despite these problems, individual collectivised enterprises were often highly successful, and anarchic organisation was in general effective:

> There is little question about the fact that, as a result of the seizure of most of the manufacturing, public utilities, and many commercial enterprises by the workers, the economy of Republican Spain began functioning as normally as wartime conditions permitted a few days after the suppression of the Rebellion there. It is also clear that the workers' collectives quickly created a war industry where none had existed before, an industry which was able to provide a substantial part of the weapons, vehicles and other military equipment which was used throughout the War by the Loyalist armed forces. At the same time, essential consumer goods such as textiles continued to be available from the factories run by the collectives. In these senses, the collectives were an economic success.[116]

At a minimum, we can say that, despite difficulties and failures, and in the face of civil war, the economy of republican Spain did not collapse under collective organisation. We do not know whether or not these organisations were sustainable in the long term, but cannot ignore their temporary success.

*Rural organisation* Village and agricultural organisation was rapidly transformed in the space opened by initial victories against the military coup. The forms this transformation and its results took varied considerably, according to local opportunities, decisions and individual peculiarities, and especially across three major ranges of difference. Anarchist and other egalitarian rural organisations varied, first, in the precise details of their administrative and social organisation. Secondly, villages differed in their relative wealth. Hugh Thomas argues that the economic situation of a village 'depended over-greatly on the situation before':[117] that is, that redistribution between poor and wealthy villages was ineffective. Third, there was wide variation in the balance of, and relations between *colectivistas* (who collectivised their land and managed it by direct local democracy) and *individualistas* (mostly small-scale peasant proprietors who remained outside the collectives, either for ideological reasons, or to wait and see how successful they were before joining). This division was exploited and widened by the republican government, and especially its communist members, for political purposes, but was often handled peaceably and reasonably on a local level.[118]

---

115 Ibid., p. 484.

116 Ibid., p. 487.

117 'Anarchist Agrarian Collectives in the Spanish Civil War', in Raymond Carr (ed.), *The Republic and the Civil War in Spain* (London, 1971), pp. 237–56, p. 254.

118 Goldman, *Vision on Fire*, pp. 64–72; Gaston Leval, *Collectives in the Spanish Revolution*, trans. Vernon Richards (London, 1975), Part Two. For examples of particular and various village organisations, see further Dolgoff, *The Anarchist Collectives*, Chapters 8–10.

Despite this variation, we can make a number of generalisations about agricultural and village organisation in the republican sector of Spain during the civil war. It was to some extent actuated by a unifying spirit: 'We wanted a terrestrial paradise, but not in the biblical sense: to live here – organized here. One man wouldn't be able to live off the work of another. It was the wish that each man work and not desire to live in luxury. One wouldn't be able to suck another's produce, and we would all eat. The world is work – intellectual and manual.'[119] That is, a spirit of levelling and activism, and not one of millennial religious mania.

The rapid transformation of class-bound and inegalitarian social forms was a bottom-up reorganisation: 'Collectivization was not (as in the Soviet Union or Cuba) imposed from above by decree, but achieved from below by the initiative of the peasants themselves.'[120]

Some administrative tactics were generally adopted by colectivistas and accepted by individualistas. A *consejo de administración* (council of administration), consisting typically of 'a president, secretary, vice-secretary and treasurer, together with a number of other *vocales* or *delegados* responsible for specific questions such as statistics, cattle, food, the olive crop and so on',[121] reported to, and was recallable by a general assembly of the whole village (that is, not usually excluding women, local individualistas, or non-agricultural workers). This assembly heard, debated and voted on all major issues for the collective and its locality. Gaston Leval gives a detailed eyewitness account of one such assembly in Tamarite de Litera.[122]

The assemblies and councils often abolished the use of state-issued currency, replacing it with common stores of goods, ration-books, work-vouchers and entitlements based particularly on how many non-working dependents (the young, old or ill) someone had to support.[123] Typically, villages organised complex systems of payments to individuals and families, based on formulas of need and work-contribution.[124]

The village collectives were probably economic successes. Although the figures for production by collectivised villages, and therefore the possibility of comparison with the system they replaced, are limited, we can say at minimum that the collectives were not economic failures. They did succeed in continuing to produce enough food, not only for themselves but for the militias at the front. According to Thomas, 'the most complete general account of a collective's finances is that of the 300-family collective of Almagro.'[125] Thomas has some doubts about the accuracy of these figures, but it appears that despite war and rapid social reorganisation, the Almagro

---

119 Anonymous anarchist quoted in Mintz, *The Anarchists of Casas Viejas*, p. 5.

120 Editor's note in Dolgoff, *The Anarchist Collectives*, p. 111.

121 Thomas, 'Anarchist Agrarian Collectives in the Spanish Civil War', p. 243.

122 *Collectives in the Spanish Revolution*, pp. 207–13.

123 Sam Dolgoff, 'Money and Exchange', in Dolgoff (ed.), *The Anarchist Collectives: Workers' self-management in the Spanish revolution 1936–1939* (New York, 1974), pp. 70–76.

124 Thomas, 'Anarchist Agrarian Collectives in the Spanish Civil War', pp. 250–51.

125 Ibid., p. 247.

collective had '75 per cent more barley … 500 per cent more wine, 200 per cent more olive oil, 80 per cent more rye, 400 per cent more peas, 300 per cent more chick-peas, [and] about 90 per cent more beans of varying sorts'[126] in store in 1937 than the village had been able to produce before collectivisation: 'The total value of the products possessed by the collective was about 50 per cent higher than in 1936.'[127] Almagro may have been unusual; but we can at least say that the production of this village, and of many others, did not collapse under collective organisation.

The social success of the collective villages is clear. In a short time, they removed or effaced considerable social and economic inequality; instituted social support of widows, orphans and invalids; organised schools, and considerably extended medical care.

Finally, collectives to some extent federalised, coordinating their production, sharing tactics and expertise, and exchanging or sometimes giving food and other goods.[128] As already noted, the redistribution towards economic equality implied by this was not entirely effective: perhaps it did not have time to be.

In general, the rural revolution was startlingly successful: 'Although these collectives varied much in their organisational structure, and their degree of "utopianism", most of them provided their members with levels of living and a feeling of self-respect which they had never before enjoyed. Many of them considerably increased the output of the land under their control.'[129] Although they were short-lived, had problems, and were having rapidly to improvise solutions in difficult circumstances, the collectives were successful in creating a situation of far greater equality and absence of domination, and making a living in it.

To sum up: in the republican sector of Spain, the opportunities and demands created by the coup, partially successful resistance and then civil war, gave rise to rapidly improvised local organisation. New networks took over the organisation of military action, urban industry, commerce and public services, and rural and agricultural life. The tactics for creating and assigning organisational, productive and other capacities they used were various, but typically included the direct democratic creation of administrative committees, responsible to and recallable by general assemblies. They also included improvisations in the face of present problems. Ronald Fraser, for instance, records how Luis Santacana, an administrator in one of Catalonia's largest textile plants, dealt with the problem of pilfering:

> [Santacana:] 'Inevitably, collectivization could not resolve all problems; there were people who lacked self-discipline, a consciousness of what was demanded of them. There was a mechanic who stole a spanner. I told him he was no longer stealing from the capitalists,

126 Ibid., p. 248.

127 Ibid.

128 Gaston Leval, 'The Peasant Federation of Levant: Extract from *Né Franco Né Stalin*', in Sam Dolgoff (ed.), *The Anarchist Collectives: Workers' self-management in the Spanish revolution 1936–1939* (New York, 1974), pp. 122–6; Thomas, 'Anarchist Agrarian Collectives in the Spanish Civil War', p. 244.

129 Alexander, *The Anarchists in the Spanish Civil War*, vol. 2, p. 1087.

> he was robbing himself and his fellow-workers. Under the old regime, he would have been sacked on the spot. "Please, please, don't steal again".' Within a fortnight the man was back and Santacana had to take disciplinary action. The collective, he said, would not sack him because he had children and needed his weekly wage. Instead, they were going to move him to a new section, the cleaning department. But that would require public notification – '"You will write your full name on the blackboard, underneath it that you have stolen two spanners and that is the reason for your move to a section where you will have no chance of further theft." "No, no," he cried, "not the blackboard." "Yes," I said, "It can't hurt you to write the truth up there." There were no more cases of indiscipline; the threat of the blackboard was sufficient.'[130]

The final and most important point about these various egalitarian organisations is that they were, in general, successful. In the middle of a crisis, and despite having to fight a war without a pre-existing military infrastructure, anarchist and other federated, minimally institutionalised, non-dominating networks managed to organise food production and distribution, munitions manufacture, fighting forces, public services, and much else: 'All these creative activities, these ventures, these changes to human relationships amounted to a "miraculous blossoming".'[131]

## Conclusion

Spanish anarchists and the Nuer differ in many ways, with the most obvious being their different technologies and ways of making a living. However, they are also importantly similar, in three major ways. First, neither exist in a social vacuum. They are examples of the political condition of 'siba', that is 'anarchy opposed to something'.[132] Both forms of life consist of bundles of minimally institutionalised networks existing in a complex relationship with, challenged by, and aware of the dangers of, much more institutionalised, hierarchical, dominating networks. So, the common belief that such anarchic social forms can only exist in unusual situations of isolation is empirically false. Secondly, neither social form can be characterised as the mere *absence* of tactics and organisations for the unequal distribution of power. Rather, both the Nuer and the Spanish anarchists used a complex and various set of tactics for creating capacities, including power over others, and for assigning it equally (or, at least, much more equally than many alternatives available to them). Third, and most generally: both the Nuer and the Spanish anarchists succeeded in creating capacities to satisfy their interests, which they share with most other humans, in food, shelter, company, continued life, and the respect of their peers. The Nuer succeeded in limiting and often resolving conflict; the Spanish anarchists were capable of organising themselves against hierarchical military aggression, with temporary success.

130 Fraser, *Blood of Spain*, pp. 218–19.

131 Skirda, *Facing the Enemy*, p. 161.

132 Gellner, *Saints of the Atlas*, pp. 1–2.

In my discussion of the Nuer, I showed that humans are capable of organising themselves to limit and resolve conflict in situations of non-domination. However, it might be argued that the Nuer's lack of (western, industrial) technology explains their success, and that our arrangements are sufficiently different that domination and hierarchy are necessary. My discussion of anarchic organisation in Spain, however, has shown that anarchic tactics and organisation have also been effective in modern industrial circumstances. Anarchic organisations can successfully organise factories and urban public services, as well as tribal conflict-resolution. We have empirical examples of humans' ability to live together, and to organise ourselves so as to satisfy our many interests, without domination.

The Nuer have been greatly changed by their encounter with states; the Spanish anarchist experiment failed. That does not mean that either was destined to be defeated, nor that their successes can be disregarded. We have the capacities and tactics available to organise ourselves in these ways. I am not making the obviously false claim that anarchic social forms are always stable, or will always win in a contest against alternative social forms. I doubt that this is true of *any* social form, anarchic or not. Rather, I am displaying this human social possibility as one amongst many others.

In this chapter, I have displayed examples of successful anarchic organisation: fragments of hope to put up against the undeniable possibilities of enslavement and violence which I displayed in Chapter 3. In my final chapter, I shall put these fragments together to show the possibility of an anarchist utopia.

## Chapter 5

# Conclusion

I began this book by promising to show that an anarchist utopia is within the bounds of human social possibility. Our route to that conclusion has so far been as follows: in Chapter One, I refuted the particularly common misrepresentation of anarchism as primitivist. I explained it as a misunderstanding of a rhetorical trope which, I claimed, is common in anarchist writing and which, I showed, is present in the otherwise very different work of William Godwin and Peter Kropotkin. This utopian trope compares our own with other social arrangements, in order to criticise the former and assert the possibility of the latter. Godwin urges comparison with an imaginary, perfected far future; Kropotkin, with real examples of past and present human life. I chose to pursue and extend Kropotkin's constructive version of the trope, which, I argued, is better suited to my own purpose of arguing for possibility than to the critical purpose which Godwin's version serves. In Chapter 2, I described and answered a challenge to this utopian ambition: the claim that the constructive cherry-picking it requires is impossible. My answer was to map social life as consisting of overlapping and interpenetrating networks of humans, who cooperatively create and assign capacities to attain and distribute goods, manage conflicts, dominate others and resist domination. In Chapter 3, I described some familiar, terrible landmarks in the landscape of human sociability: states and slavery. In Chapter 4, I described some less familiar reasons for hope: the conflict-resolution practices of the Nuer (and other acephalous groups) and the capacities for production and resistance demonstrated by anarchist groups in the Spanish civil war.

I now need to make good on my initial promise, by drawing the fragments I have collected into an account of a possible anarchist utopia. First, however, I want to say something more about my project and about the landscape of possibilities which utopia inhabits.

### The Negotiated Settlement

In my Introduction, I said that I did not intend to present my theory as the one true heir of, but wanted to come a negotiated settlement with, the anarchist tradition. I have done so by drawing on some of its threads: on a common rhetorical habit of critical and exemplary comparison; on anarchist concerns and ideas about power; and on anarchist accounts of a utopian social form. My theory is an extension of the tradition, and therefore anarchist, just because I have made this use of some of its elements. It is further specifically Kropotkinite in making use of, and extending, his version of the anarchist trope and his vision of utopia.

I have not picked out several other threads, not because they are not 'real' anarchism, but because they were not useful for my purposes. For instance, I have not made much use of Kropotkin's post-Darwinian evolutionary vocabulary (which he shares with many other nineteenth and early twentieth-century socialists[1]). This is not because I think evolution-talk mistaken, but because I have no brief to show that Kropotkin is correct in that part of his theory. For another instance, I have not taken on Godwin's perfectionism; I do think it false, but have not argued for that claim here.

My theory is anarchist, and to some extent specifically Kropotkinite, in extending the tradition in these ways. It is not, and does not need to be, 'true' anarchism: 'Interpretations … are neither good nor bad for being notionally "authentic"; they are convincing developments of the tradition, or they are not.'[2] Anarchism is various, and mine is just one anarchism among many. I believe that many anarchists will find my conclusions sympathetic, but do not suppose that all will, nor that any who did not would thereby contradict their self-identification as anarchists. I have not, then, solved the problem of the unity of the anarchist tradition; nor have I specified (necessary or sufficient) conditions for what counts as an extension of, rather than a break from, this or any other tradition. I doubt that these problems have general solutions, and do not need to solve them to carry out my project. If Bakunin can correctly be called an anarchist because he called himself one, was influenced by – as well as sometimes disagreeing with – Proudhon, and wrote texts which have family resemblances to texts by other anarchists, then I can too, by calling myself one, being influenced by – as well as sometimes disagreeing with – Kropotkin, and by writing a text which has such family resemblances. That is what I have done here.

This picture is made more complex by my having written a work of anarchist *political philosophy*. Political philosophy is a tradition (or perhaps a cluster of interlinked and nested traditions), and, as such, is subject to the same kinds of ambiguity about its unity as are other traditions. We are unlikely to be able to say what the single, unchanging task of political philosophy is: different political philosophers have had different projects and interests, and future ones might have different ones again. We can, however, distinguish two common projects in which political philosophers have been interested. There are projects which ask, What is to be done? What tactics should we use to transform our world, or to preserve it, in line with justice? This is a reasonable question, and answering it is a reasonable project, but it is not my project. On the other hand, there are utopian projects, including mine, which attempt to expand political imagination by displaying the availability to

---

1 See David Stack, *The First Darwinian Left: Socialism and Darwinism 1859–1914* (Cheltenham, 2003). See also my review in *Human Nature Review* vol. 3 (2003): 379–80 <http://human-nature.com/nibbs/03/stack.html>.

2 S.R.L. Clark, 'The Use of "Man's Function" in Aristotle', *Ethics* vol. 82 (1972): 269–83, p. 269.

us of alternative ways of life. I have been arguing that the joint social experience of humanity proves the availability to us of an anarchic utopian social form, amongst many other possibilities. I have not given an account of what means we might use, now or at any time, to realise that utopia. That was not the task I set myself, and there is nothing wrong with essays as opposed to systems.

It is worth noting some other arguments and claims which I have not made. I have not proved the *moral* claims that domination, violence, inequality and slavery are bad things, and that equality, freedom, self-determination and peace are good things. My interest has been in the factual rather than the normative side of anarchism, and I have therefore concentrated on showing that the utopian life anarchists demand is possible, not that it is morally ideal. Secondly, I have not said anything about how likely it is that the anarchist utopia will be realised, now, soon, or at any time. I do not know how to answer this question about probability for this or any other possible social form, and I doubt that anyone else does, either. Thirdly, and most importantly, I have not argued either that my utopia is inevitable, or that once achieved it would last forever. I doubt that these claims are true of any social form, utopian, adequate or disastrous. I claim only that the anarchist utopia is one among the vast range of human social possibilities, which also includes slavery and states. To paraphrase Gustav Landauer: anarchy need not come, but anarchy can come and should come, when we wish it.[3]

## Our Situation

Despite our differences, humans share some general capacities, which can be expressed in a variety of ways, and some typical interests, which are strong but can be trumped by other, less widely-shared ones. The ways in which humans have expressed their capacities, pursued their interests and lived together have varied widely. In general, however: our social activity can be mapped as consisting of multiple networks of humans interacting in various ways, creating and assigning capacities using a variety of tactics. These networks overlap and interpenetrate one another, and change in response to a range of projects and stimuli. We have not historically organised ourselves into unified and discrete social totalities, but have lived in confederal social situations. Our history is not best understood by cultural evolutionary stories, and there is no single, simple groundstate of human social life. All social networks display opposing tendencies to institutionalisation on one hand, and to resistance and interstitial emergence on the other. All are functionally promiscuous. Human sociability is typically changing and changeable, and humans are typically socially creative and plastic.

Human social life and history, then, is a flat and continuous landscape, without impenetrable boundaries. It does not have a single gradient of value or complexity; it is not divided into islands; its inhabitants do not tend either to 'evolve' in a single

3 See Russell Berman and Tim Luke, Editors' Introduction to Gustav Landauer, *For Socialism* (St Louis, MO, 1978), pp. 1–18, p. 3.

direction, or to 'collapse' back into a single groundstate. No one social form is 'more natural' than any other, and there are no 'primitive' societies.

Within this general picture, I have emphasised both long-term and transient human predicaments. States, I have argued, are far more recent and local, far less common or universal, than is often supposed. However, almost all humans *currently* live in a social situation importantly shaped by states. We are complicit in institutions which create capacity to dominate using several techniques, and which assign that capacity to hierarchical elites. We all help to create and to assign this capacity, but many of us are at the sharp end of its inequalities: we are not free. This situation is historically unusual: pristine states appear only rarely; modern states are a recent innovation; for most of the time there have been humans, there have not been states.

States are possible for us because of our evolved capacities, including our capacities for organisation, institutionalisation and violence. I have emphasised the potential for slavery, which these capacities also create, as a long-term predicament, and suggested that anarchists ought to be worried about it – perhaps more worried about it than about states.

There are many problems which humans must face in living together, whatever social form we create for ourselves. Our interests can clash, either because they differ, or because of the scarcity of goods in which we share an interest. We have propensities for violence, self-aggrandisement, dividing the world into 'we' and 'they', enslavement, weakness of will, and sheer stupidity. I have not argued that anarchy will magically solve these problems: they are general human predicaments. I claim that one of the ways in which we can approach living together, without being destroyed by these predicaments, is an anarchic utopia. No social form has ever fully solved our problems. States have not done so, and have especially failed to prevent violence: they have promoted it, perhaps more than has any other human social form. Nonetheless, humans can live together, in a variety of ways. Utopia is one of those ways.

## Utopia

In my Introduction, I characterised utopian texts as making use of a historically developed and developing vocabulary of tropes, story-fragments, and rhetorical and argumentative tactics, and argued that one could write such a text just by making use of, modifying or even alluding to or satirising that vocabulary. I then identified two pairs of important, opposing features of utopian political interventions: criticism and the expansion of imagination; storytelling and construction. I have chosen to pursue the second of each pair, and more particularly to follow Kropotkin: I intend to expand political imagination by constructing a utopia out of the real examples of human sociability I described in Chapter 4.

I ended the Introduction by quoting Kropotkin's sketch utopia; I shall do so again, to remind us of our goal. Anarchism is:

> … a principle or theory of life and conduct under which society is conceived without government – harmony in such a society being obtained, not by submission to law, or by obedience to any authority, but by free agreements concluded between the various groups, territorial and professional, freely constituted for the sake of production and consumption, as also for the satisfaction of the infinite variety of needs and aspirations of a civilized being. In a society developed along these lines, the voluntary associations which already now begin to cover all the fields of human activity would take a still greater extension so as to substitute themselves for the state in all its functions. They would represent an interwoven network, composed of an infinite variety of groups and federations of all sizes and degrees, local, regional, national and international – temporary or more or less permanent – for all possible purposes: production, consumption and exchange, communications, sanitary arrangements, education, mutual protection, defence of the territory, and so on; and, on the other side, for the satisfaction of an ever-increasing number of scientific, artistic, literary and sociable needs.[4]

The central features of this utopia have been shown, by real example, to be possible, as follows.

*Non-domination* Humans can cooperatively create capacities without creating capacities to dominate, and without unequally distributing power. Humans can create and maintain a wide variety of power distributions, using a huge range of tactics (including, but not limited to, the tactics of violence, authority and property). Some of these distributions, including those exemplified by states and slavery, are extremely unequal. Others, including those exemplified by the Nuer and the Spanish civil war anarchists, are much more equal, and tend towards actual equality. These distributions are not merely consequences of the (lucky) absence of anti-egalitarian tactics, but of the conscious use of tactics for the creation and preservation of a situation of non-domination. So, non-domination is one among a wide range of human social possibilities.

*Production and distribution* Production and distribution to satisfy human interests can be carried out by federated, minimally institutionalised, non-dominating networks of humans, rather than, for instance, by slaves working for the benefit of masters who hold extreme capacities of domination over them, or by hierarchies of owners, managers and workers who are differentially rewarded according to the dictates of property and authority discourses. In the social experiments made by anarchists and others during the Spanish civil war, we have an empirical example of the possibility of this arrangement, and its success in satisfying a wide variety of interests: food production and distribution; public services including transport, fire-brigades, education and health services; even weapons-manufacture and military organisation for self-defence. Humans in anarchic networks are capable of creating the capacities to satisfy their interests.

4 Kropotkin, 'Anarchism', pp. 233–4.

*Federal coordination* Relations between networks can be managed by federalisation and negotiation rather than by, for instance, attempts to organise all of the inhabitants of some territory into a discrete hierarchical organisation controlled from an administrative centre. As I have admitted, federal coordination between collectives in the Spanish civil war was not fully effective. But even in the short time available, and in difficult circumstances, it was partly so. Humans have been and therefore are, to some extent, capable of managing their relations with other groups by organised negotiation, by assigning the tasks of communication and coordination to representatives, and by oversight of those representatives by local general assemblies. Hierarchy is one way, but not the only way, to coordinate networks of humans. We do not know how successful Spanish anarchic federalisation would have been in the long term. In general, we do not know how far federal coordination could spread among anarchic networks, and to what extent network organisation would remain local. We do know that federalisation is a possible tactic.

*Conflict resolution* Conflict resolution can be managed by mediation, rather than by assigning coercive capacity to some institution or elite. The Nuer provide us with an empirical demonstration that, even where people have culturally-sanctioned tendencies towards violence, conflict resolution can be managed in and by anarchic networks. We can mutually organise conflict-resolution by assigning the task of mediation to ritual and coalition-forming specialists, and thereby satisfy the typical human interest in the absence or limitation of violence. One possible response to this argument is to suggest that conflict resolution by mediation may be possible in times of (relative) peace, but would collapse in war. This may be so. But as I showed in Chapter Four, war is characteristically a practice of states. Few humans are perfectly peaceful, but humans living in and with states have historically been far less peaceful than humans living without them.

*Networking* In my utopia, humans do an enormous amount of networking: they organise and maintain multiple, interacting social networks for the satisfaction of a huge variety of interests. We may worry that few would bother. Why not retreat into solitary life and let someone else do all the talking and organising? It is undeniable that this might happen in some utopian anarchic social form, and leave it either culturally and materially impoverished, or easy prey for the empire next door. However all of my descriptions of human social landmarks in Chapters 3 and 4 exemplify humans' intensely social nature. Most humans spend an enormous amount of time and effort on creating, maintaining, transforming and destroying social networks, using a vast variety of tactics for the creation and assignment of capacities, and for thereby satisfying their many interests. Some of our tactics are violent; some of the networks and institutions we form are disastrous; but social interaction is what we typically do. This fragment of my utopia is exemplified by all human history and social activity.

*Siba* It might be supposed that, even if the anarchic social form I have described is possible, its realisation would require a lucky isolation from the challenge of non-anarchic forms, and especially from states and slavery. But as I have already pointed out, we have empirical examples of 'siba',[5] of anarchic social forms existing in complex and difficult relationships with non-anarchic forms. As the egalitarian militias in Spain show, anarchic networks are capable of organising military self-defence. Further, and as I have emphasised, resistance is a permanent feature even of the most extreme systems of domination. So, it is not the case either that the realisation of my anarchist utopia would require colonising a new planet, or that such a utopia would be easy prey for the first conqueror to come along.

These are possible features of human sociability, because they are *real* features of it. Just as Kropotkin argues for the possibility of anarcho-socialism, I have argued for the possibility of an anarchic utopia, by construction out of historical and anthropological example.

One possible objection to this conclusion is that, despite the fact that my fragments are individually possible, there might be relationships, between each one of them and the wider social environment which sustains it, which make them incompatible with each other. So, these fragments could not co-exist in a single way of life. However, this response has no teeth, for two reasons.

First, it is less a criticism than a gesture in the direction of a possible criticism. It might be the case that, for instance, the form of conflict-resolution by mediation I discovered in the Nuer social form and the form of industrial production without hierarchy I discovered in the practice of Spanish civil war anarchists are incompatible, because of some features of the wider social systems in which they were embedded and on which they depended. It might be the case: but without evidence to show that it actually *is* the case, this is not a real objection. It is akin to the use of the term 'utopian', without further argument, to label something as impossible.

Secondly, and more importantly, this (gesture in the direction of) criticism misunderstands my project and its results. I have not advocated a utopian colonisation project in which we would emigrate to some isolated island and attempt to play out all of the fragments of utopia I have discovered (worse problems than the possible incompatibility of mediation and non-hierarchical factories would be facing us if we tried that, not least the difficulty of suddenly becoming quite differently socialised people). Rather, I have attempted an expansion of political imagination, by rediscovering the possibility of some features of a utopia (that is, an ideal way of life) in the joint social experience of humanity. My purpose has been to show that the anarchist utopia is available to us, not to solve all of the problems we might face in making it our own way of life.

5 Gellner, *Saints of the Atlas*, p. 1. See also Chapter 4.

## Attitudes to Utopia

The anarchic utopia is a possible way of life for us: it can be found somewhere on the same map of human sociability on which are found states, slavery, and the other, various human social possibilities. But how are we to regard it: What shall we do with this possibility? My stated purpose in demonstrating the possibility of utopia was to expand political imagination, and I denied any ambition to settle revolutionary tactics, but there is a more general question, still to be answered: How should we regard our own location relative to the real possibility of anarchy?

Before we recognise the possibility of utopia, we may regard our current predicament as inescapable, and respond with acceptance or despair. However, we now have reasons for rejection and hope. In this section, I shall consider some ways in which anarchists have elaborated on that hope. Given that utopia is possible, are we to regard it as a motivation for longing, for personal emulation, for immediate action, or what? I do not have a pat answer to this question, but several responses to it are available in the anarchist tradition.

One of the many possible taxonomies of anarchism divides it into separatist and immanentist forms. Representatives of both regard utopia as possible and desirable, but their attitudes to it differ. For separatists, utopia is on the other side of a radical break with current arrangements, whether that break is spatial (brought about by setting up new communities and colonies) or temporal (brought about by destroying those current arrangements and starting again from scratch). For the advocates both of colonisation and of ground-clearing destruction, utopia is a new design, freed from the irrationalities of tradition, historical entitlements to authority and property, and the whole paraphernalia of the old life. For immanentists, in contrast, utopia is present in seed form in, and can or will grow out from, our current arrangements. For them, utopia is concealed in the here and now.

The division between immanentist and separatist is no sharper than most other attempts at taxonomy: there is a continuum of views between the extremes. Some anarchists believe, like Marxists, that utopia is on the other side of a revolution which is immanent in our current social form. Kropotkin, for instance, regards the revolution as growing out of current arrangements, and is in that sense an immanentist, but he also distinguishes between 'the dramatic side of revolution'[6] (a necessary destructive episode) and the real revolution, which he envisions on separatist lines as the conscious organisation of utopia, by the people, in the absence of states and capitalism:

> A revolution in Europe means ... the unavoidable stoppage of at least half the factories and workshops. It means millions of workers and their families thrown on the streets ... Society itself will be forced to take production in hand, in its entirety, and to reorganise it to meet the needs of the whole people. But this cannot be accomplished in a day, or even in a month; it must take a certain time to reorganise the system of production, and during this time millions of men will be deprived of the means of subsistence ... There is only

6 Kropotkin, *The Conquest of Bread*, p. 26.

> one really *practical* solution of the problem – boldly to face the great task which awaits us, and instead of trying to patch up a situation which we ourselves have made untenable, to proceed to reorganize production on a new basis.[7]

Kropotkin is thus an immanentist about the revolution which will usher utopia in, but a separatist in how he conceives its creation.

Colonising separatists have included the founders, including Josiah Warren, of American utopian communities, including New Harmony. These utopian experiments, influenced by Robert Owen and by Charles Fourier, were an important strand of nineteenth-century American radicalism. They have been a source of inspiration for anarchists, communitarians, romantics, religious nonconformists, and others, ever since.[8] However, their separatist ideal of self-sufficient communities, organised on rational and moral grounds, operates in parallel with an immanentist ideal most clearly expressed in the experiments in non-profit community banking carried out by Warren, Benjamin Tucker and others.

Bakunin's very different separatism regards utopia as unachievable in a colony separated from the rest of humanity. Freedom cannot be achieved piecemeal: 'Man is really free to the extent that his freedom, fully acknowledged and mirrored by the free consent of his fellowmen, finds confirmation and expansion in their liberty. Man is truly free only among equally free men; the slavery of even one human being violates humanity and negates the freedom of all.'[9]

The freedom and proper authority over herself of the individual are vital to Bakunin, but they can be achieved only by everyone, not individually. The separation he believes necessary is therefore the complete destruction of current arrangements: the abolition of organised religions, monarchy and rank,

> *Abolition*, dissolution, and moral, political, and economic dismantling of the *all-pervasive, regimented, centralized State,* the alter ego of the Church ... *Abolition of all state universities ... Abolition of the state judiciary ... Abolition of all criminal, civil, and legal codes now administered in Europe ... Abolition of banks and all other institutions of state credit. Abolition of all centralized administration, of the bureaucracy, of all permanent armies and state police.*[10]

Bakunin is the most radical, or at least the most vocal, of separatists. Nothing will do for him but a complete break with the current social order: 'We must overthrow from top to bottom this effete social world which has become impotent and sterile ... We must first purify our atmosphere and transform completely the milieu in which we live ... The social question takes the form primarily of the overthrow of society.'[11]

---

7 Ibid., pp. 56–7.

8 See Pitzer, *America's Communal Utopias*. M. Night Shyamalan's film *The Village* (2004) draws on this heritage.

9 Michael Bakunin, 'Revolutionary Catechism', in Sam Dolgoff (ed. and trans.), *Bakunin on Anarchism* (Montréal, 1980), pp. 76–97, p. 76.

10 Ibid., p. 78.

11 Quoted in E.H. Carr, *Michael Bakunin* (London, 1975), p. 173.

Bakunin's thought is often unoriginal: according to Peter Marshall, it 'consists largely of Proudhonian politics and Marxian economics'.[12] His legacy to anarchists, apart from his heroic example as a revolutionary activist, has been this universal separatism. He probably inspired Buenaventura Durutti:

> We have always lived in slums and holes in the wall. We will know how to accommodate ourselves for a time. For, you must not forget, we can also build. It is we the workers who built these palaces and cities here in Spain and in America and everywhere. We, the workers, can build others to take their place. And better ones! We are not in the least afraid of ruins. We are going to inherit the earth; there is not the slightest doubt about that. The bourgeoisie might blast and ruin its own world before it leaves the stage of history. We carry a new world here, in our hearts.[13]

Other anarchists have also been optimistic about ruins, and about the utopia which will or could be built on them.

In contrast, William Godwin believed that the education and exercise of free individual judgement would lead to the gradual improvement of society from within. He rejects violent revolution and secession as means for reaching utopia, and argues instead for the steady progress of the whole through cautious deliberation:

> The true instruments for changing the opinions of men are argument and persuasion. The best security for an advantageous issue is free and unrestricted discussion. In that field truth must always prove the successful champion. If then we would improve the social institutions of mankind, we must write, we must argue, we must converse ... There are two principles therefore which the man who desires the regeneration of his species ought ever to bear in mind, to regard the improvement of every hour as essential in the discovery and dissemination of truth, and willingly to suffer the lapse of years before he urges the reducing his theory [sic] into actual execution.[14]

Rational discussion and choice will lead, gradually, to utopia.

Not all immanentists have had Godwin's faith in the progressive perfection of humanity. Many have instead relied on the readoption of power by already-existing non-dominating groups, or on the voluntary creation of alternative anarchic organisations in the interstices of our current arrangements, to replace those arrangements from within. Proudhon came to reject revolutionary separatist action in favour of gradual transformation, led by (his) economic theory, towards utopia. Hakim Bey recommends face-to-face interaction – dinner parties, quilting bees, art projects, tongs – to overcome the mediation and loneliness which he sees as the main expressions of the current distortion of human life.[15] Colin Ward argues that 'An anarchist society, a society which organises itself without authority, is always in

---

12 Marshall, *Demanding the Impossible,* p. 270.

13 Interview with Pierre van Paasen, *Toronto Star* (September 1936) <http://www.spunk.org/library/places/spain/sp000069.txt>, accessed 2 January 2006.

14 Godwin, *Enquiry Concerning Political Justice*, pp. 115–16.

15 *Immediatism: Essays by Hakim Bey* (Edinburgh, 1994).

existence, like a seed beneath the snow, buried under the weight of the state and its bureaucracy, capitalism and its waste, privilege and its injustices, nationalism and its suicidal loyalties, religious differences and their superstitious separatism.'[16]

Anarcho-syndicalists are immanentists in the sense that they regard one and the same thing, the industrial workforce organised into voluntary and federalised syndicates, as both the instrument of revolution and the form of utopia, already present within current arrangements. Despite their differences, Proudhon, Bey, Ward and the syndicalists all regard utopia as immanent in and growing out of what we have now, rather than as separated from it by destruction or colonisation, by radical fractures in time or distance.

This is not (probably, could not be) an exhaustive list of the many possible attitudes to utopia, but does identify some prominent types. Despite this complexity, the fundamental distinction is the one I started with, between immanentist and separatist: crudely, between those who think that utopia is potentially *here*, and those who think it *elsewhere*. Both attitudes could be appropriate in particular circumstances, individuals and moods. I admit to sympathy with both – although I also admit that I *am* afraid of ruins, and therefore of Popper's canvas-clearing utopian,[17] the destroy-and-build separatist. Separatism, however, is more appealing in circumstances like those which fostered More's vision of a distant island: circumstances in which there really is somewhere else to go, in which we can imagine setting up a new social design on empty land. Early utopians' imagination was fired by renaissance exploration; for us, here and now, the idea of an escape to empty land has less power, because there is no such land. So, immanentism is perhaps appropriate for us. If so, the fragments of utopia I have identified are not to be thought of as blueprints for a colony, or for a post-apocalyptic community in the ruins, but as buried beneath the snow, here.

## Conclusion

An anarchic utopia is possible. We can organise ourselves and live together in this way, amongst many other ways, and our recognition that this is the case is a widening of political imagination, with many possible motivational consequences. 'There is no final struggle'[18] for utopia, because it is as subject to impermanence as is any other human social form, but it is one of our real options. The human potential for violence and enslavement is undeniable: but we also have reasons for hope.

16 *Anarchy in Action*, p. 18.

17 See my Introduction.

18 Ward, *Anarchy in Action*, p. 29.

# Bibliography

**Books, Articles and Websites**


Alexander, Robert J., *The Anarchists in the Spanish Civil War* (2 vols, London: Janus Publishing Company, 1999).

Anderson, Benedict, *Imagined Communities: Reflections on the origin and spread of nationalism* (London: Verso, 1983).

Anderson, James, 'The Modernity of Modern States' in Anderson (ed.), *The Rise of the Modern State* (Brighton: Harvester, 1986), pp. 1–20.

Anderson, James (ed.), *The Rise of the Modern State* (Brighton: Harvester, 1986).

Anisimov, Evgenii V., *The Reforms of Peter the Great: Progress through coercion in Russia*, trans. John T. Alexander (New York: M.E. Sharp, 1993).

Avrich, Paul, 'Kropotkin's Ethical Anarchism' in *Anarchist Portraits* (Princeton, NJ: Princeton University Press, 1988), pp. 53–78.

Axtmann, Roland, 'The Formation of the Modern State: The debate in the social sciences' in Mary Fulbrook (ed.), *National Histories and European Histories* (Boulder, CO: Westview Press, 1993), pp. 21–45.

Bachrach, Peter and Baratz, Morton S., 'Two Faces of Power', *American Political Science Review* vol. 56 (1962): 947–52.

Bacon, Francis, *A New Atlantis*, in Henry Morley (ed.), *Ideal Commonwealths* (London: George Routledge & Sons, 1889), pp. 171–213.

Bakunin, Michael, 'Revolutionary Catechism', in Sam Dolgoff (ed. and trans.), *Bakunin on Anarchism* (Montréal: Black Rose Books, 1980), pp. 76–97.

—, *Statism and Anarchy*, ed. and trans. M.S. Shatz (Cambridge: Cambridge University Press, 1990).

Bales, Kevin, *Disposable People: New slavery in the global economy* (Berkeley: University of California Press, 1999).

Barber, Benjamin R., *Superman and Common Men* (Harmondsworth: Penguin, 1972).

Barclay, Harold, *People Without Government: An anthropology of anarchism* (London: Kahn & Averill with Cienfuegos Press, 1982).

Barry, Norman, 'Anarchism' in Nigel Ashford and Stephen Davies (eds), *A Dictionary of Conservative and Libertarian Thought* (London: Routledge, 1991), pp. 4–7.

Becker, L.C., *Property Rights: Philosophical foundations* (London: Routledge & Kegan Paul, 1977).

Beetham, David, *Bureaucracy* (Milton Keynes: Open University Press, 1987).

Beidelman, T.O., 'Nuer Priests and Prophets: Charisma, authority and power among the Nuer' in Beidelman (ed.), *The Translation of Culture: Essays to E.E. Evans-Pritchard* (London: Tavistock Publications, 1971), pp. 375–415.

— (ed.), *The Translation of Culture: Essays to E.E. Evans-Pritchard* (London: Tavistock Publications, 1971).

Berlin, Isaiah, 'Two Concepts of Liberty' in *Four Essays on Liberty* (Oxford: Oxford University Press, 1969), pp. 118–72.

Berman, Russell and Luke, Tim, Editors' Introduction to Gustav Landauer, *For Socialism* (St Louis, MO: Telos Press, 1978), pp. 1–18.

Bey, Hakim, *Immediatism: Essays by Hakim Bey* (Edinburgh: AK Press, 1994).

Berneri, Marie Louise, *Journey Through Utopia* (London: Freedom Press, 1982).

Blackburn, Robin, *The Overthrow of Colonial Slavery 1776–1848* (London: Verso, 1988).

—, *The Making of New World Slavery: From the baroque to the modern 1492–1800* (London: Verso, 1997).

Blassingame, John W. (ed.), *Slave Testimony: Two centuries of letters, speeches, interviews, and autobiographies* (Baton Rouge: Louisiana State University Press, 1977).

Blau, Peter M., *Inequality and Heterogeneity: A primitive theory of social structure* (New York: Free Press/London: Collier Macmillan, 1977).

Bloch, Maurice, *Feudal Society*, trans. L. A. Manyon (London: Routledge & Kegan Paul, 1961).

Blocker, H. Gene and Smith, Elizabeth S., Preface to Blocker and Smith (eds), *John Rawls's Theory of Social Justice: An introduction* (Athens: Ohio University Press, 1980), pp. vii–xii.

Bolloten, Burnett, *The Grand Camouflage: The Spanish civil war and revolution, 1936-39* (London: Pall Mall Press, 1968).

Bookchin, Murray, *The Spanish Anarchists: The heroic years 1868–1936* (Edinburgh: AK Press, 1998).

Borkenau, Franz, *The Spanish Cockpit* (London: Pluto Press, 1986).

Braddick, Michael J., *The Nerves of State: Taxation and the financing of the English state, 1558–1714* (Manchester: Manchester University Press, 1996).

Brenan, Gerald, *The Spanish Labyrinth: An account of the social and political background of the civil war* (2nd edn, Cambridge: Cambridge University Press, 2000).

Breuilly, John, *Nationalism and the State* (2nd edn, Chicago, IL: University of Chicago Press/Manchester: Manchester University Press, 1994).

—, 'The State' in Alexander J. Motyl (ed.), *Encylopedia of Nationalism* (2 vols, San Diego, CA: Academic Press, 2001), vol. 1, pp. 769–92.

Brown, Elizabeth A.R., 'The Tyranny of a Construct: Feudalism and Historians of Medieval Europe', *American Historical Review* vol. 79 (1974): 1063–88.

Bruner, Jerome, *Acts of Meaning* (Cambridge, MA: Harvard University Press, 1990).

Buber, Martin, *Paths in Utopia*, trans. R.F.C. Hull (Boston, MA: Beacon Press, 1958).

Budrys, Algis, *Some Will Not Die* (London: Mayflower-Dell, 1964).

Buisseret, David (ed.), *Monarchs, Ministers, and Maps: The emergence of cartography as a tool of government in early modern Europe* (Chicago, IL: University of Chicago Press, 1992).

Burleigh, Michael, *The Third Reich: A new history* (London: Pan, 2001).

Callinicos, Alex, *Against the Third Way: An anti-capitalist critique* (Cambridge: Polity, 2001).

Campanella, Thomas, *The City of the Sun*, in Henry Morley (ed.), *Ideal Commonwealths* (London: George Routledge & Sons, 1889), pp. 217–63.

Cannadine, David and Price, Simon (eds), *Rituals of Royalty: Power and ceremonial in traditional societies* (Cambridge: Cambridge University Press, 1987).

Canovan, Margaret, *Nationhood and Political Theory* (Cheltenham: Edward Elgar, 1996).

Carlson, A.R., *Anarchism in Germany*, vol. 1: *The Early Movement* (Metuchen: Scarecrow Press, 1972).

Carr, E.H., *Michael Bakunin* (London: Macmillan, 1975).

Carr, Raymond (ed.), *The Republic and the Civil War in Spain* (London: Macmillan, 1971).

Carter, Alan, 'Analytical Anarchism: Some conceptual foundations', *Political Theory* vol. 28 (2000): 230–53.

Carter, April, *The Political Theory of Anarchism* (London: Routledge & Kegan Paul, 1971).

Chaney, Norman, *Six Images of Human Nature* (Englewood Cliffs, NJ: Prentice Hall, 1990).

Chesterton, G.K., 'A Defence of Rash Vows' in *Stories, Essays, and Poems* (London: J.M. Dent & Sons, 1935), pp. 113–18.

Childe, V. Gordon, *Social Evolution* (London: Collins, 1963).

Chomsky, Noam, Introduction to Daniel Guérin, *Anarchism: From theory to practice*, trans. Mary Klopper (New York: Monthly Review Press, 1970), pp. vii–xx.

—, 'Objectivity and Liberal Scholarship' in James Peck (ed.), *The Chomsky Reader* (London: Serpent's Tail, 1988), pp. 83–120.

Christman, John, *The Myth of Property: Toward an egalitarian theory of ownership* (New York: Oxford University Press, 1994).

Clark, John, 'What is Anarchism?' in *The Anarchist Moment: Reflections on culture, nature and power* (Montréal: Black Rose Books, 1984), pp. 117–40.

Clark, Samuel, review of David Stack, *The First Darwinian Left: Socialism and Darwinism 1859–1914* in *Human Nature Review* vol. 3 (2003): 379–80 <http://human-nature.com/nibbs/03/stack.html> (accessed 4 January 2006).

Clark, S.R.L., 'The Use of "Man's Function" in Aristotle', *Ethics* vol. 82 (1972): 269–83.

Clastres, Pierre, *Society Against the State*, trans. Robert Hurley and Abe Stein (Oxford: Basil Blackwell, 1977).

Clendinnen, Inga, *Ambivalent Conquests: Maya and Spaniard in Yucatan, 1517–1570* (2nd edn, Cambridge: Cambridge University Press, 2003).

Cohn, Norman, *The Pursuit of the Millennium: Revolutionary millenarians and mystical anarchists of the middle ages* (revised edn, London: Paladin, 1970).

Cohn, Raymond L., 'Mortality in Transport', in Seymour Drescher and Stanley L. Engerman (eds), *A Historical Guide to World Slavery* (New York: Oxford University Press, 1998), pp. 290–92.

Conrad, Joseph, *The Secret Agent: A simple tale* (Ware: Wordsworth Classics, 1993).

Craton, Michael, *Testing the Chains: Resistance to slavery in the British West Indies* (Ithaca, NY: Cornell University Press, 1982).

—, 'Forms of Resistance to Slavery' in Franklin W. Knight (ed.), *General History of the Caribbean* vol. 3: *The Slave Societies of the Caribbean* (London: Unesco Publishing, 1997), pp. 222–70.

Creveld, Martin Van, *The Rise and Decline of the State* (Cambridge: Cambridge University Press, 1999).

Crowder, George, *Classical Anarchism: The political thought of Godwin, Proudhon, Bakunin, and Kropotkin* (Oxford: Clarendon Press, 1991).

Cunliffe, Marcus, *Chattel Slavery and Wage Slavery: The Anglo-American context, 1830–1860* (Athens: University of Georgia Press, 1979).

Curtin, Philip D., *The Atlantic Slave Trade: A census* (Madison: University of Wisconsin Press, 1969).

Dahl, Robert A., *Who Governs? Democracy and power in an American city* (New Haven, CT: Yale University Press, 1961).

—, *Democracy and its Critics* (New Haven, CT: Yale University Press, 1989).

Dandeker, Christopher, *Surveillance, Power and Modernity: Bureaucracy and discipline from 1700 to the present day* (Cambridge: Polity, 1990).

David, Nicholas and Kramer, Carol, *Ethnoarchaeology in Action* (Cambridge: Cambridge University Press, 2001).

Davis, David Brion, *Slavery and Human Progress* (New York: Oxford University Press, 1984).

—, 'Introduction: The problem of slavery' in Seymour Drescher and Stanley L. Engerman (eds), *A Historical Guide to World Slavery* (New York: Oxford University Press, 1998), pp. ix–xviii.

Dawidowicz, Lucy S., *The War Against the Jews, 1933–1945* (Toronto: Bantam Books, 1976).

Dawkins, Richard, *The Selfish Gene* (new edn, Oxford: Oxford University Press, 1989).

Derbyshire, J. Denis and Derbyshire, Ian, *Political Systems of the World* (New York: St Martin's Press, 1996).

Deutsch, Karl W., *Nationalism and Social Communication: An inquiry into the foundations of nationality* (Cambridge, MA: MIT Press, 1953).

de Groot, Silvia W. et al., 'Maroon Communities in the Circum-Caribbean', in Franklin W. Knight (ed.), *General History of the Caribbean* vol. 3: *The Slave Societies of the Caribbean* (London: Unesco Publishing, 1997), pp. 169–93.

Diamond, Jared, *Guns, Germs and Steel: A short history of everybody for the last 13,000 years* (London: Vintage, 1998).

—, *Collapse: How societies choose to fail or survive* (London: Penguin, 2005).

Dolgoff, Sam, 'Money and Exchange', in Dolgoff (ed.), *The Anarchist Collectives: Workers' self-management in the Spanish revolution 1936–1939* (New York: Free Life Editions, 1974), pp. 70–76.

— (ed), *The Anarchist Collectives: Workers' self-management in the Spanish revolution 1936–1939* (New York: Free Life Editions, 1974).

Douglass, Frederick, *Narrative of the Life of Frederick Douglass, an American Slave, Written by Himself*, ed. H.A. Baker (New York: Penguin, 1982).

Dunn, R.S., Review of Michael Craton, *Testing the Chains*, *Journal of Interdisciplinary History* vol. 15 (1984): 173–5.

Earle, Timothy C., 'Political Domination and Social Evolution' in Tim Ingold (ed.), *Companion Encyclopedia of Anthropology* (London: Routledge, 1994), pp. 940–61.

Ellul, Jacques, *Anarchy and Christianity*, trans. G.W. Bromiley (Grand Rapids, MI: William B. Eerdmans, 1991).

Eltis, David, 'Slave Trade: Trans-Atlantic trade' in Seymour Drescher and Stanley L. Engerman (eds), *A Historical Guide to World Slavery* (New York: Oxford University Press, 1998), pp. 370–75.

— et al. (eds), *The Abolition of the Atlantic Slave Trade* (Madison: University of Wisconsin Press, 1981).

Elton, G.R., *The Tudor Revolution in Government: Administrative changes in the reign of Henry VIII* (Cambridge: Cambridge University Press, 1953).

Eltzbacher, Paul, *Anarchism: Exponents of the anarchist philosophy*, trans. Steven T. Byington, ed. James J. Martin (New York: Chip's Bookshop, n.d.).

Engels, Friedrich, *The Origin of the Family, Private Property and the State: In the light of the researches of Lewis H. Morgan* (London: Lawrence & Wishart, 1972).

—, *Socialism: Utopian and scientific* (London: Bookmarks, 1993).

Engerman, Stanley L., 'Historiography: An overview', in Seymour Drescher and Engerman (eds), *A Historical Guide to World Slavery* (New York: Oxford University Press, 1998), pp. 222–7.

Esenwein, George, *Anarchist Ideology and the Working-Class Movement in Spain, 1868–1898* (Berkeley: University of California Press, 1989).

Evans-Pritchard, E.E., *The Nuer: A description of the modes of livelihood and political institutions of a Nilotic people* (Oxford: Clarendon Press, 1940).

—, 'The Nuer of the Southern Sudan', in Meyer Fortes and Evans-Pritchard (eds), *African Political Systems* (London: Oxford University Press, 1940), pp. 272–96.

—, *Kinship and Marriage Among the Nuer* (Oxford: Clarendon Press, 1951).

—, *Nuer Religion* (Oxford: Clarendon Press, 1956).

Fagan, Brian M., *People of the Earth: An introduction to world prehistory* (8th edn, New York: Harper Collins, 1995).

—, *World Prehistory: A brief introduction* (New York: Longman, 1999).

Faure, Sébastien, extract from *Encyclopédie Anarchiste* in George Woodcock (ed.), *The Anarchist Reader* (Glasgow: Fontana/Collins, 1977), p. 62.

Flannery, Kent V., 'The Cultural Evolution of Civilizations', *Annual Review of Ecology and Systematics* vol. 3 (1972): 399–426.

Flathman, Richard E., *The Practice of Political Authority: Authority and the authoritative* (Chicago, IL: University of Chicago Press, 1980).

Fleming, Marie, *The Anarchist Way to Socialism: Elisée Reclus and nineteenth-century European anarchism* (London: Croom Helm, 1979).

Fowler, R.B., 'The Anarchist Tradition of Political Thought', *Western Political Quarterly* vol. 25 (1972): 738–52.

Fraser, Ronald, *Blood of Spain: The experience of civil war, 1936–1939* (London: Penguin, 1981).

Freeden, Michael, *Ideologies and Political Theory: A conceptual approach* (Oxford: Clarendon Press, 1996).

Frye, Northrop, 'Varieties of Literary Utopia' in Thomas More, *Utopia*, ed. and trans. Robert M. Adams (2nd edn, New York: Norton, 1992), pp. 205–11.

Gallie, W.B., 'Essentially Contested Concepts', *Proceedings of the Aristotelian Society* vol. 56 (1956): 167–98.

Gamble, Clive, 'Hunter-Gatherers and the Origin of States' in John A. Hall (ed.) *States in History* (Oxford: Basil Blackwell, 1986), pp. 22–47.

Garland, David, *The Culture of Control: Crime and social order in contemporary society* (Oxford: Oxford University Press, 2001).

Gates, Henry Louis (ed.), *The Classic Slave Narratives* (New York: New American Library, 1987).

Geertz, Clifford, 'Thick Description: Toward an interpretive theory of culture' in *The Interpretation of Cultures: Selected essays* (London: Fontana Press, 1993), pp. 3-30.

—, 'Passage and Accident: A life of learning', in *Available Light: Anthropological reflections on philosophical topics* (Princeton, NJ: Princeton University Press, 2000), pp. 3–20.

—, 'The Uses of Diversity', in *Available Light: Anthropological reflections on philosophical topics* (Princeton, NJ: Princeton University Press, 2000), pp. 68–88.

—, 'The Strange Estrangement: Charles Taylor and the natural sciences', in *Available Light: Anthropological reflections on philosophical topics* (Princeton, NJ: Princeton University Press, 2000), pp. 143–59.

Gellner, Ernest, *Saints of the Atlas* (London: Weidenfeld and Nicholson, 1969).

—, 'How to Live in Anarchy' in *Contemporary Thought and Politics* (London: Routledge & Kegan Paul, 1974), pp. 87–94.

—, *Nations and Nationalism* (Oxford: Blackwell, 1983).

—, 'Soviets against Wittfogel: Or, the anthropological preconditions of mature Marxism' in John A. Hall (ed.), *States in History* (Oxford: Basil Blackwell, 1986), pp. 78–108.

Genovese, Eugene D., *Roll, Jordan, Roll: The world the slaves made* (New York: Pantheon Books, 1974).

—, *From Rebellion to Revolution: Afro-American slave revolts in the making of the modern world* (Baton Rouge: Louisiana State University Press, 1979).

Godwin, William, *Enquiry Concerning Political Justice and its Influence on Modern Morals and Happiness*, ed. Isaac Kramnick (3rd edn, London: Penguin, 1985).

—, *Collected Novels and Memoirs of William Godwin*, vol. 1: *Memoirs*, ed. Mark Philp (London: William Pickering, 1992).

—, *Thoughts on Man*, in Mark Philp (ed.), *Political and Philosophical Writings of William Godwin* (6 vols, London: William Pickering, 1996), vol. 6, pp. 31–292.

Goldman, Emma, *Vision on Fire: Emma Goldman on the Spanish revolution*, ed. David Porter (New Paltz, NY: Commonground Press, 1983).

Goodway, David (ed.), *For Anarchism: History, theory, and practice* (London: Routledge, 1989).

Gough, Kathleen, 'Nuer Kinship: A re-examination', in T.O. Beidelman (ed.), *The Translation of Culture: Essays to E.E. Evans-Pritchard* (London: Tavistock Publications, 1971), pp. 79–121.

Gray, John, 'Notes Towards a Definition of the Political Thought of Tlön' in *Enlightenment's Wake: Politics and culture at the close of the modern age* (London: Routledge, 1995), pp. 11–17.

Greuel, Peter J., 'The Leopard-Skin Chief: An examination of political power among the Nuer', *American Anthropologist* vol. 73 (1971): 1115–20.

Guérin, Daniel, *Anarchism: From theory to practice*, trans. Mary Klopper (New York: Monthly Review Press, 1970).

Hakluyt, Richard, *Voyages and Discoveries* ed. Jack Beeching (London: Penguin, 1972 [1598–1600]).

Hallowell, A.I., 'The Nature and Function of Property as a Social Institution' in *Culture and Experience* (New York: Schocken Books, 1967), pp. 236–49.

Hardesty, William H., 'Mapping the Future: Extrapolation in utopian/dystopian and science fiction' in Gorman Beauchamp et al. (eds), *Utopian Studies One* (Lanham, MD: University Press of America, 1987), pp. 160–72.

Harper, Clifford, *Anarchy: A graphic guide* (London: Camden Press, 1987).

Harré, Rom, *Social Being* (2nd edn, Oxford: Blackwell, 1993).

Harris, Marvin, 'The Economy Has No Surplus?', *American Anthropologist* vol. 61 (1959): 185–99.

—, *Our Kind: Who we are, where we came from, where we are going* (New York: Harper Collins, 1989).

Hobbes, Thomas, *Leviathan*, ed. Edwin Curley (Indianapolis, IN: Hackett, 1994).

Hobsbawm, Eric J., *Primitive Rebels: Studies in archaic forms of social movement in the 19th and 20th centuries* (3rd edn, Manchester: Manchester University Press, 1971).

—, *Nations and Nationalism Since 1780: Programme, myth, reality* (Cambridge: Cambridge University Press, 1990).

—, *Age of Extremes: The short twentieth century 1914–1991* (London: Abacus, 1995).

—, 'Bolshevism and the Anarchists' in *Revolutionaries* (London: Abacus, 1999), pp. 67–83.

—, 'Reflections on Anarchism' in *Revolutionaries* (London: Abacus, 1999), pp. 97–108.

Hoebel, E. Adamson, 'Fundamental Legal Concepts as Applied in the Study of Primitive Law', *Yale Law Journal* vol. 51 (1942): 951–66.

Hollis, Martin and Lukes, Steven, Editors' Introduction to *Rationality and Relativism* (Oxford: Blackwell, 1982), pp. 1–20.

Honoré, A.M., 'Ownership' in A.G. Guest (ed.), *Oxford Essays in Jurisprudence* (Oxford: Oxford University Press, 1961), pp. 107–47.

Höpfl, Harro and Thompson, Martin P., 'The History of Contract as a Motif in Political Thought', *American Historical Review* vol. 84 (1979): 919–44.

Horowitz, Irving (ed.), *The Anarchists* (New York: Dell, 1964).

Hospers, John, *Libertarianism: A political philosophy for tomorrow* (Los Angeles, CA: Nash Publishing, 1971).

Howard, Michael, *War in European History* (Oxford: Oxford University Press, 1976).

Hughes, Robert, *The Fatal Shore: A history of the transportation of convicts to Austrailia, 1787–1868* (London: Collins Harvill, 1987).

Hutchinson, Sharon E., *Nuer Dilemmas: Coping with money, war, and the state* (Berkeley: University of California Press, 1996).

Inikori, Joseph E., 'Capitalism and Slavery', in Seymour Drescher and Stanley L. Engerman (eds), *A Historical Guide to World Slavery* (New York: Oxford University Press, 1998), pp. 107–10.

James, Lawrence, *Raj: The making and unmaking of British India* (London: Abacus, 1997).

Joll, James, 'Singing, Dancing and Dynamite: Review of Jean Maitron, *Le Mouvement Anarchiste en France*', *Times Literary Supplement*, 10 September 1976: 1092–3.

—, *The Anarchists* (2nd edn, London: Methuen, 1979).

Kant, Immanuel, 'Perpetual Peace: A philosophical sketch' in Hans Reiss (ed.), *Political Writings*, trans. H.B. Nisbet (2nd edn, Cambridge: Cambridge University Press, 1991), pp. 93–130.

Kaplan, Temma, *Anarchists of Andalusia 1868–1903* (Princeton, NJ: Princeton University Press, 1977).

Kedourie, Elie, *Nationalism* (London: Hutchinson & Co., 1960).

Kellaway, George P., *Map Projections* (2nd edn, London: Methuen & Co, 1949).

Kelsey, Graham, 'Anarchism in Aragon During the Second Republic: The emergence of a mass movement' in Martin Blinkhorn (ed.), *Spain in Conflict 1931–1939: Democracy and its enemies* (London: Sage Publications, 1986), pp. 60–82.

Knafla, Louis A. and Binnie, Susan W.S., Editors' Introduction to *Law, Society and the State: Essays in modern legal history* (Toronto: University of Toronto Press, 1995), pp. 3–33.

Kolchin, Peter, *American Slavery 1619–1877* (London: Penguin, 1993).

Koren, J. (ed.), *The History of Statistics: Their development and progress in many countries* (New York: Burt Franklin, 1918).

Kramnick, Isaac, 'On Anarchism and the Real World: William Godwin and radical England', *American Political Science Review*, 66 (1972): 114–28.

Kropotkin, Peter, *Memoirs of a Revolutionist* (2 vols, London: Smith, Elder & Co., 1899).

—, *The State: Its historic role*, ed. and trans. G.W. [probably George Woodcock] (London: Freedom Press, 1943).

—, *Fields, Factories and Workshops Tomorrow*, ed. Colin Ward (2nd edn, London: Freedom Press, 1985).

—, *Mutual Aid: A factor of evolution* (Montréal: Black Rose Books, 1989).

—, 'Anarchist Communism: Its basis and principles' in George Woodcock (ed.), *Fugitive Writings* (Montréal: Black Rose Books, 1993), pp. 72–94.

—, *The Conquest of Bread and other writings*, ed. M.S. Shatz (Cambridge: Cambridge University Press, 1995).

—, 'Anarchism' from *The Encyclopaedia Britannica*, 11th edn, 1911, in M.S. Shatz (ed.), *The Conquest of Bread and other writings* (Cambridge: Cambridge University Press, 1995), pp. 233–47.

Kuper, Adam, *The Invention of Primitive Society: Transformations of an illusion* (London: Routledge, 1988).

Ladenson, Robert, 'Legitimate Authority', *American Philosophical Quarterly* vol. 9 (1972): 335–41.

Lambert, Malcolm D., *Medieval Heresy: Popular movements from Bogomil to Hus* (London: Edward Arnold, 1977).

Leakey, Richard, *The Origin of Humankind: Unearthing our family tree* (London: Phoenix, 1995).

Le Guin, Ursula, *The Dispossessed* (London: Grafton, 1975).

—, *Always Coming Home* (London: Victor Gollancz, 1986).

Leval, Gaston, 'The Socialization of Health Services: Extract from *Né Franco Né Stalin*', in Sam Dolgoff (ed.), *The Anarchist Collectives: Workers' self-management in the Spanish revolution 1936–1939* (New York: Free Life Editions, 1974), pp. 99–101.

—, 'The Peasant Federation of Levant: Extract from *Né Franco Né Stalin*', in Sam Dolgoff (ed.), *The Anarchist Collectives: Workers' self-management in the Spanish revolution 1936–1939* (New York: Free Life Editions, 1974), pp. 122–6.

—, *Collectives in the Spanish Revolution*, trans. Vernon Richards (London: Freedom Press, 1975).

Lewellen, Ted C., *Political Anthropology: An Introduction* (2nd edn, Westport, CT: Bergin and Garvey, 1992).

Lodge, David, *Changing Places* (London: Penguin, 1975).

Loptson, Peter, *Theories of Human Nature* (Peterborough, Ontario: Broadview Press, 1995).

Lovejoy, Arthur O. and Boas, George, *Primitivism and Related Ideas in Antiquity* (New York: Octagon Books, 1973).

Lukes, Steven, *Power: A radical view* (London: Macmillan, 1974).

Macek, Josef, *The Hussite Movement in Bohemia* (London: Lawrence & Wishart, 1965).

McGuire, Randall H., 'Breaking Down Cultural Complexity: Inequality and heterogeneity', *Advances in Archaeological Method and Theory* vol. 6 (1983): 91–142.

Mann, Michael, *Sources of Social Power* (2 vols, Cambridge: Cambridge University Press, 1986 and 1993).

—, 'The Autonomous Power of the State: Its origins, mechanisms and results' in John A. Hall (ed.), *States in History* (Oxford: Basil Blackwell, 1986), pp. 109–36.

Manuel, F.E. and F.P., *Utopian Thought in the Western World* (Oxford: Basil Blackwell, 1979).

Marshall, Peter, *William Godwin* (New Haven, CT: Yale University Press, 1984).

—, Editor's Introduction to William Godwin, *The Anarchist Writings of William Godwin* (London: Freedom Press, 1986), pp. 9–48.

—, *Demanding the Impossible: A history of anarchism* (revised edn, London: Fontana, 1993).

Martin, Rex, 'Anarchism and Skepticism' in J.R. Pennock and J.W. Chapman (eds), *Nomos XIX: Anarchism* (New York: New York University Press, 1978), pp. 140–49.

Mazower, Mark, *Dark Continent: Europe's twentieth century* (London: Penguin, 1998).

Middleton, John and Tate, David (eds), *Tribes Without Rulers: Studies in African segmentary systems* (London: Routledge & Kegan Paul, 1958).

Midgley, Mary, *Beast and Man: The roots of human nature* (Revised edn, London: Routledge, 1995).

Mill, John Stuart, *Autobiography*, ed. Harold J. Laski (London: Oxford University Press, 1926).

—, *On Liberty* in John Gray (ed.), *On Liberty and Other Essays* (Oxford: Oxford University Press, 1991), pp. 5–128.

Miller, Martin A., *Kropotkin* (Chicago, IL: University of Chicago Press, 1976).

Mills, C. Wright, *The Power Elite* (New York: Oxford University Press, 1956).

Mintz, Jerome R., *The Anarchists of Casas Viejas* (Chicago, IL: University of Chicago Press, 1982).

Moore, John, *A Primitivism Primer* <http://www.primitivism.com/primer.htm> (accessed 3 August 2005).

Moore, Margaret, 'Introduction: The self-determination principle and the ethics of secession' in Moore (ed.), *National Self-Determination and Secession* (Oxford: Oxford University Press, 1998), pp. 1–13.

More, Thomas, *Utopia*, ed. and trans. Robert M. Adams (2nd edn, New York: Norton, 1992).

Morgan, Lewis H., *Ancient Society: Or, researches in the lines of human progress from savagery through barbarism to civilization* (Chicago, IL: Charles H. Kerr & Co., 1877).

Morland, David, *Demanding the Impossible? Human nature and politics in nineteenth-century social anarchism* (London: Cassell, 1997).

Morris, William, *News From Nowhere*, in Clive Wilmer (ed.), *News from Nowhere and other writings* (London: Penguin, 1993), pp. 41–228.

Munzer, Stephen R., *A Theory of Property* (Cambridge: Cambridge University Press, 1990).

Murphy, Pat, *The City, Not Long After* (New York: Bantam, 1990).

Nettlau, Max, *A Short History of Anarchism*, trans. Ida P. Isca, ed. Heiner M. Becker (London: Freedom Press, 1996).

Nozick, Robert, *Anarchy, State, and Utopia* (Oxford: Blackwell, 1974).

Orwell, George, *Homage to Catalonia*, in Peter Davidson (ed.), *Orwell in Spain: The full text of* Homage to Catalonia *with associated articles, reviews and letters from* The Complete Works of George Orwell (London: Penguin, 2001), pp. 28–215.

Otter, Lawrence, 'Determinism and Utopianism in the Anarchist Tradition', *Anarchy* vol. 68 (1966): 305–18.

Paasen, Pierre van, Interview with Buenaventura Durutti, *Toronto Star* (September 1936) <http://www.spunk.org/library/places/spain/sp000069.txt> (accessed 2 January 2006).

Pagden, Anthony, *The Fall of Natural Man: The American Indian and the origins of comparative ethnology* (Revised edn, Cambridge: Cambridge University Press, 1986).

Paradis, James, '*Evolution and Ethics* in its Victorian Context' in T.H. Huxley et al., *Evolution and Ethics: T.H. Huxley's Evolution and Ethics with new essays on its Victorian and sociobiological context* (Princeton, NJ: Princeton University Press, 1989), pp. 3–55.

Parfit, Derek, *Reasons and Persons* (Oxford: Oxford University Press, 1985).

Parker, Noel, *Revolutions and History: An essay in interpretation* (Cambridge: Polity, 1999).

Parsons, Talcott, 'The Distribution of Power in American Society': review of C. Wright Mills, *The Power Elite*, *World Politics* vol. 10 (1957): 123–43.

—, 'On the Concept of Political Power', in *Sociological Theory and Modern Society* (New York: Free Press, 1967), pp. 297–354.

Passmore, John, *The Perfectibility of Man* (3rd edn, Indianapolis, IN: Liberty Fund, 2000).

Patterson, Orlando, *Slavery and Social Death: A comparative study* (Cambridge, MA: Harvard University Press, 1982).

Pitzer, Donald E. (ed.), *America's Communal Utopias* (Chapel Hill: University of North Carolina Press, 1997).

Philp, Mark, *Godwin's Political Justice* (Ithaca, NY: Cornell University Press, 1986).

Popper, Karl, *The Open Society and its Enemies* (2 vols, London: Routledge & Kegan Paul, 1966).

Preston, Peter, 'War of Words: The Spanish civil war and the historians' in Preston (ed.), *Revolution and War in Spain 1931–1939* (London: Methuen, 1984), pp. 1–13.

—, *A Concise History of the Spanish Civil War* (London: Fontana Press, 1996).

Rawley, James A., *The Transatlantic Slave Trade: A history* (New York: W.W. Norton & Co., 1981).

Rawls, John, *A Theory of Justice* (Oxford: Oxford University Press, 1971).

—, *The Law of Peoples* with *The Idea of Public Reason Revisited* (Cambridge, MA: Harvard University Press, 1999).

Reiman, Jeffrey, *In Defence of Political Philosophy* (New York: Harper, 1972).

Reynolds, Susan, *Fiefs and Vassals: The medieval evidence reinterpreted* (Oxford: Oxford University Press, 1994).

Richards, Vernon, Foreword to Gaston Laval, *Collectives in the Spanish Revolution* (London: Freedom Press, 1975), pp. 7–15.

—, *Lessons of the Spanish Revolution* (3rd edn, London: Freedom Press, 1983).

Ritter, Alan, *Anarchism: A theoretical analysis* (Cambridge: Cambridge University Press, 1980).

Russell, Bertrand, *Roads to freedom: Socialism, anarchism, and syndicalism* (London: Allen & Unwin, 1918).

Sahlins, Marshall D., 'The Segmentary Lineage: An organisation of predatory expansion', *American Anthropologist* vol. 63 (1961): 322–45.

Sanderson, Stephen K., *Social Evolutionism: A critical history* (Cambridge, MA: Blackwell, 1990).

Scanlon, Thomas, *What We Owe to Each Other* (Cambridge, MA: Belknap Press, 1998).

Schaack, Michael J., *Anarchy and Anarchists: A history of the red terror and the social revolution in America and Europe* (Chicago, IL: F.J. Schulte & Co., 1889).

Scott, James C., *Seeing Like a State: How certain schemes to improve the human condition have failed* (New Haven, CT: Yale University Press, 1998).

Scruton, Roger, *A Dictionary of Political Thought* (London: Pan Books, 1983).

Seed, David (ed.), *Imagining Apocalypse: Studies in cultural crisis* (Houndmills: Macmillan, 2000).

Service, Elman R., *Origins of the State and Civilization: The process of cultural evolution* (New York: Norton, 1975).

Skinner, B.F., *Walden Two* (new edn, New Jersey: Prentice Hall, 1976).

—, 'Utopianism: The design of experimental communities' in David L. Sills (ed.), *International Encyclopedia of the Social Sciences* (New York: Macmillan & Free Press, 1968), vol. 16, pp. 271–5.

Skirda, Alexandre, *Facing the Enemy: A history of anarchist organization from Proudhon to May 1968*, trans. Paul Sharkey (Edinburgh: AK Press, 2002).

Smith, L. Neil, *The Probability Broach* (New York: Ballantine, 1980).

Solow, Barbara Lewis and Engerman, Stanley L. (eds), *British Capitalism and Caribbean Slavery: The legacy of Eric Williams* (Cambridge: Cambridge University Press, 2004).

Souchy, Augustin, 'Collectivizations in Catalonia: Extracts from *Nacht Über Spanien*', in Sam Dolgoff (ed.), *The Anarchist Collectives: Workers' self-management in the Spanish revolution 1936–1939* (New York: Free Life Editions, 1974), pp. 86–98.

—, 'Workers' Self-Management in Industry: Extracts from *Collectivisations: L'Oeuvre Constructive de la révolution Espagnole*', in Sam Dolgoff (ed.), *The Anarchist Collectives: Workers' self-management in the Spanish revolution 1936–1939* (New York: Free Life Editions, 1974), pp. 78–84.

Spruyt, Hendrick, *The Sovereign State and its Competitors: An analysis of systems change* (Princeton, NJ: Princeton University Press, 1994).

St. Clair, William, *The Godwins and the Shelleys: The biography of a family* (London: Faber & Faber, 1989).

Stack, David, *The First Darwinian Left: Socialism and Darwinism 1859–1914* (Cheltenham: New Clarion Press, 2003).

Steckel, Richard H., 'Economics', in Seymour Drescher and Stanley L. Engerman (eds), *A Historical Guide to World Slavery* (New York: Oxford University Press, 1998), pp. 179–84.

Stevenson, Leslie and Haberman, David L., *Ten Theories of Human Nature* (3rd edn, New York: Oxford University Press, 1998).

Taylor, A.J.P., 'The Failure of the Habsburg Monarchy' in *Europe: Grandeur and decline* (Harmondsworth: Penguin, 1967), pp. 127–32.

Taylor, Alan, *American Colonies: The settlement of North America to 1800* (London: Allen Lane, 2002).

Taylor, Charles, 'Interpretation and the Sciences of Man', in *Philosophy and the Human Sciences: Philosophical papers 2* (Cambridge: Cambridge University Press, 1985), pp. 15–57.

Taylor, Michael, *Community, Anarchy and Liberty* (Cambridge: Cambridge University Press, 1982).

Theuws, Frans and Nelson, Janet L. (eds), *Rituals of Power: From late antiquity to the early middle ages* (Leiden: Brill, 2000).

Thomas, Hugh, 'Anarchist Agrarian Collectives in the Spanish Civil War', in Raymond Carr (ed.), *The Republic and the Civil War in Spain* (London: Macmillan, 1971), pp. 237–56.

—, *The Spanish Civil War* (3rd edn, London: Penguin, 1990).

—, *The Conquest of Mexico* (London: Pimlico, 1994).

Thompson, E.P., *William Morris: Romantic to Revolutionary* (2nd edn, London: Merlin Press, 1976).

Tilly, Charles, *Coercion, Capital, and European States, AD990-1992* (Cambridge, MA: Blackwell, 1992).

— (ed.), *The Formation of National States in Western Europe* (Princeton, NJ: Princeton University Press, 1975).

Todes, Daniel P., 'Darwin's Malthusian Metaphor and Russian Evolutionary Thought, 1859–1917', *Isis* vol. 78 (1987): 537–51.

Tucker, Benjamin, 'State Socialism and Anarchism: How far they agree and wherein they differ' in *State Socialism and Anarchism and other essays* (Colorado Springs, CO: Ralph Myles, 1972), pp. 11–25.

Turnbull, Colin M., *The Mountain People* (New York: Simon & Schuster, 1972).

Unsworth, Barry, *Sacred Hunger* (London: Penguin, 1992).

Vance, Jack, *Big Planet* (Sevenoaks: Coronet Books, 1977).

Vincent, Andrew, *Modern Political Ideologies* (Oxford: Blackwell, 1992).

Vizetelly, Ernest Alfred, *The Anarchists: Their faith and their record including sidelights on the royal and other personages who have been assassinated* (London: John Lane, 1911).

Waldron, Jeremy, *The Right to Private Property* (Oxford: Clarendon Press, 1988).

Walzer, Michael, *Spheres of Justice: A defence of pluralism and equality* (New York: Basic Books, 1983).

—, *Interpretation and Social Criticism* (Cambridge, MA: Harvard University Press, 1987).

—, *Thick and Thin: Moral argument at home and abroad* (Notre Dame, IN: University of Notre Dame Press, 1994).

Ward, Colin, *Anarchy in Action* (2nd edn, London: Freedom Press, 1973).

Wells, H.G., *A Modern Utopia*, in *Tono-Bungay and A Modern Utopia* (London: Odhams Press, no date), pp. 307–504.

Westermann, Diedrich, Introduction to Ray Huffman, *Nuer Customs and Folk-Lore* (London: Frank Cass & Co., 1970; first published 1931), pp. v–xi.

Wolf, Eric R., *Europe and the People Without History* (with a new preface, Berkeley: University of California Press, 1997).

—, *Envisioning Power: Ideologies of dominance and crisis* (Berkeley: University of California Press, 1999).

Wolff, Jonathan, 'Anarchism and Skepticism' in John T. Sanders and Jan Narveson (eds), *For and Against the State* (Lanham, MD: Rowman & Littlefield, 1996), pp. 99–118.

Wolff, Robert Paul, *In Defence of Anarchism* (2nd edn, Berkeley: University of California Press, 1998).

Woodcock, George, *William Godwin: A biographical study* (London: The Porcupine Press, 1946).

—, *Anarchism: A history of libertarian ideas and movements* (Harmondsworth: Penguin, 1963).

— and Avakumović, Ivan, *Peter Kropotkin: From Prince to Rebel* (Montréal: Black Rose Books, 1990). [Originally published as *The Anarchist Prince*.]

Yates, Frances A., *The Rosicrucian Enlightenment* (St. Albans: Paladin, 1975).

Zenker, E.V., *Anarchism: A criticism and history of the anarchist theory* (New York: Knickerbocker Press, 1897).

## Music

The Sex Pistols, ‘Anarchy in the UK’, on *Never Mind the Bollocks: Here’s the Sex Pistols* (Sex Pistols Residuals/Virgin Records), track 8.

## Film

*Fargo*, directed by Joel Coen, written by Joel and Ethan Coen (Gramercy Pictures, 1996).

*The Village*, directed and written by M. Night Shyamalan (Touchstone Pictures, 2004).

# Index